JUST PUNISHMENTS

SOCIAL INSTITUTIONS AND SOCIAL CHANGE

An Aldine de Gruyter Series of Texts and Monographs

EDITED BY

James D. Wright

JUST PUNISHMENTS

Federal Guidelines and Public Views Compared

PETER H. ROSSI and RICHARD A. BERK

ALDINE DE GRUYTER
New York

mi dwook

About the Authors

Peter H. Rossi is Emeritus Professor of Sociology at the University of Massachusetts at Amherst and past-president of the American Sociological Association. Dr. Rossi has published numerous books and journal articles.

Richard A. Berk is Professor in the Department of Sociology and the Interdivisional Program in Statistics at the University of California at Los Angeles. He also serves as the Director of the Center for the Study of Environment and Society. Dr. Berk has published on a wide variety of criminal justice topics.

ALDINE DE GRUYTER
A division of Walter de Gruyter, Inc.
200 Saw Hill River Road
Hawthorne, New York 10532

This publication is printed on acid free paper ∞

Library of Congress Cataloging-in-Publication Data
Rossi, Peter Henry, 1921–
     Just punishments : federal guidelines and public views compared /
Peter H. Rossi and Richard A. Berk.
          p.   cm. — (Social institutions and social change)
     Includes bibliographical references and index.
     ISBN 0-202-30572-4 (cloth : alk. paper). — ISBN 0-202-30573-2
(paper : alk. paper)
     1. Sentences (Criminal procedure)—United States—Public opinion.
2. Punishment—United States—Public opinion.   3. Public opinion—
United States.   4. Sentences (Criminal procedures)—United States.
5. Punishment—United States.   I. Berk, Richard A.   II. Title.
III. Series.
HV8708.R67   1997
364.6'0973—dc21   96-53324
                                                                        CIP

Manufactured in the United States of America

10 9 8 7 6 5 4 3 2 1

8/10/9 ?

In Memory of Our Mothers
Lizabeta Porcelli Rossi
Regina Clark Berk

Contents

Acknowledgments and Introduction

The research described in this book had its immediate origins in the summer of 1993, when the authors were asked by the United States Sentencing Commission to design a national sample survey. The purpose of the survey was to examine the extent of agreement between the views of the American public on the sentencing of persons convicted in the federal courts with the sentences prescribed in the commission's *Sentencing Guidelines*. We quickly accepted to undertake the task, being eager both to apply the factorial survey method, described in detail in Chapter 3, and to make contributions to criminal justice policy and criminology.

As posed by the commission staff, the research problem was uniquely suited to the factorial survey, a research method that combined sample surveys with randomized experiments, which had been initially developed by the senior author and used extensively by both authors in a wide variety of policy issues. Having specified a survey design and devised a provisional survey instrument, we pretested the approach in Los Angeles. The commission then awarded a contract to the Response Analysis Corporation to design a national household survey and collect face-to-face interviews using the survey instrument tested in the pretest.

The survey data were collected in the first few months of 1994. The authors analyzed the resulting dataset and wrote a report on the findings, submitted to the commission in September 1995. This book is based largely on that report with additional analyses added.

The authors were helped at many points by the advice and criticism of the commission staff, including Phyllis Newton, then executive director and Linda Maxfield, staff member. The Response Analysis Corporation was diligent in collecting the data and was responsible for sample design. Alec Campbell served as research assistant at UCLA and produced the graphs used in Chapter 6.

The usual authors' disclaimer applies: we are solely responsible for whatever errors appear in this book.

Peter H. Rossi
Richard A. Berk

1

Social Norms and Sentencing Felons

INTRODUCTION

In the sociology of law a central issue is whether the criminal code of a society reflects societal norms concerning how felons should be punished, as Durkheim (1953) suggested, or serves some other functions that are only coincidentally related to those norms. The alternatives to the Durkheimian interpretation include the various social control interpretations of the criminal code in which the major function of the criminal code is to serve as a deterrence to crime or as a means by which economic elites exercise control over the lower socioeconomic classes (Hart 1968).

This book makes a contribution to the sociology of law by examining the extent to which the punishments recommended to be meted out to felons convicted in the federal courts are in agreement with American norms concerning punishments to be given to such persons. American punishment norms are measured by interviewing a national sample of adult Americans to find out how each thinks persons convicted of certain federal crimes ought to be punished. The views of Americans, summarized appropriately, are compared to the punishments for such crimes as shown in the *Guidelines Manual* issued by the U.S. Sentencing Commission (1987–1993). Finding that there is close agreement lends support to Durkheim's theory by being consistent with it but does not constitute proof of its validity. Of course, if there is little or no agreement, considerable doubt is cast on Durkheim's views, but such findings do not constitute proof of alternative views.

This book also makes a contribution to the empirical study of social norms. Despite the important role that the concept of social norm plays in social science theory, there is remarkably little empirical research that attempts to give that concept a firm empirical base. The contribution we offer is to provide an empirical approach that is consistent with contemporary social measurement theory and practice.

DEFINING AND MEASURING SOCIAL NORMS

Although there are some differences among social scientists on the nature and function of norms, there is agreement on certain key features (Rossi and Berk 1985). All agree that norms consist of widely held beliefs concerning what a society or social group considers to be appropriate and inappropriate behavior in specified circumstances. Some norms apply almost universally to all members and others apply only to particular roles. For example, the norms condemning murder apply to all, whereas those pertaining to the obligations of parents toward their minor children apply only to the behavior of parents toward their children. Some norms establish the values of objects, roles, and individual qualities—for example, the norms concerning the prestige values of occupations or expressing standards of physical beauty. Norms may prescribe, proscribe, or establish the relative and absolute values of social objects. Norms not only apply to individuals but also to institutions. One can speak of the obligation of the criminal justice system to punish persons convicted of crimes in fair and evenhanded ways as well as the duty of judges to give out sentences in ways that are consistent with that obligation.

It is also agreed among social scientists that norms are recognized as binding upon members of the society to which they apply, although norms vary in the degrees to which they demand conformity. Hence the definitions of norms imply consensus concerning the content of the norms and also on the degrees of obligation accompanying them. That is, the concept of norm implies that the members of the society in question know what the norms are and agree on the strengths of obligations accompanying them. Consensus is not absolute but relative and exists in degrees.

It is important that the consensus concerns *knowledge* about the norms and does not require that members agree with the norms. Some large degree of consensus is implied over the content of the norms but how much individuals need to internalize the norms is an open question.

Norms are necessarily stated in general terms, in the sense of applying to classes of circumstances, defined fairly generally. Accordingly, there are many opportunities for disagreement to arise among members of a society over whether a norm is applicable in a specific circumstance. For example, it is likely that virtually all Americans hold that rape is prohibited behavior, but whether a specific instance of sexual intercourse is definable as rape may be unclear because the boundary between acceptable and unacceptable means of persuasion is not fixed. Indeed, a large part of the work of our legal system consists of making determinations of whether and how legal norms apply to specific instances of behavior. Accordingly, by the very nature of norms, we can expect greater consensus about them when they are stated in general terms and lesser consensus over the application of the norms to specific instances of behavior. In the present instance, we can expect more agreement among Americans about which crimes deserve harsher punishments but less agreement about the specific sentences to be imposed.

MEASURING NORMATIVE CONSENSUS

Because norms are widely held beliefs about how persons should behave and institutions should work, a critical issue in establishing the existence of a norm is that of establishing consensus. At the extreme limits, consensus is easy to establish. If every adult in the United States believed that persons convicted of murder in the first degree should be imprisoned for life, the evidence for consensus about American norms on punishing first-degree murderers would be overwhelming. However, there are strong reasons to expect that perfect agreement on most crimes will not be found. The strongest reason is that norms are general statements that have to be translated into specific beliefs concerning specific circumstances, a translation for which there may not be uniform rules. For example, the norm concerning punishment for killing someone may state that murder should be punished very severely, a statement that has to be given specific content for first degree murder. To some, very severe punishment may mean the death penalty, whereas for others life imprisonment may be very severe punishment, although no one would think that a few years in prison was appropriate. In short, although nearly everyone may subscribe to the same norm, stated generally, they each express their agreement somewhat differently. A second reason for not expecting perfect agreement is that no measurement is error-free. In the present instance, asking Americans to state what they believe to be the norms relies on individuals perceiving the norms correctly. If we asked two individuals living in Amherst, Massachusetts, to tell us how many miles it is to Washington, D.C., we could likely expect answers that agreed on the magnitude of the distance but not on the precise number of miles. Similarly, we could expect that a given norm might be perceived more or less correctly by the majority of Americans but not in precisely identical terms.

In this research, we represent the American norms concerning the punishments to be given to convicted felons by summarizing the responses given by respondents selected in a national probability sample of 1737 American households collected in 1994. One adult, 18 or over, in each household was interviewed face-to-face and asked to state the sentence he or she would give to each of a set of 42 persons, each described in a short vignette as having been convicted of one of a variety of specific criminal acts. A detailed description of the survey can be found in Chapter 3. The summary measures we will use are those that capture the central tendencies of the sentences given by respondents, usually either means or medians.

BACKGROUND OF THE STUDY

This study was undertaken on behalf of the U.S. Sentencing Commission, which also supplied the funding for it.[1] The commission was established by the U.S. Congress in 1984 with its main mission to write guidelines to be followed by the federal criminal courts in sentencing persons convicted of felonies. The legislation setting up the U.S. Sentencing Commission specified four general goals to be achieved in a schedule of sentences for convicted persons:

1. to provide effective deterrence to those who might consider violating the federal criminal code,
2. to provide just punishments for those who were convicted,
3. to ensure uniformity in sentencing across the many federal courts,
4. to make provision for departures from uniformity when justifiable.

Writing the guidelines with these four goals in mind was not an easy task. Some of the goals are not necessarily compatible with each other. Others specify goals that are vague or not easily ascertained. Chapter 2, written by former Commissioner Ilene Nagel, provides an inside view of how the commission went about the task. As she relates, the commissioners examined the actual sentencing practices of the federal courts, drew upon their own experiences, and made judgment calls about what kinds of sentences would be perceived as "just." It is clear from Nagel's account that the commission was very much concerned that the sentences recommended in the guidelines be compatible with what Americans generally believed to be appropriate punishments for the crimes in question.

The *Guidelines Manual*, first issued by the commission in 1987 and updated annually since, is the major instrument devised to reach those goals. The guidelines consist of a set of detailed and comprehensive rules for calculating sentences for persons convicted in the federal courts. The rules are tailored to the crimes committed and to certain characteristics of the convicted person, and are sensitive to circumstances that can mitigate or enhance punishments. The recommended dispositions are given in the form of a range of sentences. By following the guidelines' rules, the federal courts can each arrive at similar dispositions for similar cases. Given a crime, some description of how the crime was conducted, the harm inflicted on possible victims, and knowledge of the prior criminal record of the convicted person, almost anyone can use the *Guidelines Manual* to calculate a range of sentences for that crime.

The commission authorized and funded this study because it was concerned whether its recommendations departed in some significant way from what the American public believed to be proper punishments for violations of the federal criminal code. What are the connections between public views on sentencing and the guidelines? First of all, such views are relevant to the commission's goal of prescribing "just" sentences. A predominant interpretation of just punishment is that it is defined by popular consensus: for a schedule of punishments to be considered just, there should be some correspondence between that schedule and what the public believes to be appropriate sentences for the crimes in question. How close should such a correspondence be is another issue, although at the limits it can be said that the punishments in a prescribed punishment schedule should be positively correlated with the punishments desired by the citizens. That is, crimes treated harshly in the criminal code and the guidelines should also be considered as deserving harsh punishments by the citizenry; conversely, those treated leniently in the guidelines should also be considered as deserving minor treatment by the public. Although the commission did not phrase its concern as the degree of correspondence between the guidelines and American sentencing norms, that would be a reasonable reinterpretation of its concerns..

There are also other reasons to be concerned about the correspondence between the guidelines recommendations and the public's desires. Criminal punishment as deterrence also involves public opinion. The deterrence principle suggests that punishments for crimes ought to be set high enough to offset the gains achieved in breaking the law. For deterrence to be effective, public views of sentencing have to be related to actual punishments. Punishments regarded as too lenient arguably cannot serve as deterrents. To the extent that the public's views of just punishments are influenced by ideas of deterrence, render them relevant.

The legal and social philosophers writing about punishment and the proper rationale for sentencing make much of the contrasts among the goals of just punishments, deterrence, rehabilitation, and selective incarceration. However, actual sentencing systems typically pursue all four goals, emphasizing deterrence in some crimes, just punishments in others, making provisions for the possibility of rehabilitation for some offenders, and for lengthier incarceration of the seemingly incorrigible.[2] The sentencing rules set out in the guidelines are no exception.

The varied purposes pursued in the guidelines mean that the public's views on sentencing are relevant but not determinative. That is, to the extent that sentences are based on just punishment principles, then there should be some concern with ascertaining whether the public agrees at least with ordering of punishment severity. The other sentencing principles are not as demanding about the degree to which there should be matching between sentencing rules and the views of the public, although all at least assume that some positive popular support is needed for proper functioning. In short, some concordance between American punishment norms and sentencing rules is looked for, although the writing of sentencing guidelines should not be dominated by the aspiration to make the two coincide precisely.

There is every reason to expect that guidelines sentences and popular views on sentencing will not be far apart. According to Nagel's account, given in Chapter 2, the commission had some knowledge about popular views and in constructing the guidelines used that knowledge along with other considerations, such as existing sentencing practices. Accordingly our concern here is to uncover the specific forms that best describe the relationships between guidelines sentences and public views on sentencing. For example, it may turn out that guidelines sentences are uniformly higher or lower than those the public would prefer. Or, that there is close agreement on punishments for most crimes, but disagreement on some classes of felonies. There is a variety of possible relationships between guidelines sentences and popular views, which will be considered in the analyses.

All that said, two major points emerge: First, finding out what are just sentences in the eyes of the citizenry is important in the construction and adjustment of a sentencing system that is concerned with appearing as just. Second, public views on sentencing are not (and likely should not be) the major criterion to be used in constructing a sentencing system.

PREVIOUS EMPIRICAL STUDIES

Although there is a long-standing concern in legal and social philosophy with the issue of punishment, the empirical studies of public views on sentencing only began a few decades ago with the development of sample survey methodology. The philosophical literature deals with profound moral issues, such as the moral principles that justify punishment, the legitimate social purposes of punishment, and how equity in punishment can be achieved. In contrast, the empirical literature typically is concerned with describing citizens' views of punishment, how citizens would punish criminals, and citizens' assessments of existing criminal justice practices.

Global Assessments of Sentencing Severity in the Courts

The empirical studies receiving the widest attention are the long series of global public assessments of sentencing practices in the courts started by the Gallup Poll in the mid-1930s and continued through today by a variety of investigators. Based on answers to questions typically asking whether the courts are "too harsh, too lenient, or about right" in the treatment of convicted felons,[3] these studies have received attention because they have shown consistently that majorities of the American public believe that the courts have been too lenient in sentencing. For example, the General Social Survey,[4] an annual sample survey conducted by the National Opinion Research Center at the University of Chicago (Davis and Smith 1994), asked the following question repeatedly over the period 1972–1994, with results as shown: "In general, do you think the courts in this area deal too harshly or not harshly enough with criminals?"

Too harshly	3.7%
Not harshly enough	80.2%
About right[5]	9.6%
Don't know	5.5%
Number of persons asked	30,581

The General Social Survey findings clearly indicate a strong consensus (more than 80%) saying that the courts are not harsh enough, that the courts are too lenient in dealing with criminals, and a very small minority (4%) believing that the courts are too lenient. Furthermore, Americans have felt this way for at least two decades: the General Social Survey findings from the 1970s are not very different from the data collected in the 1990s (Stinchcombe et al. 1980).

Although these and similar findings have been cited by many advocates of harsher sentencing as strong evidence of public support for their views, that interpretation is based on the frail assumption that citizens know what actual sentencing practices are in the courts. If Americans underestimate sentences actually given by the courts, then there is little force to this argument. Because the mass media often find that it is newsworthy when lenient sentences are given to serious crimes, there may be reason to suspect that generalizations from outlier cases that appear in the media are a major force underlying this persistent finding. The public's assessments of the courts may be strongly affected by the newsworthy accounts of acquittals and lenient treatments of convicted felons.

There are other reasons to question such interpretations of the General Social Survey findings along with similar findings from other surveys. The question asked about "treatment of criminals" is ambiguous: some may have had lenient sentences in mind when they answered the question and others may have meant that too many defendants were adjudged innocent and let go.

The global assessments of sentencing are also ambiguous concerning the kinds of crimes and the types of courts being considered: do the findings mean that the American public thinks that all courts are too lenient for all crimes, that some crimes are being treated too leniently in some courts, or some other combination?

The American courts are not alone in being regarded as lenient in sentencing, but are joined by Canadian and British court systems. Walker and Hough (1988) reviewed studies made in those countries, reporting that large majorities of Canadian and British publics also believe that their courts are too lenient in their treatment of criminals. Walker and Hough (1988) also cite studies comparing the actual sentences given out by the courts to sentences desired by citizens in Canada and Great Britain. The findings indicate that the courts and citizens are not far apart in sentences desired and actual sentences given. Clearly global ratings of court leniency do not reflect widespread knowledge about actual sentencing practices. There is also evidence that there may be considerable concordance between the actual sentencing practice of the courts and punishment norms.[6]

Studies of Crime Seriousness

Given the important role played by crime seriousness or severity in some sentencing philosophies, it is not surprising that there is a strong tradition in criminological research of attempts to devise quantitative measures of seriousness. Louis Thurstone, pioneer in psychometrics, made the first study of crime seriousness in the early 1930s mainly as a vehicle for his (then) new "paired comparison" method (Thurstone 1959).

Sellin and Wolfgang (1964) studied the perceived seriousness of juvenile offenses using local samples of college students and criminal justice professionals to rate their seriousness. Rossi and his colleagues (Rossi, Bose, and Berk 1974) obtained a seriousness measure for 100 adults crimes from a general sample of Baltimore adults.

The most comprehensive seriousness study was conducted in 1977 as an adjunct to the National Crime Survey (Wolfgang, Figlio, Tracey, and Singer 1985). Some 60,000 respondents were interviewed in a national survey that asked each to judge the seriousness of a set of 25 crimes using a magnitude estimation approach. Each respondent was asked to give a numerical estimate of the seriousness of each crime relative to a standard crime—bicycle theft—given the arbitrary value of 10: Thus, if a respondent thought auto theft was four times more serious than bicycle theft, his score for auto theft would be 40. The sets of 25 crimes were varied systematically to cover a total of 204 crimes. Some of the crimes studied involved the same criminal act but varied its characteristics (for example, the degree of injury to a victim was varied).

The calculated severity scores range widely, anchored at the extremely serious end by such crimes as bombing a public building with the loss of 20 lives (72.1), rape in which the victim is killed (52.8), and a parent killing his own child (47.8), to the other extreme of trespass (0.6), vagrancy (0.3), and school truancy (0.2). Although the full crime set covers some that are handled in the federal courts (e.g., bribery, environmental crimes, and Medicare fraud), most are the kinds of crimes dealt with at high volumes in the state criminal courts. Indeed, the severity scores are built into some database computer systems maintained by state attorneys and are used to identify high-severity crimes that should receive priority treatment.

The analyses of crime seriousness data in numerous studies have found a fair amount of consensus in the American population on the ordering of crimes by severity and comparability across respondent subgroups. There are only minor ordering differences associated with respondent race, gender, and region. Furthermore, when studies taken at different points in time are compared, the relative seriousness of crimes appear to be unchanged over decades. Crime seriousness ratings appear to have all of the characteristics of normative orders (Rossi and Berk 1985) showing relative invariance over time and across major population subgroups.

Intriguing as these results may be, it is important to note that severity studies are not about sentencing (Rossi and Henry 1980). To derive desired sentences from rated seriousness it is necessary to know how the two are related, a critical issue on which the seriousness studies are largely silent. In their study of justice in sentencing, Rossi, Simpson, and Miller

(1985) show that in rating whether a sentence is just, persons take into account many more characteristics of the criminal act than the seriousness of the crime, including such elements as the harm inflicted to victims and the prior criminal record of the offender.

Studies of the Public's Sentencing Preferences

It is surprising that the direct studies of what citizens might want as punishments for convicted felons are so few in number. One of the earliest is a 1973 study of state political and criminal justice elites[7] and the potential support among them for acceptance of alternatives to imprisonment. Berk and Rossi (1977) presented elite members with samples of systematically constructed vignettes describing convicted felons, the crimes committed, previous criminal records, and some personal characteristics of the felon. Respondents were asked to provide what they personally thought would be an appropriate sentence for each vignette. Choices included only probation, part-time confinement, or imprisonment for one or several years. In addition, respondents designated what they understood to be common sentencing practices in their state for the same crimes, using the same set of alternatives. Because this was a study of state criminal justice systems, the criminal offenses were those frequently encountered in state criminal courts. Although this was not a study of sentencing by rank-and-file citizens, original plans included citizen samples. In effect, this study was a prototype of the present one.

Another sentencing study was indirectly concerned with sentencing and focused more directly on "justice." Using a factorial survey[8] design with a sample of about 800 residents of the Boston Metropolitan Area, Rossi et al. (1985) presented respondents with sets of 50 vignettes describing convicted persons. The vignettes incorporated a set of 57 different crimes, descriptions of the convicted persons and victims (if appropriate), the felons' previous records, and some of the consequences of the crimes. In addition, each vignette was randomly given a sentence. The respondents used an 11-point scale to judge whether the sentence given was "about right," "too lenient," or "too harsh." The analysis centered on the descriptions in the vignettes and the characteristics of the respondents that led to judgments that the sentences were too severe or not severe enough. In addition, the seriousness of each of the crimes was taken from the Wolfgang et al. (1985) national survey of crime seriousness, described above. Although this study did not study directly what sentences were desired by the respondents, the results clearly indicated that the seriousness of the crimes was not the all-dominating factor in respondent judgments of the appropriateness of sentences given. In particular, the consequences of the crimes, such as injury or economic loss to victims, and the previous criminal records of the criminals weighed heavily in such judgments: crimes with severe consequences and recidivists were judged as deserving of longer sentences and more severe penalties.

A major empirical study of American preferences for sentencing was undertaken by Jacoby and Cullen in 1987 with funding from the Bureau of Justice Statistics.[9] The study is based on 1920 telephone interviews with a national probability sample of telephone-owning households. Using the factorial survey approach, each respondent was read a set of eight vignettes, each describing a crime and characteristics of the criminal and of the crime victim (if any). Respondents were asked first to rate the seriousness of the criminal event described in the vignette, utilizing the magnitude estimation method employed by Wolfgang et al. (1985) in their 1977 national study, and then to designate an appropriate punishment. If imprisonment was selected, the respondent was asked to give the term of imprisonment.

The 24 crime descriptions used in the Jacoby and Cullen study were selected from 10 crime categories, mostly so-called street crimes (e.g., car theft, burglary, robbery, assault, rape, and drug trafficking). None of the crimes used involved fraud, tax evasion, or other so-called white-collar crimes and were typical of state criminal court dockets.

Jacoby and Cullen report a fair amount of consensus on the seriousness of the crimes and a fair amount of correlation between seriousness ratings and the sentences given. However, they also report that respondents varied widely in the sentences they imposed. In short, respondents translated seriousness into punishment somewhat consistently but also varied considerably around the sample consensus. The authors also suggest that because of the lack of agreement over specific punishments for specific crimes, public opinion cannot be used as a guide for establishment of sentencing guidelines.

The research efforts described above are all of citizens' judgments without any consideration of costs and emphasize conventional sentencing options. An interesting line of research indicates that respondents' choices of appropriate punishments are modified considerably, most often in the direction of less harsh treatments, when costs and additional nonconventional sentencing options are offered. Funded mainly by the Edna McConnell Clark Foundation and conducted by the Public Agenda Foundation,[10] researchers used focus groups selected to represent significant sectors of the public.[11] A number of focus groups were assembled by telephone invitations to a random sample of telephone households.

The invited persons were assembled in groups and asked to give what they considered to be appropriate sentences to each of a set of convicted offenders, described in terms of the crime committed, and the age, previous record, and gender of the offender. Only two alternatives were offered: prison term or probation. Each group was then shown a video describing prison overcrowding in the state, costs of incarceration, and descriptions of a set of less restrictive alternatives (including "strict probation," restitution, house arrest, and boot camp). A group discussion was held after the video showing. The participants were then asked to resentence the same group of offenders with the less restrictive alternatives now added to the choices offered originally. Dramatic shifts in preferences were recorded: much less incarceration for minor crimes such as shoplifting and somewhat less incarceration for major felonies such as armed robbery.

There are many technical problems with the research conducted by the Public Agenda Foundation, including potentially large sample biases and the possibility that shifts in preferences might not have been as dramatic if participants had been allowed to choose among all alternatives in the first round of questioning. All that said, the Public Agenda Foundation research stresses that choices made in the context of fuller information can vary from those made when there is little or no information.

Some Conclusions Concerning Previous Research

The review of previous research on crime seriousness and sentencing has concentrated on presenting the salient research efforts that are somewhat related to the central purposes of the study reported in the chapters that follow. Several generalizations emerge from these studies:

- Fairly strong consensus exists on the seriousness ordering of crimes, with those involving actual or threatened physical harm to victims generally considered to be the most serious and "victimless" crimes regarded as least serious.
- In giving concrete sentences to convicted persons, citizens are not guided solely by the seriousness of the crimes but also by the convicted person's previous record and the amount of damage or loss suffered by victims.
- Consensus over sentencing is weak: considerable variation can be found in the sentences given by citizens to specific crimes.
- There appears to be little structured variation in sentencing behavior: variation in sentencing is only weakly related to socio-

demographic characteristics of citizens. Although the better educated prefer more lenient sentences than the less well educated and men prefer slightly harsher treatment than women, there are no consistent differences by other socioeconomic characteristics, or by race or ethnicity.

- There is some evidence that respondent sentencing preferences can be affected, perhaps strongly, by providing a wider range of punishment choices, information on prison conditions, and the costs of incarceration.

The studies reviewed are also silent on many issues:

- All of the studies reviewed concentrated on so-called street crimes. The lack of so-called white-collar crimes limits the research's applicability to the federal criminal code.
- None of the studies grapples with the difficult problem of the dynamics of public opinion. There is no information on:
  - how the treatment of crime issues in the mass media affects public opinion,
  - perceptions of citizens views of sentencing by political leaders,
  - the role played by advocacy groups in influencing political leaders' or the general public's views on sentencing,
  - the influence of the actual sentencing practices of the courts upon public sentencing preferences.

THE AMERICAN NORMS AND SENTENCING STUDY

The research that is at the heart of this book differs in several important ways from the previous studies described in the last section. Its primary concern will be with comparing the federal guidelines sentences with the sentences desired by the American public in order to gauge how closely they match.

The study covers 89 separate crimes, ranging in seriousness from illicit drug possession to kidnaping and includes selections from the general crime categories frequently on federal court dockets. Chapter 4 presents the central tendencies and distributions of the sentences given by Americans to persons convicted of each of the 89 crimes. In addition, we examine how subgroups of the American population vary in their sentencing preferences. The study is based on an area probability sample of American households, described more fully in Chapter 3. The wide array of federal crimes studied includes drug trafficking, fraud, environmental offenses, civil rights violations, and bank robbery.

Our study also will describe how specific features of the crime committed and characteristics of felons affect sentencing decisions. Each respondent rated 42 vignettes constituting a systematically selected sample of all the federal crimes under study. Each vignette described a person convicted of a federal crime. The crime was described in concrete terms. The vignettes also contained descriptions of certain salient features of each particular criminal act and a few characteristics of the convicted person. Each adult interviewed received an independently selected sample of all the federal crimes being studied, enabling the analysis to cover a wide range of federal crimes. Because of the way in which those vignettes were constructed, described in Chapter 2, analyses can show how sentencing decisions are affected by each of the descriptive elements incorporated into the vignettes. Such analyses uncover the implicit principles used in arriving at sentencing decisions. For example, the report addresses such concrete issues as how an offender's previous criminal record or the impact on victims affects the punishment desired.

For each vignette used in the study, a guidelines sentence was calculated, making it possible to compare guidelines sentences to the sentencing preferences of the American citizenry for all the crimes studied. The comparability analysis describes what the congruency between the two sets of sentences may be and also identifies the specific crimes over which both agree and those over which there are disagreements.

Several other contemporary sentencing issues are addressed in this research. The design allowed respondents to give death sentences to crimes for which the federal statutes do not allow that sentence. Findings are presented on how much support exists for the extension of the death penalty to a wide variety of crimes.

The study also shows how much public support there may be for such measures as sharply increased prison sentences for persistent recidivists. These findings are relevant to proposed selective incarceration measures that would severely increase sentences with each additional conviction, presumably removing habitual criminals who contribute disproportionately to the crime rate. Because the present study includes descriptions of the previous record of the convicted offenders, analysis can show how much public views of sentencing are consistent with selective incarceration proposals.

Current federal sentencing practices reflect harsh statutory punishments for drug-trafficking crimes and vary sentences according to the type of illegal drug involved. This study targets these crimes—more than one-fifth of the vignettes involve a type of drug trafficking—permitting rich and detailed comparisons between guidelines and public treatment of drug-trafficking offenders.

The present study covers crimes previously receiving little or no attention: violations of laws protecting the environment, covering the manufacture and marketing of pharmaceutical drugs, or protecting civil rights. The analyses fit these crimes into the hierarchy of crime seriousness and compare public sentencing preferences with guidelines sentences.

LIMITATIONS OF THE RESEARCH

The vignettes given to the respondents are rich in comparison to those used in conventional sample surveys. The vignettes were a few sentences long, containing important information but admittedly nowhere near the amount of information reviewed by judges in court. Consequently, the sentencing tasks given to the sample can only be regarded as a skeletal simulation of actual sentencing. This is not a study of how American citizens would sentence offenders if those citizens were judges in a federal court.

The study is also centered around "typical" cases appearing in the federal courts. Those cases which attract widespread media and public attention, such as the trial of the police officers involved in the Rodney King case or the prosecution of Ivan Boesky, are represented among the crimes presented to respondents by "generic" examples stripped of the notoriety given by media treatment and the colorfulness imparted by the personalities involved. The sentencing preferences shown in this report cannot be extrapolated to such cases.[12]

The study is also limited in the punishment alternatives offered to respondents. Alternatives such as restitution, home detention, and fines were not offered. As a consequence, the study is silent on how the American public regards such measures.

The *Guidelines Manual* is a complex document providing a rich and detailed set of rules for the guidance of federal court justices. The construction of vignettes took many, but not all of those rules into account by incorporating characteristics of the crime and criminal recognized in the guidelines as relevant to sentencing. Many of the more important sets of rules were used, but there are others that were not. Accordingly, this is not a complete study of comparability but instead a study of a subset of the guidelines sentencing rules, albeit some of the more important ones.

Finally, the sentencing decisions made by respondents were made in the abstract, without any consideration of the constraints of cost or the existence of facilities to carry them out. We did not ask them to take costs as a consideration nor did we supply any information of typical costs for any of the punishment alternatives that were offered. However, it should be noted that the guidelines also do not cover cost issues either. Hence comparisons between respondents' sentencing and the guidelines are unaffected.

PLAN OF THIS BOOK

The current chapter provides an introduction to the background of the research and the major issues addressed. Chapter 2, written by Irene Nagel, who was a member of the U.S. Sentencing Commission when it wrote the original *Guidelines Manual,* describes how the U.S. Sentencing Commission went about drafting the guidelines. Chapter 3 is devoted to describing research methodology, explaining the methods used to construct the vignettes and how the sample of households was drawn. In Chapter 4, the overall distributions of sentencing preferences are shown for each crime group and for concrete examples within each group. Mean and median sentences are presented. In Chapter 5 the degrees of congruency between public sentencing preferences and guidelines sentences are shown. Chapters 6 compares how guidelines and respondents used the described features of crimes and of the convicted offender to augment or lessen punishment. In both Chapters 5 and 6, the crimes over which there are significant amounts of disagreement are identified. The remaining chapters are devoted to showing the extent to which public sentencing preferences vary by respondent subgroups: Chapter 7 describes the differences between those respondents who agree and those who disagree with the guidelines in the treatment of convicted felons. Chapter 8 shows how sentencing varies by geographic region, gender, age, race / ethnicity, and the views respondents hold on selected political issues. Finally, Chapter 9 presents a summary of major findings and their policy implications.

NOTES

1. The detailed report to the commission can be found in Rossi and Berk (1995).

2. See, for example, Martin (1983) for a description of how the Minnesota and Pennsylvania sentencing guidelines were written.

3. These studies have been summarized in Roberts (1992) and Walker and Hough (1988).

4. The General Social Survey is a general-purpose sample survey asking a wide variety of questions on issues of interest to social scientists. The survey is currently conducted annually and financed by grants from the National Science Foundation. The National Opinion Research Center is a not-for-profit affiliate of the University of Chicago engaging in social science research using sample surveys.

5. The response "about right" was not given as an alternative to respondents. Those who gave that response rejected the given alternatives and "volunteered" that response.

6. However, the evidence is not very strong. The research cited consists of local studies centering around a few crimes with respondent samples that were not very carefully selected to be representative.

7. Defined as state elected and administrative officials whose duties had close connections with the state criminal justice system. The sample accordingly included governors, heads of relevant legislative committees, judges, members of the criminal bar, and prison wardens.

8. A factorial survey employs principles of randomized experiments to construct short vignettes of "social objects"—in this case, descriptions of convicted criminal offenders—in which the characteristics of the objects are randomly associated. See Chapter 3 for a more complete description of this approach, also used in the study reported here.

9. Preliminary findings were published in Zimmerman, Van Alstyne, and Dunn (1988). With permission of the authors, this discussion is based on a longer treatment (Jacoby and Cullen 1994) now under review for publication.

10. The research has been conducted in several states using much the same approach. A good example is the research conducted in Delaware by Doble, Immerwahr, and Richardson (1991).

11. Sample sizes consisting of about 20 focus groups are typically around 400.

12. Of course, this feature is a desirable characteristic because the present study is thereby more closely applicable to the general run of criminal cases brought before the federal courts.

CHAPTER

2

Writing the Federal Sentencing Guidelines

Ilene Nagel*

The federal sentencing guidelines (USSC, 1987) were written in response to a very specific congressional mandate. The Sentencing Reform Act of 1984 created the United States Sentencing Commission as a bipartisan, independent agency within the federal judicial branch. In passing this legislation, Congress was reacting to widespread criticisms of sentencing practices in the federal courts. These criticisms centered on problems of sentencing disparity, "dishonesty in sentencing" and perceptions of undue leniency, the latter occasioned in particular by a few well-publicized cases. Empirical and anecdotal data supported the charge that persons convicted of the same criminal charges often received widely disparate sentences. Moreover, the differences in sentencing were often not random, but rather varied systematically. Data on sentencing practices showed patterns indicating that factors that should not have affected the nature or length of offenders' sentences mattered. In particular, sentences varied by the particular judge before whom a defendant appeared, by the jurisdiction in which a defendant was prosecuted, and sometimes by the race and gender of the offender.

The large differences in the time "actually served" when compared to the sentences given in court constitute the bases for the charges of "dishonesty" leveled against the sentencing system. The problem was exacerbated by the fact that the discretionary decisions of parole boards in shortening some sentences, but not others, meant that convicted felons could not know how long their sentences would last. Perhaps more im-

* Associate Provost for Research and Dean of the Graduate School, University of Maryland at College Park. Dr. Ilene Nagel was a member of the U.S. Sentencing Commission and a participant in the writing of the federal sentencing guidelines.

portant was that the public was "misled" into believing that the court sentences were the actual punishments served by convicted felons.

Charges of undue leniency were generated by widespread impressions that persons convicted of white-collar crimes were punished less severely than those convicted of other crimes: bankers embezzling large sums were alleged to be treated less severely than thieves stealing far less.

The task assigned by Congress to the commission was to write a set of mandatory guidelines to govern the sentencing decisions of federal judges for all federal offenses. The resulting guidelines were to reform sentencing in ways that would address the criticisms that had been leveled, particularly those presented to Congress. The seven commissioners appointed by the president and confirmed by the Senate were directed to write guidelines that would prescribe sentences for each of several thousand federal crimes. The enabling legislation further prescribed that the commission's draft guidelines would be submitted to the Congress and the president for their review and approval. Once approved, the guidelines would then become binding on judges in the federal courts.

Compounding the enormity of the task of prescribing sentences for the many federal criminal offenses, were the often considerable differences among commissioners in their views about how the sentencing system should be reformed. In addition, there were differences among the many constituencies who were consulted by the commission. Federal judges were apprehensive about the potential loss of their sentencing discretion. Defense attorneys were concerned about how a new sentencing scheme would affect their ability to obtain sentences favorable to their clients. Prosecutors worried about the impact of sentencing reform on plea bargaining. Probation officers were apprehensive that their role in sentencing would be altered and perhaps diminished. Groups representing the victims of crime worried that the new sentences might not reflect the seriousness of offenses or the potential dangers posed by certain offenders.

Given the complexity and size of the task, it was somewhat remarkable that the commission took less than two years to write a comprehensive set of guidelines. A draft of the guidelines was presented to the Congress in 1987. After six months of congressional review, the guidelines were approved with no changes. The guidelines went into effect in November 1987.

In seeking to implement the guidelines now enacted into law, the commission had to run a number of political gauntlets. Perhaps the most serious was an ongoing campaign by some in the federal judiciary contesting the need for mandatory guidelines, focusing on the potential for this proposed congressional action to abrogate the power of the judiciary to set sentences. As could be expected, the defense bar also campaigned against the mandatory guideline system, motivated in large part by their concern that the guidelines would reduce their ability to persuade judges to use their discretion to mete out lower sentences.

Against this political backdrop it was no surprise that congressional approval of the 1987 guidelines unleashed a torrent of lawsuits attacking their constitutionality. Nearly 300 trial and appellate court cases were filed contesting the constitutionality of the transfer of sentencing authority from judges to the commission, and the imposition of the proposed sentencing guidelines. In 1989, to the surprise of many, an eight to one decision of the U.S. Supreme Court upheld both the constitutionality of the commission and its principal work product, the Federal Sentencing Guidelines.

On reflection, it is important to note that, among other reasons, the commission's task was formidable in scope because the federal criminal code covered nearly 3000 offenses, many more than would be typical for any state. In addition, the federal legislation was clear only on directing the commission to address the issues of disparity, dishonesty, and undue leniency in sentencing. In contrast, the principles of punishments laid out by the Congress to be followed in setting sentences were a mixture of sentencing philosophies that on close examination could be characterized as partially at odds with each other. As set forth in the 1984 act, the commission was to observe the following principles in writing the guidelines:

1. Provide just punishment for the offense (as opposed to the more traditional view of just punishment for the offender).
2. Deter would-be offenders.
3. Incapacitate criminals through imprisonment.
4. Provide opportunities for rehabilitation.

The legislation did not provide a priority ranking of these sometimes contradictory principles, leaving it up to the commission to decide how to balance these multiple goals.

Perhaps the major obstacle to following these principles in writing guidelines is that they are internally contradictory. The first principle might be interpreted to suggest that the commission should follow this sentencing philosophy, as, for example, expounded by Von Hirsch (1993). Under the "just deserts" philosophy, punishments are to be set according to the gravity of the offense and the culpability of the offender. The problem, however, is that the Congress deliberately eschewed the traditional term "just deserts," substituting instead the words "just punishment," and tied the term to the offense, not the offender. The second principle invokes the utilitarian philosophy of punishments in which sentences are fixed sufficiently high to deter would-be offenders. The third principle suggests that sentencing take into account how likely the offender is to commit additional crimes, with those likely to be career criminals slated to receive longer sentences. The fourth principle suggests that sentencing include options that might rehabilitate felons, a principle whose connection to determining what is the appropriate level of sentence severity is unclear at best.

Although each of the four principles has a vast literature expounding its underlying philosophy and how it is superior to other points of view, each literature is virtually silent on how to convert those philosophical principles into concrete types and lengths of sentences. For example, none of the sentencing philosophies prescribes when to give probation, or when to give sentences or whether sentences should be for six months or for six years. Moreover, each of the principles suffers from considerable vagueness on critical points. How does one determine what is the "just" punishment for any offense? How does one determine the optimal deterrent sentence for a given offense? Is it possible reliably to predict the future criminal behavior of a felon? How is the rehabilitative potential of a criminal to be determined?

In the mid-1980s, the findings of empirical social research on these critical issues proved to be of little practical assistance. If there was any hope that crime seriousness studies would provide a way to discern what are just punishments, a review of such studies did not sustain that promise. The massive national survey of crime seriousness (Wolfgang et al., 1985) studied mainly street crimes, and only 50 crimes in all. The crimes studied were presented without any of the complexities of actual cases. Especially frustrating was that most crime seriousness studies provided no rules about how to convert seriousness measures into specific sentences.

Much the same can be said about research on the deterrent effects of punishment. Indeed, some studies showed punishments to be more severe in jurisdictions in which crime rates were high, findings that suggest that legislatures and courts raised punishments when faced by high crime rates; these observations do not support the idea that severe punishments lead to lower crime rates.

The research on incapacitation showed how difficult it was to forecast the future criminal behavior of convicted felons. It was clear that recidivists actually commit a large proportion of all crimes, but no research was able to show that recidivism could be predicted reliably at the early stages of a criminal career. Incapacitation of felons after they had demonstrated that they followed a career of criminality obviously is too late to prevent much crime.

Finally, research on the success of rehabilitative efforts did not sustain any hope that effective treatments for criminals could be found. Indeed, the influential review of evaluations of rehabilitative efforts by Lipton, Martinson, and Wilkes (1975) came to the unhappy conclusion that "nothing works."

The early period of the commission's work was marked by lively discussions as to how to go about the task of drafting guidelines sentences for so many heterogeneous offense and offender combinations. In addition, specific offenses varied widely in concrete ways that called for variation in sentencing. For example, bank robbery could be committed with a loaded weapon or without a weapon, could involve taking hostages, or might involve elaborate advance planning. These were all features of that crime that ought to involve augmenting or diminishing sentences given, in order to respond to one or another of the principles set out as guides to the commission.

As the commission began its deliberations, it became clear that pursuing the goal of "just punishment" might lead to a different set of sentences than seeking to attain the goal of deterrence or incapacitation. Accordingly, the commission opted to break into two working groups, one of which was directed to construct a sentencing system consistent with the principle of just punishment, and the other to use the principles of crime control seeking deterrent and incapacitation goals. Both working groups were directed to draft specific guideline systems, including proposed sentences for federal crimes. The just punishments working group produced an elaborate and complicated draft. The crime control group was unable to translate that theory into actual sentences. The commission circulated the just punishment draft to various constituencies for comment. The draft received virtually no support.[1]

The failure of the working groups to produce a set of acceptable guidelines suggested that the mission of the commission was explicitly defined as serving several rather than some single goal. Any guideline system that tried to implement only a single punishment philosophy was bound to fall short in serving some of the other goals given to the commission. Although the authority vested in the U.S. Sentencing Commission to determine what were just and optimally deterrent sentences seemingly was complete, the commission's statutory authority also imposed limits. The Sentencing Reform Act of 1984 was quite specific in its numerous directives to the commission. The legislation strongly called for shifting from an offender-based system to an offense-based system. The act also contained a lengthy list of factors that should be considered or which should explicitly be ignored in setting the mandatory sentencing ranges within which judges would be required to operate.

Although there was considerable debate among commissioners concerning how the commission should interpret its statutory mandate, and on what the philosophy of sentencing should be, much of the content of the debates actually focused on whether the guidelines sentences were too severe or too lenient, or about how "reasonable persons" might suggest the sentences should be. Some of the most ardent critics of the commission's work tended to ignore the fact that the commission could not disregard the statutory prescriptives under which the commission was obliged to conduct its work. Indeed, many of the more vocal guideline critics often urged the commission to expressly disobey their congressional mandates. This last request was impossible for an agency of the judicial branch.

The Sentencing Reform Act contains many directives to the commission that state, "The Commission shall." Two of these directives are particularly relevant to the commission's guidelines. In section 994(c) of the enabling legislation, Congress directed the commission to consider whether "the community view of the gravity of the offense section 994(c)(4) should be relevant to the nature, extent, place of service, or other incidents of an appropriate sentence." A comprehensive reading of the statute in its entirety, as well as its legislative history, seems to make clear that Congress intended the commission to consider "the community's view" of the gravity of the offense in determining what are appropriate sentences. The second provision, appearing in section 994(m) states, "The Commission shall insure that the guidelines reflect the fact that, in many cases, current sentences do not accurately reflect the seriousness of the offense." This provision went on to direct the commission to ascertain the average sentences served in the past for categories of offenses and offenders, but not to be bound by the findings of those studies. The inference that Congress thought that past sentences were often unduly lenient, in the community's view, was inescapable.

Curiously the commission was given no guidance as to how to determine "the community's view." As a member of the commission, I suggested early on that a sample survey be conducted to find out the sentencing preferences of the public. For a variety of reasons, time among them, this suggestion was not heeded.

Instead of a survey of public perceptions of just sentences, the staff of the commission was directed to do research on the existing sentencing practices of the courts, by offense and offender characteristics, examining aggregate data from the courts over several years and across many jurisdictions. In the end this research on past practice came to play a crucial role in the drafting of the guidelines ultimately submitted to Congress.[2]

After considerable debate, and a careful parsing of the statutory mandate, the commission opted to draft its sentencing guidelines in accordance with four principles:

First, to reduce the complexity of dealing with the thousands of offenses defined in the federal code, the commission grouped them into a score of broad categories, each composed of similar crimes—such as Fraud, Crimes Against the Person, or Antitrust. Within each of most of these broad categories, subcategories recognized important *within-*category distinctions: for example, the broad category of Drug Offenses was further subdivided into Manufacturing and Trafficking, Drug Possession, and Regulatory Violations. More than 50 such subcategories were recognized. The intent was to establish groups of similar crimes for which similar sentences could be established.[3]

Second, for each offense, the debate as to what should be the appropriate sentencing range for a crime subtype began with an examination of the staff research findings on the mean and median times served by offenders in the past, as contrasted to the sentence pronounced in court. These summary measures for each offense were calculated by aggregating federal court sentencing data from across the nation, and over a period of years. Barring a persuasive case that argued in favor of a sentence greater or lesser than the average time served in the past for a conviction for the same offense, the guidelines sentences arrived at by the commission by and large followed past sentencing practice. The result was that for the vast bulk of offenses, the commission's proposed guidelines were in fact close approximations of past practice concerning sentences actually served.

The decision to use past sentencing practice as the basis for setting the federal sentencing guidelines had the consequence of aiding the subsequent acceptance of the guidelines by the federal judiciary, while at the same time addressing the disparity issue. Using means and medians smoothed over the variations among judges, across jurisdictions, and across types of offenders that had led to the disparity criticism. It may also have provided a way of addressing indirectly the community view to the extent that we could assume that past sentencing practices expressed the collective understanding that federal judges and parole officers had concerning community views.

The commission elected to prescribe a range of sentences for each offense, clearly allowing for judicial discretion, although in a limited way. This strategy improved somewhat the acceptance of the guidelines by the federal judiciary. Probation officers and judges could choose from within an allowable sentence range permitting some discretion for individual cases.

Third, and very important, there were some few, but highly consequential notable exceptions to this drafting principle, most of which were responses to express directives from the Congress to the commission. For example around the same time as the enactment of the Sentencing Reform

Act of 1984, Congress legislated a series of new mandatory minimum sentences, primarily for drug trafficking, and those convicted of weapon offenses. Because these mandatory minimum sentences enacted by Congress were deliberately set to increase sentences substantially beyond past sentencing practice, the commission was obliged to disregard past sentencing practice data for the crimes in question, and to prescribe guidelines sentences for offenses governed by these new mandatory minimums in accordance with the new laws. As Congress intended, this resulted in guidelines sentences for these offenses being significantly more severe than past sentencing practices. The impact on sentences for drug-trafficking offenses was particularly dramatic.

The congressional mandatory minimum legislation directed that trafficking in crack cocaine should be punished considerably more severely than trafficking in other drugs, including powder cocaine. Moreover, the mandatory minimum laws specified that penalties should increase severely with the amount of drugs involved.[4] In a similar vein, the congressional mandate of very lengthy sentences for "criminal career" recidivist offenders; and those whose offenses included the use of weapons were incorporated into guidelines sentence enhancement requirements.

Fourth, for some very few offenses—e.g., car jacking, extortion, bribery —the commission was likely influenced by the focused attention on the violence, public fear, and severe consequences associated with these offenses. Several dramatic incidents that received wide attention in the media occurred while guidelines were being written. Although no decision was ever made by the commission to pay special heed to the public's view for these offenses, as compared to the public's view on other offenses, it is likely that the publicity attendant to these offenses affected the commission's determination of what was their appropriate punishment.

In a somewhat similar vein, at the time the commission was writing the guidelines, the media also contained publicity about the equity issues concerning the relatively lenient sentences given for white-collar offenses compared to sentences for other offenses. This media attention coupled with hearings on the same topics in Congress likely affected the commission's decision to impose more severe imprisonment sentences for white-collar offenses than had been imposed under past practice.

THE COMMISSION AND ITS DELIBERATIVE PROCESS

Congress created the commission with the intent of including as commissioners persons from a variety of backgrounds, thereby creating an opportunity for a multitude of perspectives to be expressed. By statute, the commission had to be bipartisan and had to include some active federal judges and some nonjudges. As the appointment process proceeded, concerns for age, race, and gender diversity were likely included in making decisions about who would be nominated. There was allegedly some demand to appoint some members who were academics, including those with legal and with social science expertise. In the end, the seven members appointed spanned a range in their philosophy of sentencing, as well as perhaps a special concern for how the guidelines might affect, among others, the judiciary, the defense bar, prosecutors, defendants, victims, and the public.

As the commission deliberated, few formal votes were taken, although a final formal vote was taken on the draft ultimately submitted for congressional review. The commission operated more on a consensus model of deliberation than on a system of voting on individual separate actions. To be sure, there were many issues on which commissioners were divided, sometimes heatedly so, but the differences so revealed typically led the commission to find some compromise alternative with which a majority could ultimately agree.

On the final formal vote, the count was six in favor of the guidelines to be submitted to Congress and one opposed. The commissioner who voted against the guidelines objected mainly to the commission's decision to write guidelines that incorporated several sentencing philosophies instead of following a single theoretical paradigm. The dissenting commissioner also objected to the guidelines' heavy reliance upon past sentencing practice. His preference was for guidelines that adhered to the philosophical principles of "just deserts."

The fact that the commission, unlike some state guidelines commissions, could ultimately come to a nearly unanimous vote of approval for its guidelines derived in large part from its extensive solicitation of views, throughout the drafting process, from those likely to be affected by the guidelines. Moreover, this solicitation of opinions from all quarters may account partially for the findings of the research reported in this monograph. The process of seeking the views of diverse constituencies undoubtedly led to the result that the guidelines are very much in line with the public perceptions of appropriate sentences.

It is notable that members of the House and Senate largely left the commission to deliberate on its own. The rare times when members of the Congress attempted to influence the commission appeared to have been the result of efforts of commission members or commission staff to rally outside support. Congress had voted overwhelmingly to transfer the authority to set sentences from itself and the federal judiciary to this newly created commission. On only a very small number of issues, and then only under extremely rare circumstances, did they attempt to negate that decision by seeking to influence commissioners.

Although in a formal sense the authority transferred to the commission by Congress to determine what were appropriate sentences was virtually complete, there were practical constraints placed on the commission because of the political context in which it had to operate. The guidelines had to be acceptable to a fiercely bipartisan Congress, with a lengthy record of bitter and acrimonious debates on sentencing. The commission also had to avoid a presidential veto: a Republican president might not go along with the Democratic majority in the Congress. Moreover, a set of guidelines that would be rejected strongly by the federal judiciary would simply be unworkable in practice. Accordingly, any set of guidelines that did not recognize these constraints would simply become part of the historical record. There was also the specter of spectacular failures by state commissions directed to impose mandatory guidelines, but whose draft guidelines had been rejected by state legislatures. The combination of prescribed but contradictory principles and enormous practical constraints presented exceedingly difficult obstacles to overcome.

Recognizing the importance of avoiding strong objections to their work on the part of various constituencies, the commission actively sought contact with the major groups concerned with sentences. The commission actively solicited the opinions (and, implicitly, the support) of the defense bar, in particular federal defenders, on virtually every aspect of guidelines drafting, from the choice of an overall structure to the basis for discretionary departures from the guidelines. During the entire drafting period, commissioners attended defense bar meetings and met with public and private defense counsel.

Federal prosecutors were also consulted. commissioners worked closely with officials in the U.S. Department of Justice, seeking their views in particular on factors which should serve to increase or decrease sentences for each offense category. Because, by statute, the attorney general was formally an ex officio member of the commission, federal prosecutors were well represented in the guidelines writing process. In contrast, the defense bar was not represented in an ex officio capacity.

The views of the federal judiciary were informally conveyed on a regular basis to commission members, especially through commissioners who were also judges, and formally to the whole commission at the numerous public hearings held on specific topics. Moreover, judges made their opinions known through the various judicial advisory groups established by and called upon by the commission to assist it in wrestling with the full panoply of issues before it.

From its inception, the commission reached out to the public for advice in a long series of public hearings. At each hearing, specially invited experts testified as did representatives of constituent groups and any member of the public. These hearings were held on a full array of topics, across the country.

In addition to the above, the commission repeatedly submitted its successive drafts to a wide array of persons for review and comment. Although the commission was sometimes criticized for sending around a series of successive drafts, the fact that each draft significantly differed from its predecessor can be cited as evidence of the commission's responsiveness to the extensive public comment it received and reviewed.

In addition to the input from the legal community, the commission apprised itself of relevant research through the creation of a Research Advisory Committee. The commission's permanent staff also included a considerable number of social scientists experienced in conducting social science research on criminal law and practice. These social scientists were recruited to be on the permanent staff of the commission, despite its being a judicial branch agency. Social science expertise consisting of the Research Advisory Committee, a social science staff, along with the presence of two commissioners who themselves were social scientists, led to extensive consultation with the community of researchers and scholars who dealt with law and social science issues, consisting of both law professors and social scientists.

In sum, this was not a commission that took the vast authority to act given it by Congress as a mandate to proceed solely on its own. Rather, this was a commission that recognized that the decision as to what is an appropriate sentence had historically been one of the most contentious issues in Congress, a question upon which the judiciary was divided, and a subject upon which reasonable persons sometimes vehemently and even violently disagreed. In recognition of this divided opinion, and the potential reasonableness of all sides, the commission sought to find a way to balance the competing views, without abdicating its responsibility to carry out its congressional mandate.

At its best, the commission's approach was to rely on a mixture of past sentencing practice tempered by contemporaneous considerations. At worst, it was a best guess at what might be right and workable in a first draft of a guidelines system. The commission realized that the draft guidelines were never intended to be fixed forever, and that they would surely benefit from the refinement and revision, which would come with time, experience, and the wisdom gleaned from reflection and research. That this patchwork of compromises reflecting past and future concerns resulted in guidelines remarkably consistent with the public's view, as finally measured (and reported in this volume), suggests that if a diverse body solicits a multitude of opinions, it can ultimately find the nation's normative pulse.

REFLECTIONS ON THE FINDINGS OF THE ROSSI AND BERK STUDY

Throughout the years following the full implementation in 1989 of the sentencing guidelines, a frequently raised issue at commission meetings focused on how closely the guidelines reflected the community view about what appropriate sentences are. The most vocal critics of the guidelines presumed without question that the guidelines were unduly harsh and went far beyond levels of severity that the public would endorse. Often these critics went on to allege that the guidelines reflected only the views of congressional representatives and senators, pandering to a public whipped into a frenzy of fear of criminal predation. Seemingly, there is an "appropriate" and an "inappropriate" public opinion, according to how closely public opinion comes to the views of those making this judgment. In the absence of any firm empirical evidence, whether the guidelines sentences exceeded, were consistent with, or were below the public perceptions of just sentences seemed to be judgments that could be made with impunity, if not credibility.

If the charge that the guidelines were wholly at odds with the community's view of appropriate sentences were true, then the study reported in this volume should report great differences between the public's view of appropriate sentences, and the sentencing guidelines. In contrast, those more willing to take a dispassionate view of sentencing might predict that the commission's sentencing prescriptions rather reflect fairly closely the public's true concern for escalating random violence, the decline of confidence in the criminal justice system to mete out appropriate punishment in accordance with the severity of the crime, and the generalized fear of crime victimization. If this is the case, we should expect the study to find a fairly close relationship between the public's views on sentencing, and the federal sentencing guidelines. Before this research was concluded, there was no way of knowing whether the commission had erred or had somehow found the nation's moral pulse.

As will be found in the chapters to follow, the latter thesis finds more support than the former, but with some notable exceptions. On the whole, the research reports an impressive degree of consistency between the guidelines sentences and public views. This finding cannot be minimized.

With some few notable and explainable exceptions, the commission did apparently manage, through its various procedures and widespread solicitation of views, to discern the central tendencies in public opinion, promulgating a sentencing system that seems highly justified, if we hold to the belief that sentencing policy should be isomorphic with public opinion.

A review of the exceptions to the above noted finding is interesting and revealing. First, Rossi and Berk find that the public does not concur with the dramatic distinctions in sentences required by Congress for drug traffickers, depending on the specific drug involved. In fact, Rossi and Berk find that the public strongly disagrees with the very severe guidelines sentences for those convicted of distributing crack cocaine. One can speculate that were the public to become informed fully about the tragic violence and community devastation more often associated with the distribution of crack cocaine versus, for example, marijuana, it might support the more severe sentences for crack traffickers mandated by Congress, especially for those engaged in ancillary violence. But of course, that would only be speculation. Moreover, the very disturbing differential racial impacts might alter public opinion. For now all we know is that there is scarce support among the public for the distinctions made in the guidelines among the several illegal drugs.

The other exceptions noted in this book involve environmental crimes, civil rights offenses, bribery, and extortion, each of which has higher guideline sentences than the public deems appropriate. The higher sentences for environmental crimes can, I believe, be explained by the publicity attendant to the *Exxon Valdez* spill during the guidelines drafting period, and the heightened concern for deterring intentional environmental pollution, a concern that characterized the late eighties. The commission was persuaded that white-collar offenses could be deterred by the threat of severe sanctions.

The differences between the guidelines and the study's findings with respect to civil rights offenses may sadly reflect a difference between publicly and privately expressed views. Those in positions of authority rightly express repugnance at civil rights violations, and deem serious sentences appropriate for those convicted of these offenses. Aggregate measures of public opinion, recorded in private, may regrettably reflect the acceptance of these offenses as not so serious, when one's views are not publicly recorded.

Finally, the hiatus between the public's view of appropriate sentences for bribery and extortion, and the guidelines is, I believe, a function of a particularly zealous argument made at the time the guidelines were being drafted, for higher sentences than were meted out in the past for these offenses, for two reasons. First, bribery often involved bribery of public officials; representatives of the Department of Justice argued convincingly to the commission that sentences for these offenders had to be severe to deter this conduct, else the government enterprise would be severely compromised. In the case of extortion, the argument was premised on the importance of several cases recently decided during the guidelines drafting period against major organized crime officials.

In sum, in all but the civil rights cases, the higher guidelines sentences were deliberate decisions by the commission to break with past practice, decisions that were probably influenced by current events. One may speculate that had the present study been conducted in 1985–1987, those differences might not have appeared. Just as the commission was likely influenced by contemporaneous reports of crime, so probably was public opinion. Of course, we do not know the extent to which public opinion changes in response to changes in the salience of particular crimes.

The remarkably high correspondence between the public views and the guidelines sentences is based on the central tendencies in Americans' views. That said, it should be noted that the variations around the means and medians are considerable. For almost every crime studied there are persons who would desire harsher punishment and some who would recommend greater leniency. Almost any view on sentencing can find some resonance among some sector of the American public. The guidelines views may come closer to where most Americans stand, but there is support for other viewpoints. The implication is that neither the guidelines nor this study will put an end to discussions about how to treat criminal offenders. And perhaps that is as it should be. Setting public policy remains a congressional responsibility. Researchers and federal agencies can only serve to inform the Congress, the ultimate arbiter and policymaker.

NOTES

1.   A detailed account of the experiences of the working groups can be found in Nagel (1990).

2.   Nagel (1990) contains a detailed account of the research undertaken by the commission staff and how the findings were used.

3.   These categories are reflected in the research reported in subsequent chapters under the terms "Crime Types" and "Crime Examples."

4.   The guidelines contain a complex detailed schedule for determining drug-trafficking sentences that recognizes fine distinctions among the amounts of drugs trafficked. No other section of the guidelines dealing with other offenses is as detailed.

3

Design and Data Analysis

INTRODUCTION

The major objective of this study was to compare guidelines rules for determining sentences and the resulting sentences with the rules and sentences preferred by the American public. The guidelines rules provide for sentencing felons according to the specific crimes committed, some of the circumstances of the crimes, and the prior records of the felons involved. Does the American public use similar rules in deciding how felons should be punished? For example, the guidelines give much longer sentences to trafficking in crack cocaine than for trafficking in cocaine in powder form. Do Americans make the same distinction? The rules for setting sentences for convicted felons prescribed in the guidelines are quite complicated. Consequently, a survey designed to ascertain whether the same (or different) rules are followed by Americans will also be complicated to a greater extent than can be incorporated easily into conventional sample surveys. As described below, we use an approach that accommodates well to the complexity of this task.

A subsidiary objective was to describe how Americans differ in their sentencing preferences. Is there a substantial amount of consensus on how convicted felons should be sentenced? Are there systematic differences in sentencing preferences by age, region, socioeconomic status, or ethnicity?

To carry out credible research bearing on these issues requires that sound measurement procedures be designed and implemented, that a representative sample of Americans be obtained, and that the data collected be properly analyzed. Sound measurement procedures are essential. If the measurement procedures are inadequate, either because they fail to capture the phenomena of interest or because they are dominated by measurement errors, then it matters little what the sample is or how the data are analyzed. If the sample does not represent the American population, one cannot draw any useful conclusions about what the American people think about federal sentencing. And if the data are improperly analyzed, there is nothing appropriate to generalize about. This chapter considers each of these methodological concerns: measurement, sampling, and data analysis.

INSTRUMENT DESIGN

As described in Chapter 1, conventional research seeking to elicit the public's views on criminal sanctions typically employs questionnaires with batteries of brief questions (Roberts 1992; Innes 1993). For example, conventional questions are often worded as follows:

"Do you favor the death penalty for people who are convicted of murder?"
"What is the appropriate sentence for bank robbery?"
"Do you favor truth in sentencing laws that require prisoners to serve their full terms?"
"Do you favor life imprisonment without the possibility of parole for offenders convicted for a third time of violent crimes?"

Although these kinds of questions may provide data of interest to politicians, administrators, and policymakers who want to understand public responses to political issues phrased as clichés that can be easily incorporated into "sound bites," such questions are not appropriate for this study. As prescribed in the guidelines, federal sentences are explicitly determined by a number of factors, including specified characteristics both of the crime and the offender. In the guidelines it matters if a firearm is used, and it matters whether the offender has had prior prison terms; sentences are adjusted accordingly. Consequently, asking a question about the appropriate sentence for bank robbery cannot cast much light on the public's agreement with the guidelines because there is no single sentence for bank robbery under the guidelines; the sentences for that crime vary with whether firearms were used, how much was robbed, and the criminal record of the convicted bank robbers.

Accordingly, for a question such as, "What do you think is the right sentence for bank robbery?" the answer that corresponds to the guidelines sentence is, "It depends!" In short, simple questions cannot be responsive to the mandate to study the correspondence or lack of correspondence between public opinion on sentencing for federal crimes and the sentences prescribed in the guidelines.

Simple "one-liner" questions about sentencing will fail to capture the views of thoughtful respondents who appreciate that, to a significant degree, sentences must vary according to the nature of the crime and the background of the offender. Individuals who might support long prison terms for individuals convicted of smuggling illegal immigrants into the United States for profit might support short prison terms for individuals who illegally smuggle family members into the United States. If the motive for the smuggling is not specified, respondents may make assumptions about circumstances or motives, with sentences ranging accordingly. Both possibilities could undermine the goals of our study. The more general point is that if you ask a simple question, you get an overly simple answer. That does not necessarily mean that the respondents are simple in their appraisal of crime events, but only that the question did not allow them to reveal the full complexity of their reasoning. That most Americans will answer simple-minded questions with matching simple-minded answers probably reflects that much casual talk about public issues remains at about that level of complexity and that conventional survey interviews are casual rather than deep interpersonal encounters.

The guidelines require that a sentencing judge take many aspects of a case into account in arriving at an appropriate punishment. Accordingly we need to know whether those aspects are important to the public and how much each should count. Our study had to be designed to provide an understanding of the rationales used by the American public when deciding on appropriate federal sentences. What are the impacts of factors that the public actually takes into account? Does it matter for the sentence given if the offender has a family to support? How important is it that the offender was the mastermind behind a savings and loan fraud as compared to simply participating in a fraud designed by others? How much does it matter if the actions of environment polluters destroy wildlife habitats or if their actions had no discernible effects on such habitats? In short, we are interested in learning how the American public thinks about crime. If the questionnaire does not give respondents the opportunity to think, the data collected will be irrelevant.

In addition, information on how people think about sentencing is relevant to theories of sentencing. For example, if the American public follows the logic of deterrence theories in sentencing white-collar offenders, that should be manifest by their giving prison terms to white-collar criminals that increase proportionately with the amount of money illegally taken. If the public's sentencing patterns are insensitive to that aspect of crime, then the reasoning of deterrence theory does not describe the way that Americans think about crime.

In summary, designing an appropriate measurement instrument requires that plausible variations in different kinds of crime be represented. It was for this reason that we decided to use the *factorial survey* approach in constructing the survey instrument for this survey. Furthermore, the factorial survey approach was devised with a primary objective of measuring norms (Rossi and Nock 1982; Rossi and Berk 1985).[1] The method is particularly suited for obtaining judgments on complex issues in a form that can be delivered to a large number of subjects.

The factorial survey is based on combining sample survey and experimental methodologies. Its base in survey methodology allows for the use of large samples that can be representative of the American population. Its roots in the experimental tradition accommodate to the complexity of issues involving norms.

In general, the factorial survey approach involves presenting to respondents short descriptions, or vignettes, of complex phenomena to be studied and asking respondents to make judgments about each vignette. Each vignette is a complex, multidimensional description of some person (in this case, a convicted felon) or event. So far the factorial survey resembles other conventional survey approaches that often use vignettes. The critical difference lies in how the vignettes are constructed and in the variety of descriptions that are permitted in the factorial survey. The factorial vignettes are constructed by systematically varying the critical features of the objects they describe. When respondents provide evaluations of each vignette, the contrasts between those evaluations provide empirical clues as to the weighting given by respondents to each vignette feature. For example, if vignettes describing crimes in which guns are used receive sentences that are on the average two years longer than vignettes describing crimes in which a gun is not used, one can estimate the average weight given by respondents to the use of a gun as two years.

Actual crimes are composed of a number of features; whether a gun is used is but one possible feature. Consequently, factorial survey methods rely on vignettes that are composed of a number of features. These features are called dimensions. Whether a gun is used could be one dimension. Whether a bystander is injured could be another dimension. How much money is taken could be yet another dimension.

Each dimension is composed of two or more categories, known as *levels*. Each level for a given dimension represents how the vignettes vary along that dimension. To repeat the gun example, a dimension called Weapon Use might have two levels: (1) used a gun, (2) did not use a gun.

The dimension called Amount of Money Taken might have five levels: (1) $100, (2) $500, (3) $1000, (4) $5000, and (5) $10,000.

The vignette dimensions are assembled just as in a factorial experiment: hence the name. The dimensions are fully crossed with one another. That is, all possible combinations of levels from each of the dimensions are represented in the set of vignettes available for use. The design is balanced, which means that the factors are by design independent of one another. This can lead to important simplifications when the data are later analyzed.

Continuing with the two dimensions discussed above, crossing the weapon dimension and the amount of money dimension leads to ten possible combinations of weapon use and amount of money taken. By adding more dimensions, fully crossed, one can build up a large number of combinations of levels that can together represent quite complicated crime descriptions. For example, one might describe a bank robbery in which the offender threatened a teller with a gun, but did not injure the teller or bystanders in any manner, and got away with $10,000. In the getaway attempt, the car jumped a sidewalk and killed a pedestrian.

Nor are we restricted to crime characteristics alone. Characteristics of the offender can be added to a bank robbery vignette. One dimension might be the offender's number of prior felony convictions, and another might be whether the offender had a family to support; both might affect the sentence respondents give.

A critical feature of the factorial survey approach is that the dimensions are combined to form vignettes by randomly picking levels out of each of the dimensions. The advantage of this procedure is the very practical gain in being able to use a relatively large number of dimensions. The more dimensions used, the richer the descriptions in vignettes.

In principle, one can keep adding dimensions, allowing for increasingly complex and richer vignettes. However, at some point the amount of information exceeds what respondents can digest. Respondents will then tend to concentrate on the few dimensions that are salient to them, ignoring the items of lesser saliency. Some respondents will have their patience tried to the extent that they will refuse to provide judgments. It is critical, therefore, to exclude all but the most important dimensions. Experience suggests that respondents can usually handle three or four dimensions with ease, and often can handle many more. Even three or four dimensions can produce very complex and realistic descriptions in some research settings. Much depends on who the respondents are and on the complexity of the material included. A factorial survey of physicians using vignettes depicting ethical dilemmas encountered in medical practice can be quite complex, because physicians are both familiar with such problems and, as a group, have above-average cognitive skills. It clearly matters whether the vignettes characterize situations with which the respondent is familiar. Respondents can generally handle more complex descriptions if the topic is one with which they are familiar. Fortunately for this survey, crimes are well known.

With just a few dimensions, the number of unique combinations possible can become very large. For example, if we study reactions to felons convicted of 50 different crimes, by offenders with from one to five previous convictions, there are 250 different combinations. If we add other dimensions, say three levels depicting the use of weapons in the crime, and five different consequences of the crimes, the number of combinations jumps to 3750. Clearly, few respondents would stand for responding to that many vignettes. Factorial surveys handle that difficulty by sampling the combinations, presenting each respondent with a separately drawn sample of all possible vignettes. Pooling the responses from many respondents results in a large sample of vignettes that can sustain analyses centering on large numbers of crimes and many dimensions describing those crimes.

Beyond the issue of vignette complexity, there will always be important wording issues. Sometimes what seem to be rather subtle differences on how vignettes are introduced or how the vignettes are phrased can affect the distribution of responses. Thus, one or more pretests are vital in order to ensure that the vignettes are properly understood by respondents who will vary in their knowledge and verbal skills.

In addition to the question of how much information respondents can evaluate in any given vignette is the question of respondent burden: how many vignettes overall each respondent can evaluate. With even a relatively few fully crossed dimensions, the number of combinations may become too large for any respondent to consider. The problem is that when the number of vignettes is too large, respondent burden becomes excessive. Depending on the complexity of each vignette, the upper bound that any one respondent may be willing and able to consider is likely to be somewhere between 20 and 50 vignettes. The factorial survey approach involving sampling vignettes makes it possible to reduce the number each respondent is asked to judge. With a large sample of respondents, quite complex vignettes can be studied without imposing an undue burden on any respondent.

Typically, a simple random sample of vignettes is presented to each respondent. This turns the factorial design into a fractional factorial design and guarantees that, on the average, there will be no association between (a) the different vignettes' characteristics and (b) characteristics of the respondent and characteristics of the vignettes. Just as in the fully crossed design, random sampling greatly simplifies later data analyses.

Choosing which dimensions should be included in a factorial survey usually involves drawing upon prior knowledge of the topic, past research, and whatever social science theory may be relevant. Because this study is concerned with comparing the public's views on sentencing with the guidelines, the relevant dimensions are given in the guidelines. Although we did not incorporate all of the dimensions that are in the guidelines, we did include most of the important ones, i.e., those that count heavily in calculating the guidelines sentences. Some of the dimensions included, such as the sex of the offender, are not used in the guidelines but were included because the commission was interested in learning how those dimensions might affect how the public weighs them in calculating sentences.

The design of the study and the feasibility of the factorial survey approach as a data collection modality were tested in a large pretest designed by the authors and fielded by the Social Science Research Institute of University of California at Los Angeles. Using a quota sample, 200 respondents were chosen to fill out a booklet containing 50 vignettes. The analysis of the pretest data led to a reduction in the size of the respondent vignette sample size and changes in the wording of alternatives. Analysis of the resulting pretest data indicated that the factorial survey approach was not only feasible but promised to provide fruitful findings.

The dimensions used in the this study are shown in Appendix A. The major dimension is Crime Type, which consists of twenty major crime categories, ranging from drug trafficking to kidnaping. These were selected from among the major federal crimes considered in the guidelines. The crime types chosen represent either a major portion of the case load in federal courts (such as drug trafficking) or are of special interest (such as environmental violations). Within each of the major crime categories, there are a number of levels, each constituting an instance of that crime category. For example, drug trafficking is represented by 20 different levels, each indicating the kind of illegal drug involved and the dollar value of the drugs trafficked.

For each crime category, there are typically one or more additional dimensions, often specific to that crime category. For example, the drug-trafficking vignettes include dimensions describing the role of the felon in drug trafficking and the use of weapons in the crime. The fraud crime category includes a dimension for the amount of money lost by victims.

In addition, each vignette also contains a short description of the convicted felon consisting of a level from each of the following dimensions: (1) Previous Felony Record, (2) Family Ties, (3) Employment, (4) Gender.

Thus, respondents are asked to take into account not only the specific offense, but also the background of the offender, before passing sentence. An offender's previous record plays an important role in the guidelines, modifying sentences for all crimes. In contrast, the other three offender attributes are not explicitly recognized in the guidelines as grounds for modifying sentences. These three offender characteristics were included because it was thought that the public might consider them relevant to sentencing.

In principle, it is desirable to allow levels in any one dimension to be picked without taking into account the other levels from other dimensions included in a vignette. In practice, it is often necessary to restrict certain combinations in order to avoid empirically impossible combinations. Although such exclusions can complicate the analysis, they avoid presenting respondents with vignettes that are bizarre or that make little sense. For example, it is not possible to have a police officer with a prior felony record, so previous record is not used with crimes in which a police officer is the perpetrator. A few such restrictions were built into the vignettes as the documentation in Appendix A indicates.

As can be seen in the vignette examples in Chapter 4 (Figure 4.1), the task given to respondents was to mark a desired sentence for each vignette. Respondents were asked to choose between (1) probation, (2) a prison term, and (3) a death sentence. For prison term, respondents were also asked to provide a sentence length in months for sentences up to a year and in years for sentences over one year. The inclusion of death sentences complicates issues and in particular, poses some difficult data analysis problems, as we address shortly. However, it was important to include the option of a death sentence. Although when the study was designed, execution was not recognized in the guidelines as a recommended sentence, for some federal crimes covered by the guidelines, judges were allowed to depart from the guidelines sentence and give a death sentence, particularly when deaths of victims or others resulted from the crime. The pretest results indicated that a small number of respondents also wanted to have the opportunity to register death as a choice. In short, the death sentence is clearly part of current public debates about punishments for some crimes and had to be addressed.

In assembling vignettes, the factorial survey approach permits specifying the probability with which each crime type appears in the vignettes and the probabilities for each dimension and each level within dimensions. To support more detailed analyses of the most common crimes, the selection probabilities were set so that the more common crimes, dimensions, and levels appeared more frequently among our vignettes. For example, the probability that a vignette would describe a drug-trafficking crime was about 0.21, whereas the probability that the vignette contain an immigration crime was about 0.052. Most of the crime probabilities were around 0.05.

In a similar fashion, the probability was fixed at 0.80 that the offender was a man and at 0.20 that the offender was a woman. We wanted the set of vignettes received by each respondent to seem plausible, and a set in which female offenders were as common as male offenders might well have seemed very unrealistic.

A total of 101,040 vignettes were generated for the study.[2] These vignettes were incorporated in 2526 independently generated booklets. Each booklet contained 40 vignettes. Respondents were asked to read each vignette, and to write the sentences they wanted for each vignette in the booklet. These booklets, in turn, were the source of the sentencing information we analyze in the chapters to follow. In addition, two vignettes were presented to the respondent before the booklet was given to acquaint the respondent with the nature of the task and to provide interviewers with an opportunity to explain the task in great detail. These two practice vignettes were identical for all respondents and represented a serious crime and a minor crime.

To better understand the rationale behind the sentences given by respondents, we also designed a brief questionnaire to obtain some biographical information on respondents and some measures of attitudes that might be related to sentencing preferences. The questionnaire was administered orally by interviewers who recorded answers on the instrument. The respondents were asked about past involvement with the criminal justice system, personal experiences with crimes, and their opinions of several related political issues, such as their views on civil liberties.

In addition, the usual assortment of background questions was asked concerning socioeconomic status and demographic characteristics. A copy of the questionnaire can be found in Appendix B.

SAMPLING AND DATA COLLECTION

Data collection for this survey took place over several months starting in January 1994. Under contract with the U.S. Sentencing Commission, the Response Analysis Corporation designed the sample for the study and deployed its field staff to conduct the needed interviews, using improved versions of the pretested survey instruments.

The sample design for the study called for 1500 face-to-face interviews with a sample representative of adults (18 years old or older) living within the continental United States and having sufficient English-language reading ability to handle the sentencing task. In designing the sampling strategy, three design issues had to be resolved: First, there was a need to balance the lower costs of cluster sampling against the loss in precision that necessarily follows from choosing households in clusters (compared to probability sampling without clustering). The overall plan was to employ a multistage cluster sample using (1) primary sampling units, usually counties or census-defined Metropolitan Statistical Areas,[3] (2) census tracts or enumeration districts, (3) blocks, (4) households, and (5) one respondent within each household. At each level, probability sampling was used. Given budget constraints, a key decision was how many secondary units to select. A reasonable compromise was to sample 100 specific locations. Fewer sites would have reduced costs, but produced less precise population estimates. More sites would have produced more precise population estimates, but at a higher price.

Second, respondents had to be selected at random within households in a manner that did not increase nonresponse. A systematic procedure was used to assure that eligible persons in the sampled households had equal probabilities of being chosen as respondents.

Third, the booklet of vignettes was to be self-administered. Consequently, literacy in English was essential. (All of the booklets were in English.[4]) Individuals who could not speak or understand English were relatively easy to identify. Individuals with limited English literacy skills were a challenge to identify. Moreover, the process of inquiring or "testing" risked alienating respondents and increasing the refusal rate.

The solution employed presented each respondent with two vignettes that were the same for each respondent. These were used to gauge the literacy of respondents and provide practice in evaluating the crime vignettes. Respondents who could not read the two vignettes readily acknowledged it. For respondents who could apparently manage the material, interviewers reviewed the sentences given for the two practice vignettes and asked about any apparent anomalies. In particular, one of the crimes was quite serious (bank robbery using a gun) and the other was much less serious (possession of a small amount of marijuana for personal use). If a longer sentence was given for marijuana possession than for bank robbery, the interviewer asked for a brief explanation. Any reasonably cogent explanation was accepted, and the respondent was encouraged to proceed. If the explanation was totally unreasonable, the respondent was asked whether he/she would be able to read and comprehend the booklet with 40 crime vignettes. If the respondent indicated an inability to undertake the task, the interview was terminated.

This method seemed to work well. Overall, designated respondents in 89% of the appropriate housing units (occupied non–group quarters) were eligible for the study. Of the ineligible, 60% did not speak English and 40% were insufficiently literate. And only 2.5% of the total needed to justify their answers to the two vignettes.

Table 3.1 shows the disposition of all the 3018 housing units chosen in the sample. Repeated attempts were made by the interviewing staff to contact all the chosen units. Some of the units (8.6%) were not usable because they were vacant or were group quarters. Others could not be contacted after many attempts (9.2%) and others (17.5%) refused to be interviewed sufficiently to determine their eligibility for the study. There were also households that were ineligible (7.2%). Counting those who completed the interview as a proportion of those who were eligible, the overall completion rate was 70.1%, an acceptable response rate by current standards.

Although the resulting sample is a probability sample, the probability of selection was not equal for all potential respondents. Because this is a household sample, respondents living in multi-adult households had smaller probabilities of selection than those who lived in single-adult households. To represent the total eligible population properly, it was necessary to devise a set of weights to compensate for those inequalities. A base weight was calculated, reflecting the probability of selection of each respondent through the various stages of selection. In brief, the base weight for each respondent was computed as the product of the inverses

Table 3.1. Sample Disposition for All Sampled Housing Units in the Study

Total Initial Sample	3018	100%
Unusable Units	262	8.6
Vacant Dwellings	218	7.2
Group Quarters	44	1.4
Usable Units	2786	91.4
Eligibility Unknown	814	26.7
No Contact	282	9.2
Initial Refusal	532	17.5
Eligible	1753	57.4
Completed	1737	57.4
Not Completed	16	0.5
Ineligible	219	7.2
Language Barrier	131	4.3
Not Literate	88	2.9
Age < 18	0	0.0
Eligibility Rate	1753 / (1753 + 219)	89
Usability Rate	2786 / (2786 + 262)	91.4
Response Rate	1737 / (1753 + 724)	70.1

of the probabilities of selection at each of the five stages. Even if the response rate had been 100%, the base weight would have been necessary; it follows from the design of the multistage sample.

In addition, a weight was computed for each respondent, to correct for differential response rates among subgroups of respondents. Respondents were each classified into one of 27 weighting classes, defined by crossing the nine census divisions with three community size strata. In effect, this strategy assumes that the characteristics of nonrespondents are the same as the respondents within each of the 27 strata. That is, the strategy assumes that nonrespondents in small towns in New England are like other small-town New Englanders. This assumption is certainly false if taken literally, but closer to being right than most other assumptions. Similar weighting strategies are routinely used in the analysis of many sample surveys.

Finally, poststratification weights were constructed. These weights force the weighted marginals to mirror a set of target marginals for the relevant population from the latest available Current Population Survey. The target marginals were for (1) age, (2) gender, (3) race (black or white), and (4) census division. For example, respondents under 30 years of age were a bit underrepresented in the sample, compared to the figures from Current Population Survey. The poststratification weight for respondents under 30 increased their representation accordingly. This assumes, of course, that the Current Population Survey is more representative than our sample. Although the larger sample size for the Current Population Survey guarantees smaller sampling errors, that leaves unaddressed non-response and response errors. Thus, we have no way of knowing whether the poststratification weights really improve matters. In any event, these poststratification weights were not used in the analyses.

In short, weights were computed that, in principle, can reduce possible biases in our sample. We stress the phrase "in principle," however. Only the weights to adjust for the probability of selection in the multistage sample are guaranteed to improve matters. The other weights rest on untestable assumptions that could conceivably make things worse. Fortunately, the results we report in later chapters change little whether weighted or not.

DATA ANALYSIS

There are three major complications that need to be considered in any analysis of the vignette crime data. Although these will be discussed in far more depth when they are faced in subsequent chapters, we discuss them initially now.

Respondents were allowed to designate one of three sentence types: probation, imprisonment, and death. If the respondent chose imprisonment, he or she was asked how long the desired sentence was. A small but significant proportion of respondents wrote "life" in lieu of designating a number of years in prison. If probation and prison are represented as sentence lengths, they may be combined into a single variable (with probation coded as 0 years in prison) and analyzed in a relatively routine fashion. Although the proper functional form and disturbance distribution remain an issue in part because of the lower boundary of zero, time in prison is a perfectly good equal-interval variable. However, life imprisonment has no fixed length, which means that the sentence length equivalent of a life sentence does not exist. In addition, a death sentence has no apparent sentence length equivalent of any kind. Hence, the first data analysis problem was how properly to fit life and death sentences into a variable representing sentencing severity.

Note that the coding problem for a life sentence and a death sentence involves sentences at the extreme right tail of the sentencing distribution. The downside is that whatever values are chosen, they are likely to have large effects on summary statistics that use all of the information in the data (e.g., means). Because whatever decisions were made about coding must be somewhat arbitrary, so are the resulting summary statistics. For example, the mean sentence for kidnaping in which the victim is killed could vary substantially depending on whether a death sentence is coded at 30, 50, or 100 years.

The upside is that summary statistics that either ignore values at the extremes of the distribution (e.g., medians) or "downweight" them (e.g., robust measures of location) provide a potential solution. To illustrate, if the sentences given for a particular crime are 5, 10, and 15 years, the median sentence is 10 years even if the sentence of 15 years is replaced by a sentence of 150 years. Of course, using medians means that some information is necessarily lost, but much of that information comes from the somewhat arbitrary coding of extremely severe sentences.

Matters are somewhat more complicated in a regression context. As outliers in the y-direction, extreme sentences will affect the intercept and goodness-of-fit measures. But when paired with outliers in the x-direction, they become potential leverage points that can dramatically affect the estimated regression hyperplane. For example, if respondents with only a grade school education are especially inclined to give death sentences for trafficking drugs, this small number of respondents can substantially affect the regression fit for the entire rest of the sample (i.e., because they are both educational and sentencing outliers). Technical fixes for leverage points are available but controversial (e.g., bounded influence regression or least median squared regression).

In the substantive chapters to follow, various options for analyzing the sentences given are considered at length. We will translate arbitrarily both life imprisonment and death into sentence length equivalents. But, when necessary, we analyze the data in a fashion so that the ordinal positions in the sentence length scale matter; we apply statistical procedures that exploit the properties of medians. Hence, the only assumptions are that life imprisonment is worse than the longest sentence in which sentence length is specified, and that death is worse than life in prison. While this takes care of outliers in the y-direction, outliers in the x-direction are more problematic. We deal with these substantively, including them in the analyses when it makes substantive sense, and excluding them from the analyses when it does not.

The second data analysis problem derives from possible nonindependence among the sentences given by individual respondents. Each respondent contributes 42 vignettes to the analysis. If individual respondents have tendencies to give sentences to their vignettes that are individually specific, such as tending to give higher or lower sentences, their vignette responses would be correlated with each other. In technical terms, one risks within-respondent correlated disturbances for almost any analysis that treats vignettes as the units of analysis. In effect, the vignette format is a repeated measures design (i.e., 40 randomly selected crime vignettes per respondent), and a hierarchical model is implied (i.e., vignettes nested with respondents).

It is well-known that correlated disturbances lead to optimistic estimates of the standard errors in which one risks underestimating the role of sampling variation. Accordingly, the effective sample is smaller than the nominal sample. In later chapters, various analytic options for countering the resulting bias are considered in detail, including statistical procedures that adjust for the optimistic standard errors. However, suffice it to say that with a nominal sample size defined as the number of respondents times the number of vignettes per respondent, the loss of power that might be caused by correlated disturbances is far too little to make an important difference. Effects that are large enough to be of substantive interest have very large t-values that would be well over 2.0 if the effective sample size rather than the nominal sample size were used.

The final data analysis problem is whether to use the vignette or the respondent as the unit of analysis. The formal solution in principle is to employ a hierarchical model in which both units are used at once. Vignettes are the micro units and respondents are the macro units. However, our response variable does not meet the assumptions of conventional hierarchical models (i.e., special cases of the general linear model). And as described in Chapter 5, our use of robust regression procedures to buffer the results against the arbitrary coding of life sentences and death sentences precludes hierarchical analyses. Unfortunately, hierarchical modeling has not been extended to the robust methods we employ.

Therefore, separate analyses are conducted for each of the two possible units of analysis. This approach is justifiable in part because, by design, each respondent receives his or her own simple random sample of vignettes. Consequently, characteristics of the vignettes are independent of characteristics of respondents, and the two kinds of units can be analyzed separately without bias.

SUMMARY

The approach used in this study to compare guidelines and public views of sentencing federal felons was to use a factorial survey. Face-to-face interviews were conducted with a probability sample of adult Americans. We measured the respondents' sentencing preferences by having each give sentences to persons convicted of a sample of federal crimes described in vignettes that described the crime in concrete details and provided information about the felon. The factorial survey approach made it possible to use fairly complex vignettes designed to facilitate the calculation of the weighting principles used by respondents in assessing the persons described in the vignettes in arriving at their sentences.

NOTES

1. The factorial survey approach has been employed successfully in studies of a variety of American norms, including kinship obligations (Rossi and Rossi 1990), distributive justice in income (Jasso and Rossi 1977), sexual harassment (Rossi and Weber-Burdin 1983), public welfare payments (Will 1993), just criminal punishments (Rossi et al. 1985), and the social standing of households and families (Rossi and Nock 1978).

2. The vignettes were produced by a computer program that printed out separate vignette booklets to be used by respondents (Weber, Sellers, and Rossi 1988). In assembling each vignette, the program routines randomly chose levels from each dimension, adding text to produce a grammatically correct vignette. The vignettes were stored as a text file, which later could be used to print out the

booklets, and as a numerically coded file, which could serve as the analysis data file when respondent answers were added. The coded data file and the text file are linked by a common identifying number.

3.   Metropolitan Statistical Areas (MSAs) are defined by the census as groups of contiguous counties and urbanized areas surrounding large cities.

4.   We considered translating booklets into other languages but the cost of doing so was prohibitive. Each booklet was unique and would have to be translated separately.

4

Sentencing Patterns for Federal Crimes

INTRODUCTION

Although the major concern of our study was to make comparisons between the ways in which the federal guidelines and the American public treat the sentencing of felons convicted of violating the federal criminal codes, there is also considerable interest in the sentencing preferences of the American public as such. Accordingly this chapter is centered around answering the question of what sentences Americans would give to those convicted of violating the federal criminal code. Of course, there is no single answer because there are many crimes defined in the federal statutes, varying in seriousness and in how those crimes affect the federal government, our major institutions, victims, and the general public. Furthermore, each crime defined in the statutes is described in a general way, whereas concrete criminal actions falling into any one general category are quite diverse. For example, larceny is defined as the wrongful appropriation of property, but there are an almost infinite variety of properties and there are many ways of thieving. It is clearly impossible to ask a sample of Americans to consider every possible act that is defined as a crime in the federal criminal code: The best we can do is to provide a relatively small number of examples, hopefully characteristic of the major federal crimes recognized in the statutes.

The selection of crimes to study was made by the commission staff and the authors. Twenty Crime Types in all were chosen, representing a limited number of general crimes. A Crime Type represents a broad crime category, such as fraud or drug trafficking, roughly paralleling the general crime categories used by the commission in writing the guidelines, as described in Chapter 2. The criteria used for selection included frequency of appearance on federal court dockets and policy significance.

Each Crime Type was represented by a number of specific examples, each describing a concrete instance of the type in question. For instance, an example of drug trafficking described the selling of a particular type of illicit drug. Descriptions were written of concrete actions believed to be clear examples of each of the types, 73 Crime Examples in all. The central feature of each vignette was a description of a Crime Example of which a person was convicted, along with some features of the criminal act and some characteristics of the criminal. As described in Chapter 3, the features of each crime and the characteristics of the criminal were randomly varied.

The 20 Crime Types and 73 Crime Examples cannot be regarded as a representative sample of all federal crimes. They were not chosen to mimic either the distribution of criminal cases in the federal courts or the distribution of felonies recognized in the federal criminal code. For that reason the overall distribution of sentences given by the respondents is not of as much interest as the distribution of sentences given to specific Crime Types and Crime Examples.

Measuring how Americans wanted criminals punished was based on asking each respondent to "sentence" 42 vignettes, each describing a person convicted of one example of one of 20 Crime Types. The Crime Types and Crime Examples are presented in Table 4.1. The phrases used for each Crime Example are the exact wordings used in the construction of the descriptive vignettes.

OVERALL SENTENCING PATTERNS

As described in Chapter 3, each of the respondents was given a booklet containing 40 vignettes describing persons convicted of crimes described by one of the phrases shown in Table 4.2. The respondents were asked what sentence "should be given" to each of the persons described in the vignettes, a wording chosen as most likely to elicit what respondents believed to be the norms governing punishment.[1] The sentencing task also assumes that issues of guilt or innocence have been previously resolved: all the vignettes described a convicted person. Each vignette also contained information about how the crime was committed and, in some cases, some of the consequences of the crime. In addition, for all crimes, the convicted person is described in terms of gender, family status, employment status, and previous record. All of the information included was randomly varied for each crime example used. Appendix A contains lists of the additional descriptive phrases that were used in connection

Table 4.1. Crime Types and Crime Examples Used in Study[a]

I. DRUG TRAFFICKING
 1. has been convicted with several others of taking part over a four-month period in the selling of powdered cocaine.
 2. has been convicted with several others of taking part over a four-month period in the selling of crack cocaine.
 3. has been convicted with several others of taking part over a four-month period in the selling of heroin.
 4. has been convicted with several others of taking part over a four-month period in the selling of marijuana.

II. MINOR FRAUD
 5. has been convicted of writing bad checks on an account opened using false identification.
 6. has been convicted of using a stolen credit card.
 7. has been convicted of soliciting donations for a nonexistent charity.
 8. has been convicted of obtaining a mortgage by making false claims about assets and income. The defendant had no intention of paying back the mortgage.[b]

III. MAJOR FRAUD
 9. has been convicted of obtaining a mortgage by making false claims about assets and income. The defendant intended to pay back the mortgage.[b]
 10. , a company officer, has been convicted of making personal gain from inside information learned before the information was made public. The officer bought stocks for HIS/HER personal account knowing that the stock price would go up when the information was made public. [Gender varied according to offender gender chosen.]
 11. has been convicted of being responsible for the failure of a savings and loan association by lending money to borrowers HE/SHE knew could not pay back. [Gender varied according to offender gender chosen.]
 12. has been convicted of selling worthless stocks and bonds as valuable assets.
 13. has been convicted of selling defective helicopter parts to the federal government endangering the lives of helicopter personnel and passengers. The seller knew the parts to be defective.
 14. , a doctor, has been convicted of submitting false Medicare claims to the government.

IV. FIREARMS
 15. has been convicted of illegally owning a handgun because of a prior felony conviction for theft.
 16. has been convicted of illegally owning a hunting rifle because of a prior felony conviction for theft.
 17. has been convicted of possessing sawed-off shotguns, a prohibited weapon.
 18. has been convicted of selling firearms to a known felon.
 19. , a licensed dealer, has been convicted of selling firearms without maintaining required sales records.

(continued)

Table 4.1. (Continued)

V. LARCENY
   20. has been convicted of stealing property
   21. has been convicted of stealing mail containing checks
   22. has been convicted of buying and selling goods HE/SHE knew were stolen. [Gender pronoun was varied to match gender of convicted offender.]
VI. IMMIGRATION
   23. has been convicted of smuggling unauthorized aliens into the U.S. for profit.
   24. has been convicted of smuggling family members who were unauthorized aliens into the U.S.
   25. has been convicted of illegally entering the U.S. using false papers.
   26. has been convicted of illegally reentering the U.S. after a previous deportation.
   27. has been convicted of smuggling unauthorized aliens into the U.S. for profit in a way that endangered the safety of the aliens.
VII. BANK ROBBERY
   28. has been convicted of robbing a bank. The robber gave a note to the teller demanding money but did not threaten any harm. The robber did not have a weapon.
   29. has been convicted of robbing a bank. The robber pointed a handgun at a teller and demanded money. The gun was not fired.
   30. has been convicted of robbing a bank. The robber pointed a handgun at a teller and demanded money. The robber fired the gun at the ceiling but no one was hurt.
   31. has been convicted of robbing a bank. The robber pointed a handgun at a teller and demanded money. The robber fired the gun at the teller who suffered a minor wound.
   32. has been convicted of robbing a bank. The robber pointed a handgun at a teller and demanded money. The robber fired the gun at the teller who was seriously wounded.
   33. has been convicted of robbing a bank. The robber gave a note to a teller demanding money and threatening to blow up the bank. No one was hurt.
VIII. STREET ROBBERY
   34. has been convicted of robbing a convenience store.
   35. has been convicted of taking a car by forcing the driver out of the car.
IX. EMBEZZLEMENT
   36. , a bank employee, has been convicted of stealing bank funds.
   37. , a bank vice president, has been convicted of stealing bank funds.
   38. , a postal worker, has been convicted of stealing from the U.S. mails.
X. CIVIL RIGHTS
   39. , a police officer, has been convicted of beating [STATUS][c] motorist who was found driving a car with no registration and with expired license plates.
   40. , a police officer, has been convicted of beating a motorist who was found driving a car with no registration and with expired license

(continued)

Table 4.1. *(Continued)*

_____

plates. The motorist resisted the police officer's attempts to examine HIS/HER license and registration. [Gender pronoun varied to match gender of motorist.]

41. , a police officer, has been convicted of beating a motorist who was found driving a car with no registration and with expired license plates. The motorist did not resist the police officer's attempts to examine HIS/HER license and registration. [Gender pronoun varied to match gender of motorist.]

42. has been convicted of trying to get [STATUS]^c couple who just moved into the neighborhood to move out by burning a cross on their lawn.

43. has been convicted of painting threats and obscenities on a [DENOMINATION]^d.

XI. ANTITRUST

44. has been convicted of conspiring with other companies to fix prices for soft drinks.

45. has been convicted of agreeing with competitors to rig bids for government contracts in order to control the market and guarantee higher profits for the companies involved.

XII. FOOD AND DRUG VIOLATIONS

46. has been convicted of adding poison to 17 packages of over-the-counter drugs

47. has been convicted of putting a drug on the market falsely claiming that the drug was adequately tested and had no dangerous side-effects.

48. has been convicted of putting a new drug on the market, concealing evidence that the drug had potentially dangerous side-effects in users.

XIII. ENVIRONMENTAL VIOLATIONS

49. has been convicted of illegally logging on federal lands.

50. has been convicted of failing to install proper antipollution devices on factory smoke stacks.

51. has been convicted of killing a bald eagle, protected by law as an endangered species.

52. , a plant manager, has been convicted of violating the terms of the plant's water discharge permit by discharging waste water that was 20 degrees warmer than allowed into a stream.

53. , a plant manager, has been convicted of violating the terms of the plant's water discharge permit by discharging waste water containing a toxic chemical.

XIV. TAX

54. has been convicted of tax evasion for underreporting income on tax returns

55. has been convicted of failing to file income tax returns

56. has been convicted of promoting an illegal tax shelter to the public

XV. EXTORTION AND BLACKMAIL

57. has been convicted of (either) (a) extorting money from a victim by threatening to kill a family member. (or) (b) blackmailing a prominent person by threatening to reveal a sexual indiscretion.

_____

(continued)

Table 4.1. (*Continued*)

XVI.	BRIBERY

    58. , a government purchasing agent, has been convicted of accepting a bribe to award a supply contract.

    59. has been convicted of bribing a county commissioner to obtain a contract.

    60. has been convicted of bribing a company purchasing agent to obtain a supply contract.

    61. , a county commissioner, has been convicted of accepting a bribe to award a contract.

XVII. DRUG POSSESSION

    62. has been convicted of possessing a small amount of powdered cocaine for personal use.

    63. has been convicted of possessing a small amount of crack cocaine for personal use.

    64. has been convicted of possessing a small amount of heroin for personal use.

    65. has been convicted of possessing a small amount of marijuana for personal use.

XVIII. FORGERY / COUNTERFEITING

    66. has been convicted of counterfeiting U.S. currency.

    67. has been convicted of writing bad checks on an account opened using false identification.

    68. has been convicted of making purchases using illegally obtained credit card numbers.

XIX. MONEY LAUNDERING

    69. , a rare coin dealer, has been convicted for failing to file forms required when receiving a cash payment of more than $10,000.

    70. , a rare coin dealer, has been convicted of arranging large cash purchases by criminals. The dealer provided the criminals with rare coins which they could then sell and appear to have earned the money lawfully.

    71. , a bank official, has been convicted of arranging deposits of large sums of money in ways that avoided the requirement that cash transactions of more than $10,000 be reported.

XX. KIDNAPING

    72. has been convicted of kidnaping a person, demanding ransom. The kidnaped person was not harmed.

    73. has been convicted of kidnaping a person, demanding ransom. The kidnaped person was killed.

[a] Roman numerals indicate Crime Types. Arabic numerals are used for Crime Examples. The phrases describing each crime example are exactly as they appear in the vignettes used.

[b] These two crime examples were misclassified as minor and major, respectively. However, in the detailed analyses of crime examples, we do not distinguish between major and minor fraud, minimizing the effects of this misclassification.

[c] In these vignettes, the minority status of the victim is systematically varied. (See Appendix A.)

[d] In these vignettes, one of several denominational places of worship is shown. (See Appendix A.)

with each of the Crime Types and Crime Examples, and the crimes to which they pertain.

An illustrative example of a vignette is shown in Figure 4.1. Note that respondents were asked to indicate which of several alternative sentences should be given to the convicted person. The choices were as follows:

Probation—no time in prison
Prison term for less than a year and the number of months to be served
Prison term for one or more years and the number of years to be served
Death penalty

In addition to these choices, some respondents wrote in "life" as the number of years to be spent in prison and a few entered "deportation" as the sentence to be given in response to some of the immigration law violations. Although interviewers were instructed to discourage such responses, some respondents seemingly had such strong preferences for life sentences that they could not be encouraged to convert those preferences into years of imprisonment. It is also possible that when interviewers checked over completed vignette booklets, they failed to detect such responses when they were written in. In any event, it appears likely that the proportion of life sentences in this study is below what might have been obtained had we allowed for life sentences to be an acceptable alternative to specified years of imprisonment.

Table 4.2 presents the distribution of responses over the four choices as described above. In a very small proportion of vignettes, less than 1 percent, no responses were made at all. These nonresponses most likely represent vignettes inadvertently skipped as indicated by their random

A man has been convicted of robbing a bank. The robber pointed a handgun at a teller and demanded money. The robber fired the gun at the ceiling, but no one was hurt. $19,000 was taken.

The defendant is married and has a spouse and two children. The defendant is currently unemployed and has served 2 previous sentences, each more than a year.

What sentence should be given in a case like this? **CIRCLE EITHER 1, 2, 3 OR 4:**

1 **PROBATION** No time in prison	2 **PRISON** Less than 1 year # Months ___	3 **PRISON** 1 Year or more # Years ___	4 **DEATH** Penalty

Figure 4.1. Illustrative Vignette Rating Task

Table 4.2.   Distribution of Types of Sentences Given to All
         Vignettes

Sentence given	Number	Percentage
Unanswered	633	0.9
Probation	10,160	13.9
Prison less than 1 year	8,843	12.1
Prison: 1 year or more[a]	51,379	70.4
Death penalty	1,915	2.6
Deportation	24	0.03
Total	72,954	100.0

[a] Includes life sentences written in by respondents.

distribution among Crime Types.[2] Imprisonment for a term greater than a year was clearly the most popular sentence, being given as a response in more than 70% of the vignettes. Probation and prison terms less than a year were given respectively to 14 and 12% of the vignettes. The least popular were death sentences, given in only 3% of the vignettes.[3]

Some vignettes were given prison sentences but the respondents did not indicate the prison term desired, with the consequence that 801 vignettes could not be used when we consider the full distribution of the amounts of imprisonment, as shown in Table 4.3. Probation was given to slightly more than 14% of the vignettes and in another 19% prison terms of less than one year were meted out leading to about one in three of the vignettes being given the "minimal" sentences of either probation or prisons terms less than a year. Indeed, half of all the sentences were 3 years or less, as indicated by the median sentence of 3.0. However, there were many longer sentences, with 15% being over 10 years, life, or death sentences. Life sentences were written in as responses to 2.5% of the vignettes and death sentences were given to 2.7%.

The analysis strategy pursued relies heavily on using respondent sentencing means and medians. In order to calculate the mean or median sentence given, it was necessary to translate probation, life, and death into numbers of years of imprisonment. By definition, probation understandably represents zero years of imprisonment and was so coded. The other two qualitative responses, life and death, required making somewhat arbitrary judgments. We rejected the alternative of omitting them from sentencing analyses on the ground that too many vignettes would be dropped from the analysis. We adopted the convention used in the sentencing guidelines, translating life sentences into 39.2 years, the actuarial life expectancy for persons at the average age at which federal felons are convicted. Following that line of reasoning we also treated sentences given by respondents that were greater than 39 years as 39.2 years.

Death sentences presented a greater translation problem. In a literal sense, a death sentence might mean a relatively short period of imprisonment until the sentence was carried out, but there is obviously no way a short sentence followed by release can be made equivalent to the same sentence followed by execution. Reasoning that a death sentence was a more drastic punishment than life imprisonment and hence should be represented by a higher number, death penalties were coded as 80 years of imprisonment, an admittedly arbitrary translation.

Using those translations, the mean sentence meted out to the vignettes was 8.85 years. The considerable difference between this number and the median, 3.0 years, reflects the heavy influence of extreme values in the calculation of the mean of a highly skewed distribution. These distributional properties of the sentences given present problems in how to summarize the findings properly. Ordinarily means are convenient summary measures but in this case the mean is far from the typical sentences given: more than 70% of the vignettes were given sentences that were smaller than the mean.

The mean sentence is highly affected by how life and death sentences are represented numerically. The decisions made, discussed earlier, are admittedly arbitrary: other choices would also affect the means. Several alternatives were tried: first, all life and death sentences were deleted, resulting in a mean sentence of 6.2 years and a median of 3.0; second, we recoded all sentences above 39.2 years to that value, resulting in a mean of 7.2 years and a median of 3.0. Clearly the mean is strongly affected by how life and death sentences are translated into sentence years, although the medians remain identical. Note also that in either of these two alternative translation modes, means and medians are still very far apart. However, median sentences are unaffected by these decisions. For that reason, many of the analyses use medians as central tendency measures.

In many of the analyses we also present data on life sentences and death sentences as well as means and medians in order that the reader can have information on those responses. When comparing guidelines and respondent sentencing patterns, as in Chapter 5, we adopt a different convention for handling death sentences, as explained in detail in that chapter.

Suspecting that a few respondents with highly divergent sentencing patterns were playing an important role in producing the skewed distribution, we investigated that possibility. We found a number of respondents who were either considerably more punitive or considerably more lenient than typical for all others. There were 34 respondents who gave out more than 10 death sentences, a few giving as many as 30. At the other extreme, 23 respondents gave out more than 20 probation sentences. It is difficult to imagine that either these very punitive or very lenient respondents had taken the sentencing task seriously, although we have no direct evidence to that effect.[4] All told, we identified 101 respondents —5.8% of all respondents—whose patterns of responses to vignettes can only be regarded as bizarre. Removing these extreme cases from the data set noticeably lowered the resulting average to 8.1. In subsequent calculations, the 101 outliers are removed from the analysis.

As can be discerned in Table 4.3, when giving sentences longer than a few years, respondents showed a decided tendency to favor sentences that were multiples of five, e.g., 5, 10, 15, 20, and to slight sentences that fall in between. We believe that it is reasonable to interpret this "bunching" of sentences as indicating that respondents do not clearly differentiate between sentences that are just a year or so apart when dealing with longer sentences above five years. Under this interpretation, a 10-year sentence is not very different from an 8-, 9-, 11-, or 12-year sentence.

A graphical representation of the overall sentencing pattern is given in Figure 4.2 as a "box and whisker" graph. The rectangular box spans the

Table 4.3.   Distribution of Sentences Given (Unweighted)

Sentence Given	Percentage	Cumulative Percentage
Probation	14.2	14.2
1 year or less	19.2	33.4
2 years	9.6	43.0
3 years	7.0	50.0
4 years	2.5	52.5
5 years	14.1	66.6
6 years	1.3	67.9
7 years	1.1	69.0
8 years	1.4	70.3
9 years	0.2	70.5
10 years	10.7	81.2
11–19 years	4.2	85.5
20–29 years	6.4	91.9
30–39 years	1.4	93.3
39.2 years[a] (life)	4.0	97.3
Death	2.7	100.0
Total N	71,470[b]	

[a] Includes all sentences over 39.2 years and all "life" sentences written in.

[b] Invalid responses in which respondents indicated imprisonment as a sentence but did not specify the number of years were removed. Note that percentages vary from those shown in Table 4.2 for that reason.

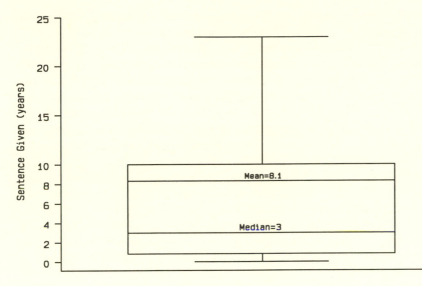

Figure 4.2.   Box Plot of All Sentences Given

interquartile range, within which lie 50% of the sentences, in this case spanning from 0.83 to 10.0 years. The two lines within the box represent respectively the locations of the mean and median. The "whisker" extending from the top of the box marks the range over which sentences given are continuous and exceed the upper end of the interquartile range, and the bottom whisker does the same for sentences given that were below the bottom value of the interquartile range. Sentences above and below the two whiskers are not plotted.[5]

RELIABILITY ESTIMATES

How consistent are respondents in their sentencing? A unique feature of the factorial survey design used permits a direct estimate of consistency (or reliability). All of the respondents were given two "practice" vignettes, one describing a marijuana possession crime and the other a bank robbery. These practice vignettes, reproduced in Appendix C, were identical for all respondents. Because the 40 vignettes incorporated into the booklets were randomly chosen, some of the booklets contained vignettes that were identical to those used in the practice vignettes.

For the 463 individuals who gave sentences to marijuana possession twice, the correlation between the two sentences was +.76, representing a fairly high level of reliability. Respondents (69%) typically gave the same sentence to both marijuana vignettes. Clearly, response reliability at this level was quite acceptable.

Only 48 respondents received bank robbery vignettes in their booklets that were identical in all respects to the practice bank robbery vignette. In order to get a reasonably stable reliability estimate, we matched the practice vignette with any other vignette that described the same criminal act and a felon with the same prior record as shown in the practice vignette. This meant that some vignettes described crimes with amounts robbed that were different from the practice vignette and described a felon of different marital and employment status. Accordingly, reliability was not quite as good for the bank robbery vignette. For the 248[6] respondents receiving two vignettes describing the same bank robbery Crime Example, the correlation between their two sentences was +.63. Identical sentences were given by 47% of the respondents.

Although the two correlation coefficients indicate reliability levels that are modestly high,[7] it is also clear that many respondents gave different sentences to the same Crime Example. However, the differing sentences were not far apart. We interpret these discrepancies to bolster the interpretation given earlier that respondents did not clearly differentiate among sentences that were of the same magnitude. That is, a 5-year imprisonment sentence was not seen as clearly different from a 4-or 6-year sentence. The main implication of this interpretation is that we cannot expect that comparability will be high between the sentences given by individuals and guidelines sentences. For a given vignette, the guidelines sentence is constant, whereas respondents vary and are somewhat inconsistent. However, summary measures such as means and medians which tend to smooth out such matters may produce higher levels of comparability.

CRIME TYPES

In Table 4.4, the sentences given to each of the general Crime Types are summarized, along with the sentences given to all crimes combined. For each crime, five summary measures[8] are shown: median and mean years, percentage given probation, percentage given life sentences, and percentage given death sentences. In the first row the summary measures

Table 4.4. Sentences Given to Crime Types: Outliers Removed [a]

| | Sentences Given to General Crime Types | | | | | |
Crime Type	Median Years	Mean Years	Probation (%)	Life (%)	Death (%)	N[b]
All Vignettes	3	8.1	13.8	3.2	2.0	67,286
Kidnaping	25	36.4	0.5	10.9	32.2	1,396
Drug Trafficking	10	15.2	2.2	8.6	4.0	13,413
Food & Drug	9	16.8	5.2	7.7	8.4	1,989
Bank Robbery	5	10.1	1.1	4.1	1.3	5,499
Street Robbery	5	9.6	1.9	4.1	0.9	1,328
Extortion/Blackmail	5	9.1	6.3	4.1	1.3	683
Counterfeiting/Forgery	5	6.3	4.9	1.6	0.0	2,049
Major Fraud	3	6.5	13.5	1.9	0.4	4,035
Money Laundering	3	5.1	13.2	0.9	0.0	1,995
Larceny	3	5.0	10.3	1.2	0.1	1,908
Firearms	2	5.0	15.6	1.1	0.4	3,370
Antitrust	2	4.8	15.9	0.1	0.0	1,353
Embezzlement	2	4.8	9.4	0.9	0.0	1,945
Immigration	2	4.5	19.6	0.8	0.0	3,333
Tax	2	4.4	15.3	1.2	0.0	4,014
Minor Fraud	2	4.4	11.8	0.8	0.0	2,097
Environment	1	3.5	24.9	0.1	0.0	3,315
Civil Rights	1	3.3	20.7	0.0	0.0	3,343
Bribery	1	3.0	20.5	0.4	0.0	2,597
Drug Possession	0.5	2.0	41.3	0.0	0.0	7,012

[a] Crime Types arranged in descending order of medians with ties broken by means.
[b] All respondents with outlying patterns of responses (N = 101) removed before calculations. Unrated vignettes not included.

are given for all vignettes combined. Subsequent rows are arranged in order of decreasing median sentences, with ties broken by the average sentences.

There are several outstanding features in the findings of Table 4.4: First, respondents clearly differentiated among Crime Types. Kidnaping crimes received the most severe punishments, with a median sentence of 25 years. At the other extreme, the possession of a small amount of illegal drugs received the least punishment, with a median punishment of 0.5 years (6 months). All told, the 20 Crime Types account for about 21% of the variance in sentencing.[9] Second, Crime Types that resulted in the actual or potential death of victims were the crimes most severely punished. One of the crimes included in Kidnaping involved the death of the kidnaped person and one of the Food and Drug violations involved placing poison in over-the-counter drugs with a resulting death. These two Crime Examples raise the means considerably for those Crime Types.

Third, the several summary measures of sentencing tend to be consistent. Crimes with high proportions of death penalties tend also to have high percentages of life sentences and very low percentages of probation sentences.[10] Conversely, crimes likely to be given probation sentences are very unlikely to get long prison sentences. Fourth, the average sentences are typically higher than median sentences, by magnitudes varying from about 1.5 to 3 or 4, indicating that for every Crime Type, there are always some, although usually very few, who want to give long prison sentences. Even for the drug possession Crime Type, there were a few who recommended the death sentence.[11]

A graphic representation of sentencing by Crime Types is shown in Figure 4.3. The distribution of sentences given to each Crime Type is displayed as a "box and whisker" graph, arrayed from left to right in order of decreasing sentencing severity.[12] Kidnaping is at the one extreme and Drug Possession at the other. The boxes whose upper edge is the 75th and lower edge the 25th percentile show the wide range of sentences given to the Crime Types. Note that the boxes are longer for Crime Types with higher medians, indicating that sentence enhancing characteristics of the vignettes count more when the crimes committed are more serious. For example, a long prior record leads to a greater sentence enhancement for a convicted bank robber than for someone convicted of a minor fraud.

Table 4.4 and Figure 4.3 both indicate that there is considerable varia-

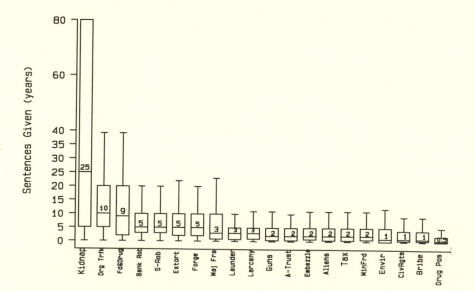

Figure 4.3. Sentences by Crime Types

tion in sentencing among respondents for each of the Crime Types. This variation partially represents the fact that respondents give different sentences to the same Crime Type. In addition, some of the variation is generated by the additional dimensions that are incorporated into the vignettes. For example, each of the vignettes describing Fraud Crime Types describes convicted persons with different previous criminal records, committing different kinds of specific frauds, and whose crimes involved different amounts of money. We will show in later chapters that sentencing varies according to these additional descriptive dimensions. When all of the dimensions included in the vignettes are taken into account the variation shown in Table 4.5 and Figure 4.3 is considerably reduced. In short, the sentencing variations shown are not to be interpreted as measuring how great the lack of consensus over sentencing is among the public.

CRIME EXAMPLES

Table 4.5. Sentences Given to Crime Examples: Medians, Means, Percentage Given Probation, Percentage Given Death Sentences[a]

	Sentences Given By Respondents					
Crime Example[b]	Median Years	Mean Years	Probation (%)	Life (%)	Death (%)	N
Kidnaping: victim killed	80	58.6	0.0	16.6	60.0	724
Poisoning over-the-counter drugs	15	26.6	0.7	12.2	16.6	681
Bank robbery: teller seriously wounded	15	19.9	0.5	13.2	4.8	635
Crack trafficking	10	16.0	1.4	9.7	4.3	3,281
Cocaine trafficking	10	15.9	1.7	9.4	4.1	3,387
Heroin trafficking	10	15.8	2.1	9.2	4.2	3,359
Bank robbery: teller suffered minor wound	10	15.4	0.0	8.9	2.4	616
Selling defective helicopter parts to U.S.	10	11.9	1.9	4.3	1.7	672
Marijuana trafficking	8	13.1	3.5	6.0	3.5	3,386
Kidnaping: victim not harmed	6	12.5	1.0	4.8	2.7	672
Marketing drugs concealing side effects	5	13.4	5.5	6.7	4.8	631
Carjacking	5	10.4	2.0	4.1	1.5	732
Marketing drugs with false safety claims	5	10.0	9.3	4.1	3.6	677

(*continued*)

Table 4.5.   (Continued)

| Crime Example[b] | Sentences Given By Respondents | | | | | |
	Median Years	Mean Years	Probation (%)	Life (%)	Death (%)	N
Extortion/blackmail	5	9.1	6.3	4.1	1.3	683
Bank robbery: bomb threat but no injury	5	8.9	2.1	3.6	0.6	666
Robbery of convenience store	5	8.5	1.6	4.0	0.3	596
Bank robbery: weapon fired but no harm	5	8.2	0.7	1.8	0.9	2,240
Bank robbery: weapon used but not fired	5	8.2	0.1	2.5	0.1	681
Counterfeiting U.S. currency	5	7.6	3.3	2.0	0.0	704
Selling firearms to known felon	5	7.5	7.5	1.7	1.0	657
Selling worthless stocks and bonds	5	7.5	3.3	18	0.3	680
Smuggling aliens endangering their safety	5	7.1	4.0	1.5	0.0	727
Doctor filing false Medicare claims	5	6.9	7.3	2.3	0.0	684
Coin dealer laundering criminal money	4	6.8	7.0	1.5	0.1	669
Using illegally obtained credit card numbers	4	6.1	4.6	2.4	0.0	664
Bid rigging on government contracts	4	6.0	10.2	1.1	0.3	642
Smuggling aliens for profit	4	5.9	6.12	1.4	0.3	649
Bank robbery no weapon used	4	5.8	3.4	0.6	0.3	661
Bank official causing S&L failure	3	6.1	8.9	1.8	0.0	660
Firearms dealer failure to keep sales records	3	6.1	13.7	1.5	0.1	722
Postal worker stealing from U.S. mail	3	5.6	5.2	1.3	0.1	672
Stealing U.S. mail	3	5.5	7.5	1.1	0.0	636
Writing bad checks on false accounts	3	5.0	6.7	0.3	0.0	681
Stealing property	3	5.0	10.7	1.1	0.3	653
Soliciting for nonexistent charity	3	4.9	10.1	1.1	0.0	661
Writing bad checks on false account	2	4.6	12.6	1.3	0.0	719

(continued)

Table 4.5. (Continued)

Crime Example[b]	Sentences Given By Respondents					
	Median Years	Mean Years	Probation (%)	Life (%)	Death (%)	N
Illegal logging on federal lands	2	4.6	15.3	1.2	0.0	650
Bank official concealing large cash deposits	2	4.5	13.4	0.9	0.0	666
Owning illegal sawed-off shotgun	2	4.5	19.5	1.2	0.3	670
Buying and selling stolen goods	2	4.5	12.8	1.3	0.0	619
Police officer beating unresisting motorist	2	4.4	12.9	0.4	0.4	675
Tax: evasion by failure to file returns	2	4.4	17.9	1.3	0.1	1,341
Tax: evasion by underreporting income	2	4.4	15.2	1.3	0.0	1,340
Company official using insider information	2	4.4	15.7	0.5	0.0	661
Bank employee embezzling bank funds	2	4.4	10.2	1.0	0.3	610
Bank officer embezzling bank funds	2	4.3	13.0	0.3	0.0	663
Promoting illegal tax shelter	2	4.3	12.7	1.1	0.1	1,333
Using stolen credit card	2	4.2	9.4	0.6	0.0	701
Factory discharging toxic wastes into stream	2	4.2	21.3	1.3	0.4	664
Police officer beating minority motorist[c]	2	3.8	12.8	0.1	0.3	709
False mortgage application: no intent to pay	2	3.8	15.4	0.0	0.0	628
Coin dealer failing to file required forms	2	3.8	19.0	0.4	0.0	660
Convicted felon owning handgun	2	3.7	12.8	0.4	0.0	691
Bribing county commissioner	2	3.5	16.2	0.7	0.0	686
Bribing company purchasing agent	2	3.3	19.8	0.6	0.1	657
Factory failure to install antipollution device	1	3.8	23.2	0.4	0.0	674
Price fixing conspiracy	1	3.7	21.0	0.4	0.3	711
Smuggling alien family members	1	3.5	24.1	0.7	0.3	668
Harassment of minority neighbor[c]	1	3.4	21.2	0.3	0.3	650

(continued)

Table 4.5. (Continued)

| Crime Example[b] | Sentences Given By Respondents | | | | | |
	Median Years	Mean Years	Probation (%)	Life (%)	Death (%)	N
Convicted felon owning hunting rifle	1	3.0	25.4	0.1	0.0	627
Crack possession for personal use	1	3.0	25.1	0.5	0.2	1,361
Illegal reentry after deportation	1	2.9	30.3	0.0	0.0	631
County commissioner accepting bribe	1	2.6	22.5	0.0	0.0	615
Government purchasing agent accepting bribe	1	2.6	23.9	0.1	0.0	639
Vandalism of house of worship	1	2.6	23.3	0.6	0.1	673
Illegal entry into U.S.	1	0.7	35.6	0.1	0.0	658
Cocaine possession for personal use	0.9	2.9	30.0	0.6	0.1	1,329
Heroin possession for personal use	0.9	2.6	29.5	0.5	0.0	1,368
Killing endangered bald eagles	0.9	2.5	28.3	0.1	0.1	669
Factory discharging hot water into stream	0.7	2.2	36.4	0.3	0.0	658
Police officer beating resisting motorist	.5	2.1	34.7	0.5	0.3	636
False mortgage application: intent to pay	0.5	2.1	43.5	0.6	0.0	678
Marijuana possession for personal use	0.0	1.0	59.5	0.0	0.0	2,954

[a] Crimes arranged in order of decreasing median sentences, with means used to break ties: outliers removed. (Respondents who gave 10 or more death sentences, 10 or more life sentences, or 20 or more probation sentences are deleted.)
[b] The exact wordings used are shown in Table 4.1.
[c] The motorist or the neighbor in these vignettes is described as one of the following: "an African-American," "an Hispanic-American," "an Asian-American," or "homosexual."

The Crime Types are admittedly coarse categories, each consisting of many quite different specific criminal acts. In lumping those diverse acts into a single category, important distinctions among crimes are undoubtedly lost. The Crime Examples were designed to capture some of those distinctions. For example, there are many ways to commit a Major Fraud. In the vignettes, the Major Fraud Crime Type is represented by six examples including insider stock trading violations, selling defective helicopter parts, filing false Medicare claims, and causing a savings and loan bank to fail. In writing the Crime Examples, we picked those we believed to be well-known, so that most respondents would recognize them.

The sentences given to each Crime Example are shown in Table 4.5 arranged from top to bottom in order of decreasing median sentences, with ties broken by means.

Heading the table are kidnapings in which the victims are killed, with a median sentence of 80 years, reflecting the fact that than three out of five (60%) of the respondents wanted a death sentence for this crime (represented as a sentence of 80 years). Note that this kidnaping Crime Example received significantly greater punishment than the next in line. The second-ranked crime, poisoning over-the-counter drugs, receives a median sentence of 15 years, many years less[13] than kidnaping. At the other extreme is the possession of "a small amount" of marijuana with a median sentence of zero years, reflecting that about three in five respondents gave probation as a sentence.

Some general tendencies can be discerned in Table 4.5:

First, crimes involving the actual or potential death of victims or serious harm to victims tend to be at the top of the list, receiving harsher sentences.

Second, respondents apparently desire relatively harsh penalties for trafficking in illegal drugs, as shown by the four drug-trafficking crimes being among the top 10 crimes. In the next chapter, we will show that the sentencing guidelines are significantly harsher than our respondents' sentences. In contrast, possession of small amounts of the same illegal drugs for personal consumption is clearly viewed as among the least serious crimes, all four drug possession crimes appearing among the bottom 13 least serious crimes.

Third, for most Crime Types, the specific examples belonging to the crime groups do not cluster closely together. For example, environmental crimes are distributed over a wide range, from rank 44 to 69; civil rights crimes range from 41 to 71; and fraud crimes range from 8 to 72. Respondents apparently weigh heavily the consequences of a crime in their sentencing. Examples drawn from the same Crime Type that vary in their consequences for the safety of people are regarded more seriously. Accordingly, the fraud crime involving selling defective helicopter parts to the government is among the most serious of all crimes (rank 8), whereas making a false mortgage application with the intention of paying back is among the least serious (rank 72). Similarly, crimes that do not have specific victims or do not directly threaten the physical well-being of individuals are treated less harshly. (The differences within Crime Types are described in greater detail in Chapter 6.)

HOLDING CRIME CONSTANT

Because each of the crime groups is made up of several examples and each vignette contains information in addition to the crime of conviction, clear consensus on the sentences to be given to Crime Types or Crime Examples is not to be expected. All of the vignettes contained varying information on the offender's previous record and many contained varying information on the gravity of the offense. For example, each of the fraud vignettes contained information on the amounts of money obtained fraudulently. These additional dimensions affected the sentence given to each vignette to some degree. The impact of such information on sentencing will be analyzed in detail in Chapter 6. We can anticipate those findings by indicating that the respondents did vary their sentencing behavior, as those descriptions varied.

Although 40 of the vignettes were constructed according to the procedure described in Chapter 3 in which the Crime Examples and other information were randomly assembled, two vignettes were included in the study that did not vary from one respondent to another.[14] These were the two vignettes used to provide practice in the sentencing task, to give the interviewers opportunities to provide instruction to respondents, and to assess respondent literacy skills. The two standard vignettes differ in the gravity of the offenses described. One of the standard vignettes describes a person convicted of the possession of a small amount of marijuana for personal use and the other describes a bank robbery in which the offender threatens a teller with a handgun, and fires the gun with no resulting injury.

These standard practice vignettes provide an opportunity to examine the degree of consensus among respondents when confronted with identical crime descriptions. The sentences given to the two standard vignettes are shown in Table 4.6, along with the sentences given to those vignettes when used as randomly assembled vignettes. The randomly assembled vignettes contained varied information on the convicted offender, especially that concerning the offender's previous criminal record. Contrasting the sentences given to the standard vignettes with the randomly assembled vignettes provides an appreciation of the amount of

Table 4.6. Sentences Given to Practice Standardized Vignettes and Randomly Constructed Vignettes of the Same Crime Example (Outliers Removed)

Crime Example	Median (Years)	Average (Years)	Interquartile Range	Probation (%)	Life (%)	Death (%)	N
Practice Marijuana Possession	0	0.45	0–0.25	69.9	0	0	1,588
Random Drug Possession	0.25	1.6	0–2	46.4	0	0	1,366
Standard Bank Robbery	5	7.8	3–10	0.5	1.6	0.9	1,636
Random Bank Robbery	5	8.9	3–10	1.0	2.2	1.0	703

variation in sentencing behavior contributed by the descriptive dimensions added to each vignette. Figure 4.4 also provides a graphic view of the differences between standard and randomly constructed vignettes.

As expected, there was more consensus concerning the two standard vignettes than concerning the randomly constructed counterparts. Indeed, the standard marijuana possession vignette gets close to unanimity, with about 7 out of every 10 vignettes receiving probation sentences. In contrast, less than half of the random marijuana possession vignettes are given probation sentences. Much the same can be said of the standard bank robbery vignettes. In short, although the crime itself may dominate the process, sentencing is responsive to other information about the crime and the criminal when included in the vignette descriptions.

SUMMARY

The overall sentencing patterns of the respondents were described in this chapter. Several important generalizations emerge:

1. Most respondents took the sentencing task quite seriously, making clear distinctions among Crime Types and Crime Examples in their sentencing of convicted criminals. There is some evidence that a small minority were very severe in imposing punishments on each Crime Type and Crime Example, making most members of the sample seem relatively moderate in comparison.

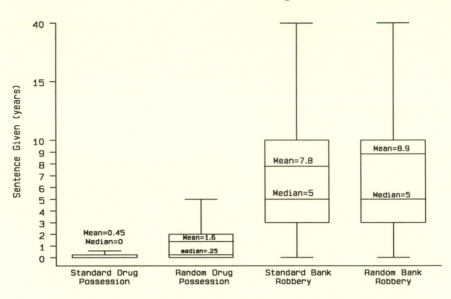

Figure 4.4. Standard and Random Vignettes Compared

2. The reliability of respondent sentences was found to be fairly high.
    When respondents rated the same crime example twice, the sen-
    tences given were of the same magnitude.
3. Although only the most serious and the least serious crimes re-
    ceived anything close to the same sentence from all respondents,
    nevertheless there was some degree of convergence among re-
    spondents, an issue that we will return to time and time again in
    later chapters.
4. Respondents saw many distinctions among specific criminal be-
    haviors that are formally grouped together. Within Crime Types,
    specific Crime Examples often received widely different sentenc-
    ing. Respondents distinguished among specific examples of gen-
    eral crime categories. It appeared that respondents were more
    sensitive to the consequences of crimes for the physical safety of
    victims than they were to the economic losses suffered. In short,
    any indication of violence to persons tended to be met with
    harsher sentences.

The findings shown in this chapter also describe the structure of American norms concerning what should be appropriate punishments for convicted criminals. We believe that the findings are clear evidence that a
normative structure exists. The respondents' sentences are not idiosyn-

cratic but vary according to both broad types of crimes and specific examples of those types. The sentences do have measures of central tendencies, means and medians, that represent typical responses. Measurement errors admittedly obscure the clarity of the normative structure. Taking such errors into account, there is firm evidence of a normative structure upon which the responses of individual Americans converge.

NOTES

1.   Alternative wordings such as "the sentence you would give" or "the punishment you would prefer" were rejected on the grounds that their use might elicit personal preferences rather than norms.

2.   In addition, there were 801 vignettes to which respondents indicated prison terms were to be given but neglected to write down the sentence lengths. Obviously, these vignettes also cannot be used in any analyses based on sentence lengths. Thus the overall valid response rate for vignettes was 98%: 71,470 usable vignettes out of a total of 72,594.

3.   A small number, 24, of the vignettes were given the write-in sentences of "deportation." We have chosen to treat these responses as equivalent to being placed on probation and hence as zero prison time. When life sentence was written in as a response, it was given a special code. There were 1802 life sentences written in, covering 2.5% of all vignettes.

4.   An alternative explanation is that these outliers did not completely understand the sentencing task.

5.   These sentences, amounting to about 6% of all vignettes, are omitted in the interest of simplifying the graph.

6.   The difference between the numbers of respondents receiving identical vignettes for the two different practice vignettes reflects the greater complexity of the bank robbery vignettes and the different probabilities assigned to the two Crime Types. Drug Possession appeared twice as frequently in the vignette distribution.

7.   Reliability measures for typical survey questions range from .6 to .7. Reliability measures for multiple item tests are typically above .85.

8.   Measures of response dispersion, such as standard deviations or the interquartile range, are not shown because most of the variation around the mean or median is caused by the dimensions that are included in each vignette. For example, all of the vignettes contain a statement about the prior record of the convicted felon, a vignette feature that influences strongly the sentences given. The interquartile ranges are shown in the box-and-whisker plots in Figure 4.3.

9.   Calculated by regressing sentences given on the 20 Crime Types, each represented by a binary dummy variable. The resulting R^2 is .21.

10.   The correlations of the mean and median sentences with percentage life

and percentage death are about +.95 and approximately −.65 with percentage probation.

11.   Note that Table 4.4 has been purged of the 101 outliers discussed earlier.

12.   The data used are purged of the 101 outliers discussed above and weighted to compensate for sampling disproportionalities. In addition, it was necessary to code the top sentences as 40 years because the full scale of sentences would have produced graphs that were unreadable.

13.   Because so many death sentences were given to kidnapings, this difference does not have any real meaning.

14.   The two standard vignettes (reproduced in Appendix C) were given on a sheet separate from the booklet containing the randomly constructed vignettes in order to orient the respondent to the sentencing task and to provide the interviewer with an opportunity to explain the task, if the respondent appeared uncertain about how to proceed, as described in Chapter 3. The standard vignettes were chosen to represent crimes differing widely in gravity in order to induce a common response set to the sentencing task.

5

Guidelines and Sample Sentences Compared

INTRODUCTION

An important issue in the sociology of law concerns the extent to which the legal code of a society mirrors the normative structure of that society. To the extent that federal sentencing guidelines represent the legal codes of our society, our dataset can provide some empirical findings relevant to that issue by comparing respondent sentences to those required in the guidelines. The sentences given by our sample were shown in detail in the previous chapter. The major goal of this chapter is to compare those sentences to those prescribed in the sentencing guidelines.

In addition to important issues posed in the sociology of law, there are also several policy reasons for making these comparisons. First, as related in Chapter 2, the guidelines were written in response to a legislative mandate requiring the commission to be guided in some significant measure by the relative seriousness of criminal offenses. Serious crimes were to be given harsher sentences and crimes of lesser seriousness were supposed to be treated more leniently. The several social science studies of public beliefs about the seriousness of crimes reviewed in Chapter 1 have shown that the public has well-structured views about relative seriousness: there is a fair amount of consensus on the seriousness ordering of crimes. How well was that consensus transformed into respondents' recommended sentences?

Unfortunately, the existing studies of crime seriousness could not have been of much help to the commission in attempting to ascertain what the American consensus is on sentencing. The crimes studied were mostly those dealt with in the state criminal courts and many federal crimes, especially white-collar crimes, were not studied at all. For example, Wolfgang et al.'s (1985) national study was concerned mainly with "street" crimes. In addition, seriousness does not translate easily into sentences.

As Rossi et al. (1985) have shown, the seriousness of a crime may be the main factor in judging the appropriateness of sentences, but respondents also take into account prior criminal record and the consequences of the crime for victims and the public.

Second, there is the issue of public confidence in the fairness and equity of the criminal justice system. Although there is no strong reason why guidelines sentences should be patterned precisely after public preferences, it would be a matter of concern were the two to be found far apart. A criminal justice system risks losing its legitimacy if it provides sentences that are much harsher or much more lenient than what the majority of its constituents believe to be just.

For these reasons we can expect some degree of correspondence. However, there are also good reasons to expect differences between guidelines sentences and those desired by the public. Such differences are bound to occur because sentencing policy also reflects other goals besides maximizing legitimacy. Among many other considerations, some involve possible deterrence effects of sentencing, fiscal implications of the costs of prosecution and imprisonment, and the ease or difficulty of running the courts.

Accordingly there are no clear expectations about how closely comparable guidelines sentences and those given by the public should be. The degree of acceptable comparability may be largely a matter of judgment.

In addition, there are also technical considerations. As shown in Chapter 4, Americans cannot be considered to be of one mind on sentencing for almost all of the crimes studied. There were some respondents who were in favor of each of the alternatives in sentencing offered for almost every crime. The critical issue is how best to summarize what were central tendencies in sentencing, a difficult decision when average and median values for most crimes were far apart.

Finding consensus or lack thereof requires deciding how to measure comparability. A stringent definition is one in which comparability is defined as identical sentences. A less demanding definition of comparability requires only close rank orderings of sentences for crimes, in which it is possible for the public views and guidelines sentences to rank crimes the same way but to differ systematically in the sentences imposed. Several approaches to measuring comparability will be considered, from which the reader can choose.

Finally, comparability can be explored at different levels of aggregation. At the finest level, the sentences given by individual respondents to specific vignettes can be compared to the calculated guidelines sentences for the same vignettes. This comparison assesses the extent to which individual respondents agree with the guidelines in giving sentences to specific vignettes. Aggregating respondent sentences by calculating mean or median sentences provides another way of making comparisons in which guidelines sentences are contrasted with the central tendencies found in public opinion. Several levels of aggregation will be explored in this chapter.

As discussed in Chapter 4, respondents may have had in mind a rather fuzzy magnitude when giving sentences to the vignettes. A two-year sentence may be not very different in their minds from a three-year sentence. In contrast, there is little fuzziness in the guidelines. Accordingly, we can expect that individual respondents may not agree precisely with the guidelines, although mean and median sentences computed over the entire sample may be much more comparable when contrasted with the guidelines.

CALCULATING GUIDELINES SENTENCES

In essence, the guidelines consist of a set of rules for arriving at sentence ranges for persons convicted in the federal courts. The guidelines take into account both the crime of which the defendant was convicted and the actual nature of the criminal conduct by assigning a "base offense level" (a number) that serves as a starting point in assessing the seriousness of an offense. This base offense level can be increased or decreased based on the circumstances of the case. The factors that modify the base offense level (such as use of a weapon, presence of more than minimal planning, or amount of loss) are enumerated in the guidelines. Many such factors are specific to a given class of crime and a few apply to all crimes.

A base offense level, modified by the specified circumstances and other general adjustments (such as role in the offense), forms one axis of a table used to determine sentence ranges. The other axis reflects the defendant's criminal history as expressed in one of six categories. The point at which the adjusted offense level and criminal history category intersect in the table determines a range of sentences for an offender. Ordinarily a federal judge must choose a sentence from within the designated guidelines range unless the court can identify a relevant factor not covered in the guidelines; in this case, the judge may depart from the guidelines range and must provide a reason for so doing.

The guidelines are carefully documented and permit a person with knowledge of the relevant statutes and the details of an offense to compute the guidelines sentence range recommended. For example, by following the guidelines structure carefully, one can calculate that a sentence range of 46 to 57 months would apply to a person with no previous criminal history who was convicted of extorting $19,000 from a victim by threatening to kill someone in the victim's family.

The fact that there are parallels between the vignettes and the guidelines is, of course, no accident, but part of the vignette design strategy. Many of the dimensions built into the vignettes paralleled provisions in the guidelines.[1] For example, the guidelines indicate that sentences for drug-trafficking offenses should vary in specific ways according to the drug in question, the amount of the drug involved, the role played by the defendant in the transaction, and the presence or use of weapons associated with the transaction. Accordingly, the vignette design for drug-trafficking calls for vignettes to vary the type of illegal drug, the amount of drugs involved, the role played by the convicted person in the drug trafficking, and weapon use. Most important of all, the parallels make it possible to calculate a guidelines sentence for each of the vignettes used in the study.

The translation of the crimes and dimensions used in this study into recommended sentences was done by staff members of the U.S. Sentencing Commission. Their familiarity with guidelines made the translation of the vignette dimensions into guidelines sentences as faithful as possible. However, the translation was not without problems: First, the guidelines definitions are more precise than many of the vignette descriptions. For example, the guidelines include an adjustment for "aggravated role" if a defendant's criminal behavior included organizing or managing criminal activity involving five or more participants. However, the corresponding vignette dimension did not specify the number of persons managed by the defendant; it was unclear whether this substantial adjustment should have been applied.

Second, some offense details included in the guidelines affect sentences by way of judicial discretion at the time of sentencing. For example, the guidelines permit the judge in conservation and wildlife cases to depart from the guidelines sentence range when the quantity or seriousness of damage is "not adequately" measured by the guidelines sentence. Consequently vignettes describing such crimes can be given guidelines sentence ranges, but actual sentences imposed can often fall above those ranges.

A special problem is posed by the way in which death sentences are treated in the guidelines. Although death sentences are allowed in the federal criminal code in a limited number of federal crimes, particularly those that can be prosecuted as first-degree homicide, the guidelines regard death sentences as allowable departures from the guidelines and do not provide a numerical interpretation for death sentences. The most severe guidelines sentence is imprisonment for 39.2 years, the equivalent of a life sentence. A kidnaping in which the victim is killed has a guidelines-recommended sentence of 39.2 years, but the guidelines also state that the death penalty is an allowable departure.

There are two crimes included in our study for which the death sentence is an allowable departure: kidnaping when the victim is killed and food and drug violations that result in deaths. We were not able to decide with great confidence how to handle the death sentences given by respondents to those two crimes. Looked at in one way, such sentences are congruent with the guidelines; looked at in another way, they are also departures. Accordingly, we decided to regard respondent death sentences given to those crimes in which the guidelines allow death sentences as 39.2 years. In all other cases, death sentences were given the numerical value of 80 in order to capture the fact that such sentences are far from the recommended guidelines sentences. In Chapter 8 a special analysis of the use of death sentences by respondents is presented.

As a consequence of the two ambiguity factors, the mapping of guidelines sentences on vignettes was not always easy and was in some cases impossible. It is important to understand that, aside from death sentences given by respondents, these translation difficulties applied mainly to dimensions that modified the two major features of the vignettes, the crimes committed and the offenders' prior records, the main determinants of guidelines sentences. The crimes committed and the offenders' prior records together accounted for 92% of the variation in guidelines sentences.[2] In short, for the most important features of each vignette, the assignment of guidelines sentences was accomplished typically with little ambiguity. However, for some of the minor other dimensions incorporated into some of the vignettes, the translation of levels into sentence enhancements could not be accomplished with great confidence.

A guidelines-recommended sentence for an offense consists of a range of sentence lengths. The midpoint of the guidelines sentencing range for each crime description in a vignette was used to represent the recommended guidelines sentence and attached to the crime as described in each vignette. Accordingly, the extortion crime used as an example above was given a guidelines sentence of 51.5 months or 4.2 years. Each of the vignettes studied was given a guidelines-recommended sentence that varied according to the crime described, the levels of crime dimensions used, and the previous record of the convicted offender. For example, the calculated guidelines sentences for vignettes involving extortion crimes ranged from 0.58 to 10.3 years, the differences among sentences reflecting varying amounts of money extorted and the previous record of the convicted offender. It should be borne in mind that the calculated guidelines sentences are based only on the information contained in the vignettes and that sentence enhancements were sometimes translated with some uncertainty.

Actual cases coming before the courts are much richer and more detailed: Hence guidelines punishments for concrete cases would take into account features of cases that were not incorporated into the design of vignettes. Furthermore, the guidelines recommend a range of sentences of which we have taken the midpoint. Accordingly, the results shown in this chapter are based on a comparison of respondent sentences with guidelines sentences as calculated with some uncertainty, believed to be minor in nature.

It is also important to keep in mind that we did not ask the respondents to act as if they were judges nor did we ask them to take into account the fiscal or other implications of their sentencing decisions. Actual judges sentencing actual cases are given, we hope, more information on cases and more time to decide on sentences. Accordingly, the comparisons made are not with how the courts treat convicted felons but with how the guidelines treat cases with limited information on the cases.

ANALYSIS STRATEGY

The dataset permits several kinds of comparisons between guidelines sentences and those made by respondents. At the most disaggregated level, comparisons between guidelines and respondent sentences can be made for each of the close to 70,000 vignettes. At the vignette level, the comparisons are of how close the 70,000 respondent sentences are to the guidelines sentences for those vignettes. At the most aggregated level, we can compare how close respondent sentences come to guidelines sentences for the 20 Crime Types consisting of broad classes of crimes, using the mean or median sentences given by respondents. Comparisons on this level indicate the extent to which, say, the mean or median guidelines sentence for larceny crimes compares to the mean or median sentence given to those crimes by respondents. A third level of intermediate aggregation centers around the 73 Crime Examples, each being a concrete instance of one of the Crime Types. A fourth approach is to consider each crime example as modified by the prior criminal record given to the offender. There are 175 combinations of unique examples and prior crime records that can be used.[3]

Because of the considerable amount of interrespondent variability in sentencing (as shown in Chapter 4) least comparability can be expected at the vignette level, and greater amounts of comparability at the level of Crime Types, Crime Examples, and the combinations of Crime Examples and prior records. Using means or medians simply reduces interrespondent variability.

Each mode of analysis is useful. For example, if it is assumed that a citizen's level of satisfaction with the federal criminal justice system is related to the differences between how he or she would sentence criminals compared to the guidelines sentences, then the study of the distribution of satisfaction is well served by the comparisons at the level of individual vignettes. However, if we are concerned with whether the guidelines sentences minimize differences with individual citizens in the aggregate, then comparisons at more aggregated levels of Crime Types or Crime Examples may be more appropriate.

Levels of aggregation also are relevant to the study of norms. Once we are above the level of measures made on individual persons, we are dealing with characteristics of social groups and other social aggregates. Hence norms are best represented by aggregate measures. In the sociological literature contextual measures or measures of group characteristics are typically means or medians or other measures of central tendencies.

Comparisons at each level of aggregation will be presented in this chapter. We start with comparisons at the level of individual vignettes and end with analyses at the level of Crime Examples as modified by the convicted felons' prior criminal records.

DISTRIBUTIONS OF GUIDELINES AND RESPONDENT SENTENCES GIVEN TO VIGNETTES

After removing the vignettes rated by outliers, as discussed in Chapter 3, there remain 68,712 vignettes for which we have a sentence given by a respondent and also a guidelines sentence, constituting the dataset for the analyses presented in this chapter.

Considering the means and medians of guidelines and respondent sentences, it would appear that the American public would like to see convicted felons receive longer sentences than are recommended in the Guidelines. As shown in Table 5.1, the mean sentence given by the public was 7.2 years in contrast to the average guidelines sentence of 5.7. However, differences between guidelines and sample medians were not as great, 3 vs. 2.5 years. Using the differences between the averages, it appears that the sample wanted felons to serve sentences about 1.5 years

Table 5.1. Means, Medians, and Interquartile Ranges of Guidelines and Sample Sentences[a]

	Sentence in Years	
Measure	Guidelines	Sample
Mean	5.7	7.2
Median	2.5	3
Interquartile Range	1.1 to 6.5	0.83 to 10

[a] N = 68,712. Respondent outliers were removed from this table and in other tables in this chapter.

longer, but considering the medians, the difference in desired sentence lengths was 0.5 years. Not surprisingly, the interquartile ranges also differ, with the sample sentences spanning a wider distance than the guidelines sentences.

These samples-guidelines differences in overall means and medians are based on the specific crime examples and the distribution of vignettes included in the study. A different selection or a different distribution could alter the differences significantly because, as will be shown below, there are crime examples over which there is substantial disagreement in either direction. In addition, the means and medians are overly influenced by how the vignettes were distributed among Crime Types. For example, slightly more than 1 in 5 of the vignettes depicted a drug-trafficking crime and almost 1 in 10 were concerned with drug possession crimes for a total of close to 30% of all vignettes relating to illicit drug crimes. Consequently, the overall means and medians for both respondent and guidelines sentences are strongly influenced by the sentences given to drug crimes, especially drug trafficking.

In many instances means and medians do not reveal all that should be known about a dataset because these measures tell us little about how individual values are distributed. The full distribution of guidelines sentences is shown in Figure 5.1 and that of the sample in Figure 5.2. There is an overall resemblance between the two distributions, with sentences in both clustering toward the left sides of the two histograms, indicating that most vignettes were given short sentences by respondents and that most crimes were treated that way as well by the guidelines. However, there are also important contrasts: First, the histogram for sample sentences is more irregular, brought about because sentences in multiples of 5 years were favored over intervening sentences lengths. i.e., respondents tended to favor sentences of 5, 10, 15, 20 (etc.) rather than intermediate lengths. Second, sample sentences tended to be both more lenient and harsher,

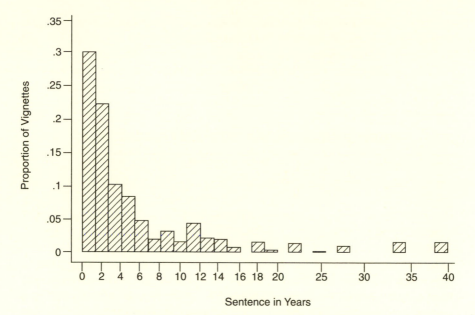

Figure 5.1. Distribution of Guidelines Sentences

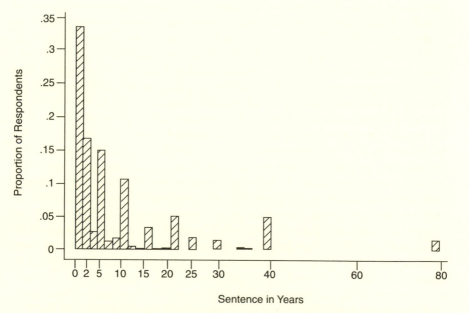

Figure 5.2. Distribution of Respondent Sentences

with more sentences under 1 year in length and also more sentences at the extreme of 39.2 years.

Computing the difference for each vignette between sample and guidelines by subtracting the respondent sentence from the guideline for that vignette, we can examine the distribution of those differences, as displayed in the histogram in Figure 5.3. Because the death sentences given by respondents produced high negative numbers distorting the histogram, death sentences have been omitted from Figure 5.3.[4]

In Figure 5.3 a normal curve with the same mean and standard deviation as the distribution of sentencing differences is superimposed on the histogram. The contrast between the normal curve and the histogram shows that the distribution of differences is at the same time more peaked and more dispersed. Half of the differences lie between +1.8 and −3.5, with a median value of 0 and an average of 1.3. About 30% of the values are between −1 and +1, indicating that in almost one-third of the vignettes the differences between guidelines and sample sentences are a year or less apart. There is also a slight tendency for the sample sentences to be more lenient, with 59% of the differences that are less than a year being negative.[5]

In short, there is a fair amount of agreement between respondents and the guidelines.

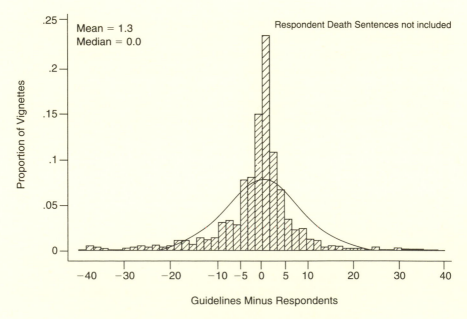

Figure 5.3.   Guidelines-Respondent Differences

VIGNETTE LEVEL REGRESSION ANALYSIS

As a first step in the analysis of comparability, the guidelines and respondent sentences for each individual vignette are compared, answering the question of how closely the respondents' sentences correspond to those recommended in the guidelines at the most disaggregated level, individual vignettes. To make this comparison, regression analyses were made in which the guidelines sentences were regressed on the respondent sentences for each vignette. In effect, this approach compares the two measures over the more than 67,000 vignettes.

Two regression models were employed, with results as shown in Table 5.2. Panel A presents a classic least squares regression equation, and Panel B contains a median regression.[6] Each approach locates a straight line running through points in a plane representing the pairs of guidelines and respondent sentences that minimizes the differences between the sentences and that line. The model in Panel A minimizes the squares of those differences and that in Panel B minimizes the absolute values of those differences. In the least squares regression, extreme values strongly influence the location of the line, whereas in the median regression extreme values do not play so important a role. Given that respondent sentences do contain many extreme values, the median regression line may represent more closely the general relationship of guidelines and respondent sentences.

The interpretation of the coefficients is quite straightforward. In both models, if the guidelines and the respondent sentences were identical for each vignette, the value of the regression coefficient would be 1, the intercept term would be 0, and the R^2 value for the equation would be 1. Departures from those values indicate systematic discrepancies. For ex-

Table 5.2. Regressions of Guidelines Sentences on Respondent Sentences (Units Are Vignettes)[a,b]

A. OLS Regression
   $$S_{gi} = 3.6 + 0.28S_{ij}, \quad R^2 = .18, \quad N = 67,286$$

B. Median Regression
   $$S_{gi} = 1.5 + 0.25S_{ij}, \quad \text{Pseudo } R^2 = .08, \quad N = 67,286$$

[a] All coefficients are significantly different from 0 at better than the .0001 level. In addition, the regression coefficients are also significantly different from 1.00 at better than .0001.
[b] S_{ij} designates sentence given to vignette i by respondent j; S_{gi} designates guidelines sentence for vignette i.

ample, a calculated value of the regression coefficient departing from 1 means that the two values increase at different rates: for example, a coefficient of 1.5 means that on the average respondents gave an additional 1.5 years for each additional year given by the guidelines. The intercepts indicate the constant value by which guidelines sentences differ across the board from respondent sentences: For example, a regression constant of 2.5 indicates that guidelines sentences on the average exceed respondent sentences by 2.5 years. The R^2 values are an overall measure of how closely the values cluster around the regression line, 1 indicating that all the values are on the line and 0 indicating that the points are randomly located. The "pseudo R^2" shown for the median regression also has a similar interpretation. In any event, values lower than .5 indicate very modest clustering about the regression line.

The classic regression in Panel A accounts for 18% ($R^2 = .18$) of the variance, with an intercept of 3.6 and a regression coefficient of 0.28. The intercept can be interpreted as the constant difference between sample and guidelines sentences and the regression coefficient shows the increment in sample sentences that is associated with each unit change in guidelines scores. These results indicate that guidelines sentences are systematically higher than respondent sentences by a constant of about 3.6 years. However, a one-year increment in respondent sentences is only accompanied by a 0.28-year increment in guidelines sentences. In other words, the guidelines start off with higher sentences than the respondents and guidelines sentences increase by about 0.38 years for each additional year of respondent sentences. It should also be noted that the least squares regression line does not fit the points very well: R^2 is a very modest .18.

The median regression shown in Panel B of Table 5.2 is an equation that uses the medians of the sample sentences and the guidelines sentences. Because this approach is based on minimizing the absolute deviations around the regression line, it is much less sensitive to extreme values than the classic regression. The median regression equation has a smaller intercept, 1.5, and a regression coefficient, 0.25. In other words, the median regression results indicate that the guidelines give higher sentences than respondents, about 1.5 years more, and that guidelines sentences increase by 0.25 years for each additional year of respondent sentences. The median regression results do not show the guidelines as being harsher to the same degree as the classic regression results because outliers are not given as much weight. Note also that the predictive power of the median regression is much less than that of the classic regression, the pseudo-R^2 being .08.

All of the regression results shown in Table 5.2 are highly significantly different from zero with standard errors that are many magnitudes smaller than the coefficients, about 20 times smaller for the regression constant and 120 times smaller for the regression coefficient. In short, these findings are extremely unlikely to be the result of sampling variation.[7]

The regression coefficients in Panel A and B are very much alike, indicating that it makes little difference whether we consider means or medians as measures of central tendencies in either guidelines or respondent sentences. The main difference between them lies in the values of the intercepts. The ordinary least squares equation, influenced by the death sentences given by some respondents, has a relatively large intercept. Overall, both regression equations show that on the level of vignettes, the correspondence between sample sentences and guidelines sentences is not very high. Although the two kinds of sentences tend to go hand in hand, there is also a lot of variation in that overall correspondence, with many respondents giving sentences that are higher and many that are lower than the guidelines sentences for the same crimes.

An important source of the considerable variability of respondent sentences is that they are not very reliable: that is, when the same vignette is rated twice by the same respondent, the sentences given tend to differ. As described in Chapter 4, the correlation between the two responses given to the same vignettes by respondents was about .60–.70, a modest degree of reliability at best, although quite similar to typical reliability values for survey items.

A reasonable interpretation of the modest degree of reliability in respondent sentencing is that respondents did not distinguish clearly among sentences that are of the same magnitude. A sentence, say, of four years is not seen as very different in severity from a sentence of six years. This interpretation is bolstered by the fact that respondent sentences tended to cluster around sentences that were multiples of five, as shown in Figure 5.1 earlier. Respondents were consistent only in giving the same sentence magnitude and not the same number of years when rating the same vignette twice. In short, at the level of individual respondent sentencing behavior there is evidence that "measurement error" is large enough to account for much of the discrepancy between the guidelines and public opinion.

TAKING RESPONSE SETS INTO ACCOUNT

In the analysis of the preceding section, the implicit assumption was made that all respondents had the same understanding of the sentencing metric: that is, a year in prison means the same to one respondent as a year in prison to any other respondent. That assumption may not be justified. Perhaps respondents had different interpretations of prison time, some holding, for example, that a year in prison was a very severe sentence and others holding that a year was not very severe. This might lead some respondents to give longer sentences than others even though all wanted to impose sentences of the same severity. In that event, some portion of the differences between respondent and guidelines sentences might well be due to varying "response sets," systematic differences from respondent to respondent in the calibration of sentences. In other words, one respondent may have a general tendency to give long sentences whereas another may be inclined to give generally short sentences.

Although we do not have a very satisfactory way of measuring such response sets, we can take advantage of the two practice standard vignettes discussed in Chapter 4. Because the two vignettes were administered to each respondent and hence depict the same crime and offender, we can use the sentences given to the vignettes by each respondent as a proxy for each respondent's response set, reasoning that because they were the same for all respondents, the sentences given to that vignette reflect that respondent's response set at least in part.

Table 5.3 shows how the regression equations presented in Table 5.2 are modified when the sentences given to the standard bank robbery vignette and the standard drug possession vignette are held constant. Note that the standard vignettes are excluded from the dependent variable. Although the regression coefficient for the guidelines sentences is virtually unchanged, varying only in the second decimal place, the regression constants are influenced by being increased slightly. The regression coefficients for the proxy standard vignettes are not of much interest in themselves, although they are statistically significant and small, providing some evidence that weak response sets were at work.

Table 5.3. Regressions of Sample Sentences on Guideline Sentences Holding Respondent Response Set Proxies Constant [a]

A. OLS Regression
$$S_{gi} = 3.9 + 0.29S_{ij} - 0.06B_j + 0.03P_j, \quad R^2 = .18, \quad N = 64{,}161^b$$

B. Median Regression
$$S_{gi} = 1.6 + 0.25S_{ij} - 0.02V_j + 0.01P_j, \quad \text{Pseudo } R^2 = .08, \quad N = 64{,}671 \ ^b$$

[a] S_{ij} designates sentence given to a nonstandard vignette i by respondent j; S_{gi} designates Guidelines sentence given to i; B_j is the sentence given by respondent j to the standard bank robbery vignette; P_j is the sentence given by respondent j to the standard drug possession vignette. All coefficients are significant at better than the .0001 level.
[b] All standard vignettes involving bank robbery or drug possession were removed.

The findings of Table 5.3 indicate that respondent response sets probably play only a minor role in the difference between guidelines sentences and those given by respondents, at least to the extent that the sentences given to the standard vignettes reflect such phenomena: the resulting R^2 is only slightly higher for the least squares equation and not at all so for the median regression equation. This finding means that the variability from respondent to respondent is not simply a matter of different sentence calibrations. Rather the differences are due to other causes.

SENTENCES FOR CRIME TYPES

The vignettes were designed to represent specific concrete cases describing convicted felons and their crimes. At that level, the fit between what the respondents want as sentences and what the guidelines prescribe is not very close. Although the two tend to go hand in hand, there were differences of kind and degree between the two. However, it can be argued that it is not necessary to have close agreement about specific cases between individual Americans and the guidelines as long as there is fairly close agreement among the central tendencies of sentencing about classes of crimes. That is, agreement about the median or mean sentences may be what is most important.

Table 5.4 lists the guidelines and respondent sentences for the 20 different Crime Types included in the study. To simplify presentation, the Crime Types are ordered by the median sentence given under the guidelines. In the first column, one can see that kidnaping is the most heavily penalized crime in the guidelines schedule (39.2 years), bank robbery is the second most heavily penalized crime (11.3 years), and so on. The second column shows the median sentences given by respondents. For example, the median respondent sentence for kidnaping is 25 years, the mean respondent sentence for bank robbery is 5 years, and so on. Columns 3 and 4 show the mean sentences given under the guidelines and by respondents respectively.

Respondent sentence measures in Table 5.4 differ from values shown in Chapter 3 because of the truncation of extreme sentences described earlier.

Note that respondent sentences have means and medians that are generally far apart. We favor using the medians of respondent sentences for further analyses because they will be unaffected by the arbitrary coding of life and death sentences (which fall at the tails of the sentencing distri-

Table 5.4. Sentences for Crime Types: Guidelines and Sample Sentenced Compared. Crime Types Arranged in Descending Order of Median Guidelines Sentences

Crime Type	Median (Years) Guidelines	Median (Years) Sample	Means (Years) Guidelines	Means (Years) Sample	Interquartile Range Guidelines	Interquartile Range Sample	N
Kidnaping	39.2	25	25.7	23.6	27.8	34.2	1,396
Bank Robbery	11.3	5	10.9	10.1	4.5	7	5,499
Street Robbery	9.1	5	9.7	9.6	6.8	7	1,328
Drug Trafficking	7.3	10	12.5	15.2	19.5	15	13,413
Food & Drug	6.5	9	7.3	14.1	10.9	18	1,989
Civil Rights	4.3	1	3.1	3.3	3.2	3.65	3,343
Major Fraud	3.5	3	3.5	6.5	3	9.2	4,035
Extortion/Blackmail	3.1	5	3.8	9.1	4.8	8	683
Money Laundering	3.1	3	3.8	5.1	4.1	4.2	1,995
Firearms	2.5	3	2.5	5.0	2	4.5	3,370
Bribery	2.5	1	2.1	3.0	1.4	3.5	2,597
Tax	2.2	2	2.5	4.4	1.8	4.5	4,014
Environment	2	1	2.9	3.5	3.4	5	3,315
Antitrust	2	2	2.3	4.8	0.5	4.5	1,353
Forgery/Counterfeiting	1.8	5	2.4	6.3	2.3	8	2,049
Minor Fraud	1.8	2	1.8	4.4	1.3	4.2	2,709
Larceny	1.2	3	1.7	5.0	1.5	4.1	1,908
Embezzlement	0.9	2	1.3	4.8	1.7	4.2	1,945
Immigration	0.75	2	0.8	4.5	0.6	4.5	3,333
Drug Possession	0.25	0.5	0.6	2	0.5	2	7,012

bution). In contrast, the medians and the means for guidelines sentences are much closer together, a consequence of the fact that the guidelines sentences as calculated for some specific crime were not free to depart from some fixed number. Accordingly, guidelines sentences are quite well represented by their means.[8]

Finally, the next two columns show the interquartile ranges for the guidelines sentences and the respondent sentences. As shown in the interquartile ranges, by and large there is more variability in the respondent sentences, which is not surprising. Variation in the guidelines sentences is solely a function of vignette characteristics, while variation in respondent sentences is a function of vignette characteristics *and* respondent characteristics. The only exception to the general pattern is for drug trafficking, where the interquartile range for respondent sentences is a bit smaller. The less variable respondent sentences reflect the fact that respondents did not treat the four kinds of drugs as differently as the guidelines. In particular, respondents did not regard trafficking in crack cocaine as being especially heinous compared to trafficking in powder cocaine, heroin, or even marijuana, whereas in the guidelines crack trafficking is punished more severely.

Comparing the two series, it is clear that sometimes guidelines sentences are more lengthy and sometimes respondent sentences are more lengthy. For example, the guidelines sentence is longer for drug trafficking and bank robbery, but shorter for extortion and forgery.

Figure 5.4 shows the same data in a scatterplot format. Median respondent sentences are represented on the horizontal axis and mean guidelines sentences are represented on the vertical axis. The diagonal line is the least squares line resulting when mean guidelines sentences are regressed on median respondent sentences. The two lines banding the regression line indicate where guidelines sentences would fall two standard errors above and below the predicted regression values. Points lying outside the bands are identifiable as statistical outliers, which are distant from the regression line far beyond chance expectations.

Crimes with deviations lying outside the "confidence band" are labeled. No crimes fall below the confidence band and only two Crime Types lie above the band: bank robbery and street robbery, both Crime Types for which guidelines sentences are much higher than respondent sentences.

The first impression is that there is, on the average, remarkable comparability between mean guidelines sentences and the median sentences desired by the public for Crime Types. A more precise evaluation can be obtained by testing the null hypothesis that the intercept of the regression line is 0.0 and the slope of the regression line is 1.0. If the intercept is 0.0,

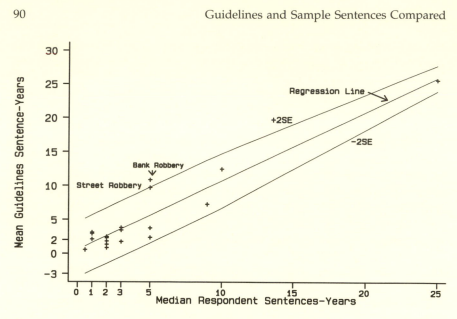

Figure 5.4. Crime Types Scatterplot

there is no systematic tendency over the full set of Crimes Types for mean guidelines sentences to be longer or shorter than median respondent sentences. If the slope is 1.0, a one-year increment in median respondent sentence length is associated on the average with a one-year increment in median guidelines sentence; on the average, the two sentencing distributions move in step with one another over the full set of Crime Types and in that sense, the *structure* of the sentencing is the same. The estimated regression equation has a regression coefficient of 1.0 and an intercept of 0.54, neither statistically different, respectively, from 1.0 and 0.0. The departures are small in practical terms. Stated differently, given a respondent median sentence for a Crime Type, the best predicted guidelines sentence is the actual calculated mean guidelines sentence.

The fit is also impressive, with an R^2 for the equation of .78 A key implication is that when there are departures from the regression line, they tend to be small. At the Crime Type level of aggregation, one can "explain" most of the variation in median guidelines sentences from in formation about median respondent sentences.

Because kidnaping, the upper right-hand point of Figure 5.4, receives sentences that are much longer than any of the other Crime Types, one could suspect that much of the overall correspondence is dominated by the Crime Type of kidnaping. However kidnaping is not particularly influential. The least squares regression lines with and without kidnaping are virtually identical: Without kidnaping the intercept is 0.42 and the slope is 1.02, whereas the regression line with kidnaping included has an intercept of 0.54 and slope of 1.0.[9]

Perhaps the major lesson from Figure 5.4 is that there is fairly strong agreement on aggregated sentences for Crime Types. However, as a unit, Crime Types are coarse; overall conclusions heavily depend on how the vignettes were designed and then aggregated. For example, we suspect that if the design had allowed for the killing of a teller or witness in some of the bank robbery vignettes, the median sentences for bank robbery might have looked a lot like the median sentences for kidnaping. But most important, in the real world, sentences are given out for specific offenses and not for the broad categories represented by Crime Types. These considerations argue for looking at the correspondence between guidelines and respondent sentences using more specific offenses.

CRIME EXAMPLES

The 20 Crime Types are each composed of several examples. Each example is a description of a concrete instance of one of the Crime Types. (The actual Crime Example descriptions used in the vignettes are presented in detail in Table 4.1.) A strong argument can be made that it is the degree of correspondence concerning examples that should be a matter of concern, because the examples are closer to the way in which crimes are perceived by the public. Accordingly, a finer-grained approach to comparing guidelines and sample sentences is to examine that correspondence at the level of the 73 Crime Examples used.

Table 5.5 shows mean and median sentences under the guidelines and the mean and median given by respondents for the 73 crime examples. Overall, going to the more specific crime examples produces greater heterogeneity in both guidelines and respondent sentences. In addition, there are more and sometimes greater disparities between the mean guidelines and the median respondent sentences.

In Table 5.5, by far the largest disparity between the mean guidelines sentences and the median respondent sentences is for trafficking in crack cocaine; the guidelines sentence (either median or mean) is about 12 years longer than the respondent median sentence and 6 years longer than the respondent mean sentence. Interestingly, the disparity for trafficking in marijuana is also large, but in the opposite direction: respondent mean sentence is 13.1 years versus 4.4 years as the mean guidelines sentence.

Table 5.5. Guidelines and Sample Sentences Compared for 73 Crime Examples. Crimes ranked in descending order by median Guidelines Sentences

Crime Type	Median (Years)		Means (Years)		N
	Guidelines	Sample	Guidelines	Sample	
Kidnaping: Victim killed	39.2	39.2	39.2	33.9	724
Drug Trafficking: Crack	22	10	21.8	16.0	3,281
Bank Robbery: Teller seriously wounded	17.6	15	17.5	19.9	635
Bank Robbery: Teller had minor gunshot injury	14.1	10	14.1	15.4	616
Kidnaping: Victim unhurt	11.3	6	11.5	12.5	672
Street Robbery: Carjacking	11.3	5	11.4	10.4	732
Bank Robbery: Weapon fired at ceiling	11.3	5	11.3	8.2	2,240
Food & Drug: Poisoning OTC drugs	9.4	15	10.5	21.8	681
Drug Trafficking: Cocaine	9.1	10	12.1	15.9	3,387
Drug Trafficking: Heroin	9.1	10	11.8	15.8	3,359
Bank Robbery: Weapon used but not fired	8.1	5	9.2	8.2	681
Environment: Discharging toxic wastes	8.1	2	8.6	4.2	664
Money: Coin dealer laundering criminal funds	7.3	4	7.3	6.8	669
Street Robbery: Convenience store	6.5	5	7.6	8.5	596
Bank Robbery: Bomb threatened but not used	6.5	5	6.9	8.9	666
Bank Robbery: No weapon used	4.8	4	5.6	5.8	661
Fraud: Bank officer causing S&L failure	4.8	3	5.4	6.1	660
Civil Rights: Police brutality of motorist	4.3	2	4.3	4.4	675
Civil Rights: Police brutality of minority motorist	4.3	2	4.3	3.8	709
Civil Rights: Police brutality resisting motorist	4.3	0.5	4.3	2.1	636
Forgery: Counterfeiting US currency	3.8	5	4.7	7.6	704
Fraud: Selling defective helicopter parts	3.8	10	3.7	11.9	672
Extortion/Blackmail	3.1	5	3.8	9.1	683
Bribery: Bribing county commissioner	3.1	2	3.4	3.5	686
Firearms: Owning sawed-off shotgun	3.1	2	3.4	4.5	670
Fraud: False mortgage: Intent to repay	3.1	0.5	3.0	2.1	678
Fraud: Doctor filing false Medicare claims	3.1	5	2.9	6.9	684

Fraud: Selling worthless stocks and bonds	3.1	5	2.9	7.5	680
Fraud: Company officer; insider trading	3.1	2	2.9	4.4	661
Firearms: Dealer selling guns to felons	2.8	5	3.0	7.5	657
Drug Trafficking: Marijuana	2.5	8	4.4	13.1	3,386
Environment: Discharging hot water into stream	2.5	0.7	2.8	2.2	658
Firearms: Dealer keeping poor sales records	2.5	3	2.6	6.1	725
Tax: Failure to file returns	2.5	2	2.5	4.4	1,341
Tax: Failure to report income	2.5	2	2.5	4.4	1,340
Bribery: County commissioner accepting bribe	2.5	1	2.5	2.6	615
Money: Coin dealer not reporting big purchases	2.2	2	2.4	3.8	660
Firearms: Felon owning handgun	2	2	2.5	3.7	691
Antitrust: Bid rigging	2	4	2.3	6.0	642
Antitrust: Price fixing	2	1	2.3	3.7	711
Larceny: Buying and selling stolen goods	2	2	2.3	4.5	619
Fraud: Soliciting for fake charity	2	3	2.2	4.9	661
Environment: Factory polluting air	2	1	2.2	3.8	674
Food & Drug: Marketing drug with side effects	1.8	5	5.9	11.7	631
Food & Drug: Marketing drug false testing	1.8	5	5.4	8.6	677
Tax: Promoting illegal tax shelter	1.8	2	2.3	4.3	1,333
Fraud: False mortgage no intent to repay	1.8	2	1.8	3.8	628
Money: Bank official laundering criminal funds	1.8	2	1.7	4.5	666
Embezzlement: Postal worker	1.8	3	1.7	5.6	672
Fraud: Using stolen credit card	1.5	2	1.7	4.2	701
Fraud: Writing bad checks	1.5	2	1.6	4.6	719
Forgery: Writing bad checks on false account	1.3	3	1.2	5.0	681
Larceny: Stealing US mail	1.2	3	1.7	5.5	636
Civil Rights: Harassment of minority neighbor	1.1	1	1.3	3.4	650
Civil Rights: Vandalism of house of worship	1.1	1	1.3	2.6	673
Bribery: Bribing company purchasing agent	1.1	2	1.2	3.3	657

(continued)

Table 5.5. (Continued)

Crime Type	Median (Years)		Means (Years)		N
	Guidelines	Sample	Guidelines	Sample	
Firearms: Felon owning hunting rifle	1	1	0.7	3.0	627
Embezzlement: Bank officer	0.9	2	1.3	4.3	663
Immigration: smuggling aliens for profit	0.9	4	1.1	5.9	649
Immigration: Smuggling aliens endangering safety	0.9	5	1.1	7.1	727
Forgery: Using illegally obtained credit cards	0.9	4	1.1	6.1	664
Larceny: Stealing property	0.8	3	1.2	5.0	653
Bribery: Govt. purchasing agent accepting bribe	0.8	1	1.1	2.6	639
Drug Possession: Heroin	0.8	0.9	0.8	2.6	1,368
Immigration: Illegal re-entry into US	0.8	0.9	0.8	3.0	631
Drug Possession: Crack	0.8	1	0.8	3.0	1,361
Embezzlement: Bank employee	0.6	2	0.9	4.4	610
Environment: Killing bald eagle	0.4	0.9	0.6	2.5	669
Immigration: Illegal entry into US	0.4	0.7	0.6	2.5	658
Immigration: smuggling alien family members	0.4	1	0.6	3.5	668
Drug Possession: Cocaine	0.4	0.9	0.5	2.9	1,329
Environment: Illegal logging on federal lands	0.3	2	0.5	4.6	650
Drug Possession: Marijuana	0.3	0.0	0.3	1.0	2,954

The guidelines make an decided distinction between trafficking in crack cocaine compared to marijuana. The public agrees that trafficking in crack is more serious than trafficking in marijuana, but only a little bit more serious.

There are additional crime examples in which the guidelines means are noticeably larger than respondent means, including carjacking, bank robbery, several environmental crimes, and one of the civil rights crimes. There are also examples in which the public apparently wants more severe sentences than the guidelines, including several immigration crimes and the sale of defective helicopter parts to the federal government. Overall agreement is clearly tempered by strong differences surrounding specific offenses.

Figure 5.5 graphs the relationship between the two series. The two lines above and below the regression line form a "confidence" band representing two standard errors above and below the regression line. Falling far above and outside the band is the Crime Example of trafficking in crack cocaine, clearly representing the greatest disparity between the guidelines and the respondents. Also above the confidence band were the Crime Examples involving a bank robbery in which a gun was fired but no one was injured, carjacking in which the victim is not injured, and the environmental violation in which toxic wastes were released into a stream.

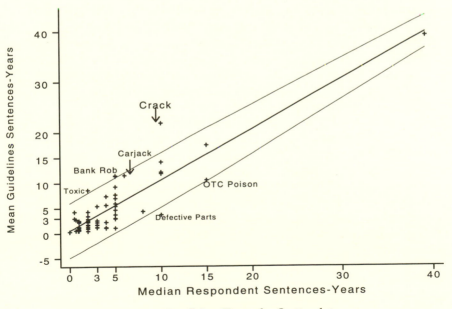

Figure 5.5. Crime Examples Scatterplot

Crimes falling at or below the lower line of the confidence band are Crime Examples in which respondents gave much longer sentences than the guidelines. Only two Crime Examples are so identified: a fraud crime in which defective helicopter parts were sold to the government and adding poison to over-the-counter drugs. Significantly, both these Crime Examples involve potential physical danger to persons.

Despite these divergences, there is remarkable overall consensus between mean guidelines sentences and median respondent sentences. The regression line has a intercept of 0.54 and a slope of 1.00, values that are not statistically different from 0.0 and 1.0, respectively.[10] In addition, the adjusted R^2 for the regression is .78;[11] the few striking departures from the regression line still left a very good fit intact. In short, on the one hand, we find once again that overall the guidelines map well onto the public's views. On the other hand, the few departures seem all the more anomalous by contrast.

COMBINING PRIOR RECORD AND CRIME EXAMPLES

At the very end of the process of determining guidelines sentences, each crime is combined with the convicted person's prior record of felony convictions. The design of the vignettes also followed that process, with each vignette randomly assigned a prior record of either none, two, or four felony convictions. This provides an opportunity for a much finer aggregation by combining crime examples and prior record. There are 175 such combinations,[12] too many to show in a table. However, a scatterplot can be more easily comprehended: it is shown as Figure 5.6.

Figure 5.6 has the same structure shown in prior figures. It plots the mean guidelines sentence and the median respondent sentences for each of the 175 combinations. Three lines are shown, the upper line representing sentences two standard errors above the predicted guidelines sentence, the middle line being the regression line, and the lower line representing two standard errors below the regression line. Points at or outside the confidence band are identified and named, the number in parentheses representing, respectively, a prior record of four previous convictions (3), prior record of two previous convictions (2), and no prior record (1).

The least squares regression line has an intercept of 0.45 and a slope of 1.02. As before, we cannot reject the hypothesis that the intercept was 0.0 and the slope 1.0. Once again, the structure of the two sentencing distributions is, on the average, the same. The adjusted R^2 for the regression is

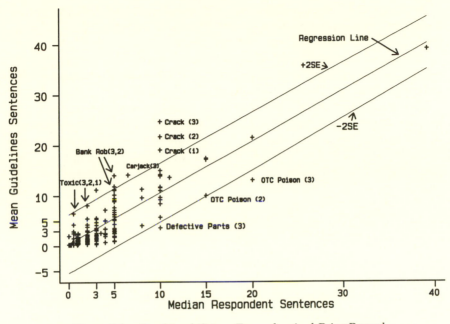

Figure 5.6. Combined Crime Examples And Prior Record

.80, about the same as for the crime examples. In short, taking the effects of prior record into account, the correspondence between guidelines and respondent sentences remains high and perhaps slightly higher. This finding also indicates that the respondents and the guidelines agree on prior record adjustments to sentences.

All that said, there are 12 combinations that lie outside the confidence band, nine of which are offenses to which the guidelines give much higher sentences than the respondents. Conspicuous among the outliers are the three crack-trafficking offenses, all of the combinations involving that crime. Clearly the guidelines sentences for this crime are much harsher than respondents desired and even more so for offenders with prior records. The other combinations in which guidelines are harsher than respondents include carjacking committed by an offender with four prior convictions but with no resulting physical harm to the victim; bank robbery in which the robber has four prior convictions, in one case brandishing a gun and in the other case discharging the gun harmlessly into the bank ceiling; and the environmental crime of discharging toxic chemicals into a stream (all levels of prior convictions).

There are three combinations in which respondents give much longer sentences: two involving felons with either two or four prior felonies putting poison into over-the-counter drugs, and the other a fraud in which a manufacturer sold defective helicopter parts to the government.[13] In the latter example, respondents were likely reacting to the potential for physical harm to helicopter passengers.

Overall, median respondent sentences were close matches to the mean guidelines sentences, suggesting that the public agrees with the guidelines about the weights to be given to prior criminal records as well as the punishments to be meted out for crimes. (This issue is taken up in greater detail in Chapter 6.)

SUMMARY AND CONCLUSION

We return to the central question posed in the beginning of this chapter. To what extent do the U.S. Sentencing Commission's guidelines correspond to the public's views on the sentencing of persons convicted of violating the federal penal code? The findings presented indicate that the guidelines map rather well onto the central tendencies of public wishes. In each instance when we examined aggregate respondent data, we were unable to reject the null hypothesis that the two sentencing distributions had the same structure. Furthermore, because the federal criminal courts deal with crimes of quite a different mix compared to the state courts, which are more likely to receive attention from the mass media, one might expect that the federal crimes might be less well-known and hence views on sentencing of such crimes might not be very well structured. In this light, the similarities between the guidelines and public views are remarkable.

We also found that agreement varied widely depending on level of aggregation. Fairly close agreement exists when the means and medians of sample sentences are considered but is much more modest when we consider individual sentences. An interpretation of the differences among levels of aggregation is that there is considerable "error" in individual respondent sentences. There is apparently no clear public consensus on an absolute scale of severity of punishment that corresponds directly to lengths of prison sentences. One person's two-year sentence may be the equivalent of another's four-year sentence. In addition, the differences between sentences are not distinct: respondents who gave a four-year sentence on one occasion to a specific crime may give a different sentence on another occasion to the same crime. In other words, the punishment norms of our society are only dimly apprehended by respondents. These "errors" tend to cancel out when responses are aggregated as shown in our analyses at the Crime Type and Crime Example levels of aggregation. In line with this interpretation is the finding that respondents with more formal education have smaller "errors" in their sentences than those with less education.[14]

With the major exception of drug-trafficking crimes, it was also found that the factors considered by the guidelines as grounds for specific kinds of sentence enhancements were also regarded as grounds for such changes in sentencing by the public. Especially important was the close agreement over sentence enhancements justified by the prior criminal records of the offender.

Yet, within the remarkable correspondence between the guidelines sentences and respondent sentences, there were several striking disagreements. In particular, the guidelines and the public differ strongly on trafficking in illegal drugs. The guidelines favored very severe punishments for dealing in crack cocaine, whereas the public does not regard trafficking in that drug as more serious than dealing in either powder cocaine or heroin. At the same time, the public desired somewhat longer sentences for trafficking in marijuana. The message from the public may be that trafficking in any illegal substance is a major felony, but trafficking in crack cocaine should not be singled out for especially severe punishments.

As related in Chapter 2, the guidelines sentences for drug trafficking were established by the commission in a different fashion than the other crimes. Congress had mandated a specific set of penalties for drug-trafficking crimes, which were incorporated into the guidelines. Unlike the procedures used in setting sentences for other crimes, the commission disregarded past sentencing practices for drug-trafficking crimes as well as whatever understanding the commissioners may have had concerning the preferences of the American public. Our findings show that the congressional mandates departed strongly from those preferences.

Less striking, but still important, is that the public appears to regard crimes that endanger the physical safety of victims and bystanders as more serious than the guidelines, as, for example, the Crime Example of adding poison to over-the-counter drugs. In general, concerns about the safety of individuals drive a lot of the variation in sentences for both the guidelines and the public, but these concerns translate more readily into longer sentences when the public's preferences are elicited.

Finally, the guidelines treat environmental crimes, violation of civil rights, and certain bribery and extortion crimes more harshly than the public. It is difficult to see what these crimes have in common, and we fail to find any general lessons.

At a more general level, our data are consistent with a view that the guidelines are substantially structured by the central tendencies of public opinion. At the same time, there is significant variation around these central tendencies, so that particular individuals are unlikely to see in the guidelines a fully accurate reflection of their own preferences; the structure of correspondence only becomes apparent in the aggregate. Thus, there is ample room for visible and heated criticisms of the sentences prescribed by the guidelines even though the guidelines map rather well onto what the public "wants" on the average.

NOTES

1.   Some of the dimensions used in the study are not recognized in the guidelines as grounds for sentencing decisions. For example, the vignettes vary the gender of the offender but the guidelines do not recognize gender as a factor to be used in sentencing. These dimensions were included because there was concern that respondents might take them into account.

2.   This estimate was calculated by regressing the guidelines sentences for each vignette on the crimes and prior records of each vignette, entered as dummy variables. The resulting R^2 was .92.

3.   Using the lower or upper boundaries of the guidelines sentence ranges was also considered. Preliminary analyses indicated that using these alternatives did not affect results markedly. For example, using the lower boundary in regression typically affected the intercept values but not the regression coefficients.

4.   Including respondent death sentences shifts the mean of differences from −1.3 to −2.0 and produces a long left tail. However, the median is not affected noticeably.

5.   This finding may be an artifact caused by taking the midpoint of the ranges of guidelines sentences. Respondents were allowed to give probation sentences of 0 years, but taking the midpoint of the most lenient guidelines range meant that there were no guidelines sentence that were exactly 0. However, an alyses using the lower bound of the guidelines sentencing range indicate that only slight differences occur in most calculations.

6.   Median regression is a special case of quantile regression methods. The general approach is recommended when the distribution of values of the dependent variable is skewed. An extended discussion of this approach can be found in Manski (1988).

7.   Because each respondent contributed 42 vignettes, the vignette sets of each respondent are not completely independent. That is, the vignettes rated by a

respondent were more likely to be treated somewhat the same way by that respondent and differently from other respondents. The mean correlation between pairs of sentences given to pairs of vignettes by the same respondent is .22. As a consequence, standard errors computed in the traditional way tend to be underestimated.

To gauge the impact of the possible intrarespondent dependence, four random samples of vignettes were drawn, each consisting of one vignette from each respondent. The least squares regression results follows:

Replicate	Constant	b	R^2	N
1	3.5	.27	.17	1.596
2	3.3	.30	.20	1.596
3	3.7	.28	.16	1.602
4	3.7	.28	.17	1.609

In each replicate the standard errors are very small, all coefficients are significant, and, as to be expected not very different from the results in Table 5.2. Whatever intrarespondent consistency may exist cannot account for the highly significant results shown in Table 5.2, even though the true standard errors for the coefficients tend to be 10 to 20% higher.

8.   Because guidelines sentences are fixed for all identical vignettes, there are no outliers in these sentences. Hence the mean is a good descriptive measure of their central tendencies. In addition, the findings in the analyses of the next few pages are not strongly affected by whether means or medians are used to represent guidelines sentences.

The kidnaping Crime Example constitutes an exception, with a median sentence of 39.2 years and a mean of 25.7, values that are far apart. This discrepancy occurs because there are slightly more kidnapping Crime Examples in which the victim is killed, for which the guidelines sentence is 39.2 years, than Crime Examples in which the victim is unhurt, for which the guidelines sentence is 11.3 years. Because more than 50% of the kidnaping vignettes describe the former Crime Example, the median is 39.2 years. In this instance the median does not serve well as a measure of central tendency.

9.   The adjusted R^2 for the equation including kidnaping is .78 whereas that for the equation excluding that crime is .58. Although kidnaping does not meaningfully influence the location of the least squares line, it adds dramatically to the explained variance.

10.   The regression results using the median guidelines sentences were very close; the intercept was 0.23 and the slope 0.98, not statistically different from 0.0 and 1.0, respectively.

11.   We also tested for regression line differences when the crime example of kidnaping and killing the victim was omitted. The resulting regression equation was virtually identical to the line computed when that crime example was included, although the adjusted R^2 for that line dropped to .58.

12.   For some of the crime examples involving persons in occupations denied

to those who have prior felony convictions, e.g., bank officials, elected officials, or police, vignettes were given the no prior record description. Hence only one combination was possible for such vignettes.

13.   This Crime Example was one in which no prior record was given to all vignettes with this example.

14.   Quantile regressions of guidelines sentences on respondents sentences for those with college degrees produced a pseudo R^2 more than twice as large as that for respondents who never completed high school.

6

Sentence Enhancements:
Guidelines and Respondents Compared

INTRODUCTION

The guidelines allow for sentences for crimes to be enhanced in certain specific ways, depending in some instances on how the crime was committed, on the kinds of losses inflicted on victims, and on the previous record of the offender. Some of these enhancements were included systematically in the vignettes given to the respondents. In Chapter 5, we compared respondents and guidelines sentences primarily on how both gave sentences for crimes, disregarding the other features of the crime as described in the vignettes. In this chapter, we compare the two according to how much sentences were affected by the other features of the crime and offender as described in the vignettes.

The overall conclusion of Chapter 5 was that, with a few important exceptions, there was remarkable agreement on crimes. Perhaps the most significant exception was for drug trafficking, where guidelines sentences were far more punitive than respondent sentences, especially for trafficking in crack cocaine. However, such overall comparisons reveal little directly about the specific sources of agreement and disagreement. In the case of drug trafficking, for instance, was the disparity a result of differences in how crack and powder cocaine were viewed? Or was it the role of the offender in the crime, the amount of economic gain, or the salience of violence? Or perhaps was it some combination of the weights given to each?

Similar issues can be raised when there was apparent agreement between the guidelines sentences and average respondent sentences. For example, in the case of bank robbery, one could imagine counterbalancing effects in which the guidelines treated the threat of violence more severely than the respondents did, but the respondents treated actual violence more severely than the guidelines did. As a result, overall agreement can actually mask important differences in how the vignette dimensions affected the sentences given by respondents.

In this chapter, we will directly address the ways in which the vignette dimensions were evaluated by the guidelines and the respondents. For each of the Crime Types for which comparisons can be made, we will graphically compare the weights given by the guidelines and respondents to various features of the vignettes in the determination of overall sentence. For example, is the importance of using a firearm the same for respondents and the guidelines when sentences are given? Such comparisons between the weights will allow us to disentangle the sources of agreement and disagreement in the overall sentences given. That is, we will show what the weights are for both the guidelines and respondents and, in so doing, identify agreements and disagreements.

The issues considered in this chapter are also relevant to the structure of American sentencing norms. Such norms may also prescribe how sentences for crimes may be augmented or diminished in the same or different ways from those required by the guidelines. If our results indicate that respondents pay no attention to the crime features used by the guidelines in modifying sentences, then we have evidence that American sentencing norms do not support the guidelines. Other findings might mean that there is agreement between the norms and the guidelines, or that the norms weight those features differently.

ANALYSIS STRATEGY: BANK ROBBERY AS AN ILLUSTRATIVE EXAMPLE

We begin with the crime of bank robbery. Because bank robbery is a familiar crime and one that has several interesting dimensions, it provides a good vehicle for an exposition of the graphical methods we will employ for all of the analyses, along with the statistical reasoning underlying the approach. Comparisons between the guidelines weights and the average respondent weights for this crime are likely to be especially meaningful because respondents' understanding of the issues was likely to be quite good. The issues are considerably less familiar for less common federal crimes such as bribery and embezzlement. For such crimes, one might anticipate that comparisons between the weights would be complicated by respondents' lack of familiarity with the crimes in question and reflected in relatively great variability in sentencing.

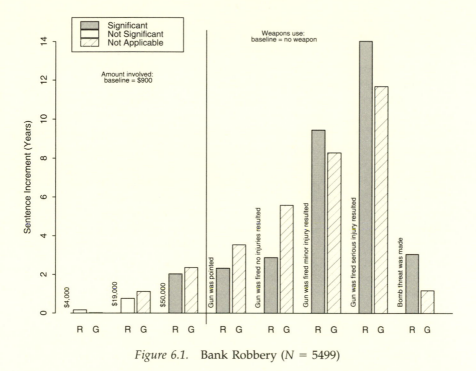

Figure 6.1. Bank Robbery (*N* = 5499)

Figure 6.1 shows two sets of bar graphs. The capital letter beneath each bar designates whether the bar above refers to respondents (R) or guidelines (G) sentences. The vertical axis, Sentence Increment (Years), is calibrated in years, but they are years added to (greater than zero) or subtracted from a defendant's sentence (less than zero) associated with the enhancement feature in question. Note that the bars are not the total length of the sentence given but the *increase* or *decrease* associated with the crime feature in question. The left panel contains the increments given by respondents and the guidelines associated with the amount of money taken in a bank robbery. The right panel contains the increments given by respondents and the guidelines associated with the descriptions in the vignettes of how a weapon was used in the bank robbery. How these increments were calculated will be addressed shortly.

Consider first the left panel. Compared to the baseline of $900 taken in a bank robbery, one finds that for both respondents and the guidelines, taking greater amounts of money leads to longer sentences: a few months longer for taking $4,000, about a year for taking $19,000, and about two years longer for taking $50,000. Since the bars for respondents and the guidelines are about the same size, there is substantial agreement on the weights given. Finally, the shaded bars for respondents are statistically significant in that we are able to reject the null hypothesis that the increment is zero at the .05 level. As discussed briefly below, statistical inference is not relevant for the guidelines weights because no sampling is involved.

The right panel shows how the ways weapons were used in the robbing of of a bank adds to the sentences given to the vignettes. Compared to the baseline, no weapon used, we see that ordering of the increments is the same for both respondents and the guidelines. From the smallest to the largest increments the order is (1) bomb threat, (2) pointing a gun, (3) firing a gun with no injuries, (4) firing a gun with minor injuries, and (5) firing a gun with major injuries. It is also clear that the variation in sentence increments is substantial: 2 to 3 years for a bomb threat and 12 to 14 years when there are major injuries as a result of using a firearm. Importantly when an injury results from the use of a weapon, respondents give larger increments than the guidelines, and when no injury results the guidelines seek longer sentences than the respondents. These differences range between about one year and three years.

How were these increments calculated? The respondent increments are nothing more than regression coefficients. As such, they represent average effects on sentence length of each of the levels in an enhancement dimension. We regressed the sentence given in all of the bank robbery vignettes on all of the levels (minus one within each dimension, preventing linear dependence) for each relevant dimension. The omitted level is referred to as the baseline in the graph. The sample size N (shown on the title line of the graph) is the number of bank robbery vignettes evaluated. The graph shows the ordinary least squares results.[1] The same formulation was then applied to the guidelines sentences,[2] and a second set of regression coefficients was computed.[3]

Statistical significance for the respondent weights was determined from the regression results.[4] Respondent increments that are statistically significant are shown in shaded bars, whereas those that are not are unshaded were not statistically significant. Statistical tests for the guidelines increments are not really necessary because they are fixed and constant for each level and therefore the guidelines increments have no sampling error: there is no need to worry about the luck of the draw if there is no draw. All of the guidelines bars are shaded using diagonal lines. As for differences between the two sets of increments, we will emphasize differences of one year or more, which we take to be large enough to be substantively important. Such differences are also statistically significant, treating the guidelines weights as fixed. Again, sampling error cannot be a concern if there is no sampling.

The overall findings shown in Figure 6.1 indicate broad agreement between the respondents and the guidelines with some interesting quantitative disparities. The disparities have implications that are both substantive and methodological. On the substantive side, respondents place more weight than the guidelines on the concrete consequences of crime. In particular, putting bank tellers at risk or injuring them is weighted more heavily by respondents, shown by larger increments for respondent sentences. For the guidelines, using a weapon deserves a larger increment but the resulting injuries are not weighted as important as for the respondents. On the methodological side, it is apparent that respondents were able to make sense of the vignette dimensions. The increments given to the bank robbery characteristics are orderly and sensible.

We turn now to the other crimes in this study using the graphical approach described above. Most of the other crimes have enhancement dimensions that are specific to the crimes in question. Accordingly, each crime has to be treated somewhat differently. In the remainder of this chapter we will group crimes that are similar and discuss each group separately. We start with "street crimes," a group of crimes that are well-known and contain some of the most frequent crimes committed.

STREET CRIMES

We have already discussed one of the best-known street crimes, bank robbery. We will proceed to deal with the remaining crimes in this group.

Robbery of a Convenience Store

Convenience stores are robbed so frequently that the evening TV news only pays attention to those in which significant harm occurs. The newspapers also provide little coverage of these crimes. Although most such robberies are handled by state and local criminal justice agencies, some come under federal jurisdiction and are tried in the federal courts. The close to 600 vignettes describing this crime contained dimensions describing the dollar amount stolen, whether the offender used a weapon, and whether injuries were inflicted.

Figure 6.2 shows the sentencing increments given for each of the dimensions. The left panel indicates that, compared to the baseline of $400, the amount of money taken is unimportant. The increments given by

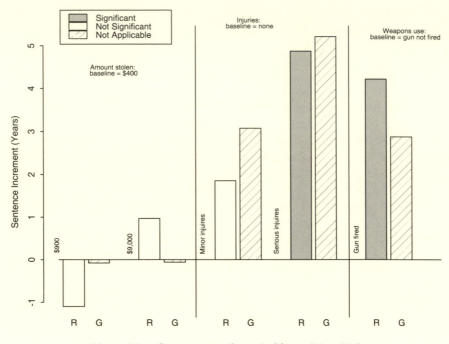

Figure 6.2.   Convenience Store Robbery (*N* = 596)

respondents for the amounts stolen are not significantly different from the baseline. That is, one cannot reject the null hypothesis that the regression coefficients are zero.

The middle panel shows that in contrast, when there are injuries to robbery victims,[5] both the guidelines and respondents react. When there are minor injuries, the respondents add nearly two years to the sentence and the guidelines add around three. For serious injuries, both add nearly five years. Overall the respondents are bit less punitive than the guidelines.

The panel on the right refers to the use of a weapon in the commission of the robbery. When a gun is fired, as opposed to simply used to coerce, respondent and guidelines sentences get longer. Respondents add nearly four years, and the guidelines add nearly three years; respondents are a bit more punitive. Overall, however, the major message is substantial agreement in the weights given.

Kidnaping

As shown dramatically in earlier chapters, kidnaping is a crime that both the guidelines and respondents react to very severely. The only descriptive dimension used in the vignettes containing this crime concerns the death of the victim. The enhancements for killing the victim, shown in Figure 6.3, are quite dramatic. For both the guidelines and respondents, there is a very large increment in sentence length when the victim is killed: an average of over 21 years for respondents and around 28 years for the guidelines.

It is important to keep in mind that there are a substantial number of death sentences represented in the respondent sentence increments shown in Figure 6.3. As described in Chapter 5, we are following the convention of defining death sentences for kidnaping given by respondents as agreement with the sentencing guidelines. Therefore, death sentences were coded the maximum allowable value of 39.2 years. The guidelines penalty was fixed also at 39.2 years. A key consequence is that the difference between the bars in Figure 6.3 may more instructive than the length of each bar. Restated, it is the *difference* between the sentence increases that is most instructive, not the sentence increases themselves. That difference is about seven years. The guidelines sentences increases are somewhat larger.

Still, the overall conclusion is straightforward. When the victim is

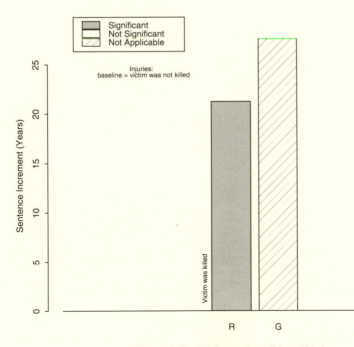

Figure 6.3. Kidnapping ($N = 1396$)

killed, both respondents and the guidelines increment sentence length dramatically. Indeed, the increments are the largest we will see for any of the crimes we shall consider.

Drug Possession

The description of drug possession was "a small amount of [drug] for personal use." What was varied was the kind of illegal drug involved. Accordingly, the key issue addressed in the drug possession vignettes is the impact of different kinds of narcotics. Figure 6.4 shows that, compared to marijuana, the possession of cocaine, crack, or heroin leads to longer sentences from both the respondents and the guidelines, but overall, respondents would increase the sentence by about a year for all three narcotics. The increments called for by the guidelines are only about four months for crack and heroin, but there is virtually no guidelines increment for powder cocaine. Clearly, the public is less tolerant of drug possession but in practice, the differences are not especially large. The real

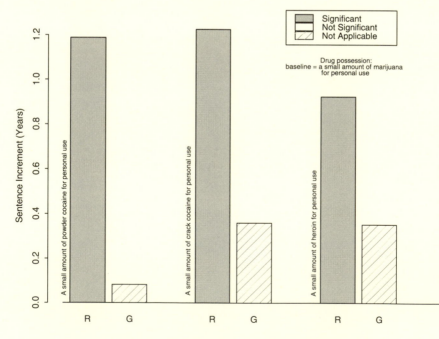

Figure 6.4. Drug Possession (*N* = 7012)

action revolves around drug trafficking, where the federal role is clearly more central. The drug "problem," as seen by both guidelines and respondents, apparently is with the supply side; demand is essentially unimportant. In this light, we turn to drug trafficking.

Drug Trafficking

Because of the considerable policy interest in drug trafficking, there are more dimensions describing this crime than any of the others used in the study. Writing the guidelines rules concerning this crime could not proceed as with the others because, as described in Chapter 2, the commission had to implement the sentencing rules explicitly set by Congress for this crime. To support the analysis of the increments in sentences associated with those dimensions, the study design allocated about one in five vignettes to drug trafficking. There are four main dimensions used in drug-trafficking vignettes; the increments associated with each are shown in Figures 6.5 through 6.8.

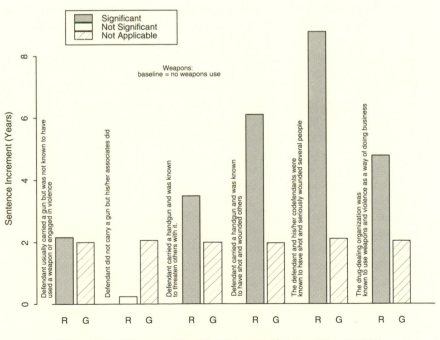

Figure 6.5. Weapons Used in Drug Trafficking ($N = 13,413$)

An important issue in drug trafficking is that the crime is often accompanied by violence. Illegal businesses typically resort to violence in competing for market shares, and in enforcing illegal agreements with others. The impacts of levels of the violence dimension are shown in Figure 6.5. Each level of the violence dimension is contrasted with drug trafficking in which no weapons were used. Overall, the increase in guidelines sentence length is two years for the involvement of weapons in drug trafficking, and the guidelines do not distinguish between the different forms of violence accompanying weapons use. In contrast, respondents made very important distinctions among the different ways weapons were used in drug trafficking.

Indeed all of the findings of interest in Figures 6.5 concern the increments respondents gave. Compared to the baseline, where the defendant did not use or carry weapons of any kind, respondents gave no sentence increment if the offender did not carry firearms but his/her associates in drug trafficking did. However, for respondents carrying a handgun, even when there was no violence involved in the crime, added an average of about two years to the sentence. Threatening with that gun added an average of about three years. Working for a drug organization known for violence added an average of about five years. Using firearms to shoot and wound others added six years. And when the defendant and others with him/her used firearms to shoot and wound others seriously, the sentence was nearly nine years longer. Once again, putting people at risk is of especially great concern to respondents, while the guidelines seemingly ignore such issues.[6]

As Chapter 2 relates, Congress was quite explicit in linking sentence severity in drug trafficking to the amounts of drugs involved. The vignette dimension described both the dollar value and the amount of the drug. The sentence increments in dollar amounts are shown in Figure 6.6. As Congress decreed, the guidelines sentences increase dramatically with the dollar amount trafficked. The respondents also lengthened sentences as the drug amount and economic gain from the drug-trafficking offense increased. In writing the guidelines for drug trafficking, the commission was concerned about deterrence as well as just deserts. Respondents reacted similarly but not as steeply in line with drug amounts. In each instance save one ($1000), the sentence increases from the guidelines are substantially greater. Compared to the baseline of a $100 economic gain, a $1 million economic gain drew a 22-year increment from the guidelines, but only an 8-year increment from the respondents. The difference is 14 years. For an economic gain of $100,000, the difference between respondents and the guidelines is nearly 10 years. For a $20,000 economic gain, the difference is about 5 years. Clearly, the

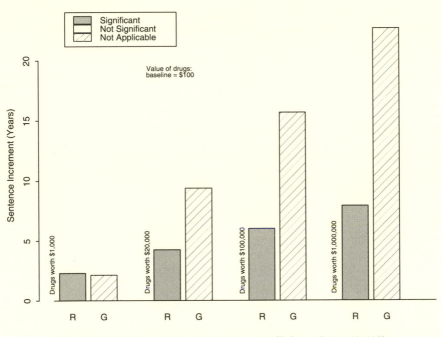

Figure 6.6. Value of Drugs in Drug Trafficking (*N* = 13,413)

guidelines take the amount trafficked far more seriously than do the respondents.

The guidelines make striking distinctions in sentencing according to the kind of drug involved. Respondents clearly disagree on how trafficking in different kinds of narcotics should be punished. Figure 6.7 shows that respondents increase sentences by about 3 years for cocaine, crack and heroin, compared to the sentence for trafficking in marijuana. The increment is modest and consistent. In stark contrast, the guidelines add about 8 years for trafficking in cocaine or heroin, and 17 years for trafficking in crack, all compared to trafficking in marijuana. Thus, the disparities between respondent sentence increments and guidelines sentence increments range from about 5 to 14 years. Clearly the public makes fewer distinctions among drugs and is far less punitive. Put another way, to the respondents there is nothing very special about crack cocaine. Alternatively, the results of Figure 6.7 may reflect a difference in focus. What may matter most about drug trafficking to the respondents is the violence that may be associated with it.

There are many different specific roles that a defendant may take in the complex crime of drug trafficking. The final dimension we will consider,

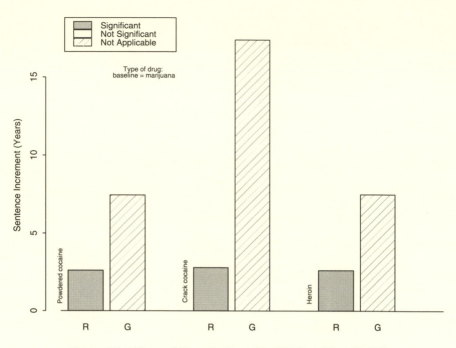

Figure 6.7. Type of Drug in Drug Trafficking (*N* = 13,413)

as in Figure 6.8, consists of a set of levels describing various degrees of involvement ranging from peripheral to central roles in drug trafficking. Although the overall patterns for respondents and the guidelines are rather similar, the guidelines call for much larger sentence enhancements. The baseline level is a defendant whose apartment was used for drug sales. The role of drug courier drew an increment of about six months from respondents and two years from the guidelines. The role of street-level dealer drew an increment of effectively zero from respondents and about four years from the guidelines. The role of bodyguard also had no impact for respondents, but increased guidelines sentences by approximately two years. The role of financial backer produced about a two-year increment for respondents and about a four-year increment for the guidelines. Finally, being a leader of the trafficking operation added approximately two years to the respondent sentence if the drug-dealing organization was small (6 people) and about four years if the drug-dealing organization was big (50 people). The comparable figures for the guidelines were increments of about seven years regardless of the size of the organization. In short, the respondents and the guidelines agreed quite well qualitatively about the importance of the different drug-trafficking roles.

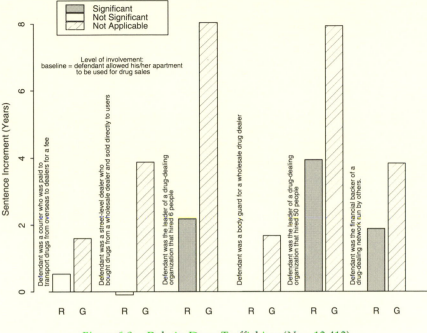

Figure 6.8. Role in Drug Trafficking (*N* = 13,413)

However, in each instance, the guidelines provided for somewhat greater sentence increases.

In summary, the public takes more seriously and makes important distinctions between different kinds of violence associated with drug trafficking. The guidelines also respond to violence, but not nearly so dramatically and in such detail. As a result, the sentence increases are greater for respondent sentences when violence is the issue.

Both respondents and the guidelines take the size of drug transactions into account: greater drug amounts are associated with greater sentencing increases, but the guidelines increases are much larger. To help put this in context, trafficking in drugs worth $20,000 leads to a larger increment in the guidelines sentences than when the defendant was known to have shot and seriously wounded people in the past (roughly 10 years to 8 years, respectively). For respondents, the sentence increases are about the same (roughly 4 years).

The public treats cocaine, crack, and heroin with about equal and moderate seriousness, compared to marijuana. The guidelines concentrate on crack in particular and overall treat trafficking in cocaine, crack, and heroin as far more serious than trafficking in marijuana. Finally, there is broad agreement between the respondents and the guidelines with respect to increments determined by the role of the defendant. However, once again, the guidelines sentences increments are larger.

Carjacking

Carjacking consists of the forcible seizure of a car from its occupants. Distinguished as such, carjacking is a crime that has achieved some prominence in public attention over the last decade. As Ilene Nagel's account relates, at the time the commission was writing the guidelines, the Washington mass media gave considerable attention to several instances of carjacking. Her account suggests that the commissioners were led by that publicity to treat carjacking more harshly than other forms of robbery. Indeed, the reason this crime was included in our study was because of the continued interest of the commission and its staff in it. Three descriptive dimensions were included in carjacking vignettes as shown in Figure 6.9. The left panel indicates that the value of the car matters a bit. Com-

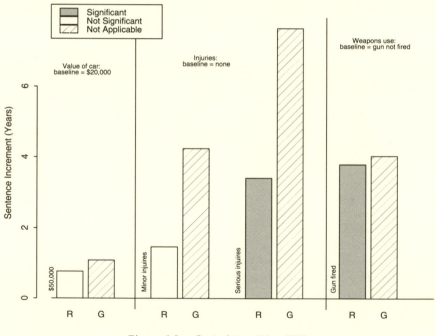

Figure 6.9. Carjacking ($N = 732$)

pared to a car valued at $20,000, taking a car valued at $50,000 adds about a year to the guidelines sentence. The increment for respondents is nearly a year, but is not statistically significant. For this reason, one cannot reject the null hypothesis that the two weights are the same.

The middle panel shows that injuries make a more substantial difference than the value of the car involved. Compared to the baseline of no injuries, minor injuries add about four years to the guidelines sentence and nearly two years to the respondent sentence. But again, the respondents' average sentence increase is not statistically significant, although this time the difference between guidelines and respondents weights is significant. The guidelines call for a larger increment than the respondents. When the injuries are serious, the guidelines increase is around seven years and the respondent increase is around four years. It seems fair to conclude that for this crime, the guidelines are more responsive to public safety than respondents.

Finally, the right panel shows that compared to when no gun is fired, firing a gun during a carjacking adds nearly four years to the sentence for both the guidelines and respondents. There is nearly perfect agreement.

The overall conclusion we can draw about the various street crimes is that there is strong qualitative agreement between respondents and the guidelines in how various crime features are to be factored into sentencing. Typically, the dimension levels are ranked in the same way, even with those dimension levels that are quite complicated. In other words, for street crimes there seems to be not just substantial agreement in the overall sentence given, but in how that sentence is constructed. Perhaps the major exception is for drug trafficking. The public seems more concerned than the guidelines about drug-related violence and less concerned than the guidelines about singling out trafficking in crack cocaine for especially long sentences.

OFFENSES OFTEN LINKED TO STREET CRIMES

We turn now to offenses that are often associated with street crimes: extortion, the illegal possession or sale of firearms, money laundering, and larceny. We suspect that given the central role all have played in media coverage of crime, the public will have views that can be captured in our vignettes; these will turn out to be familiar crimes.

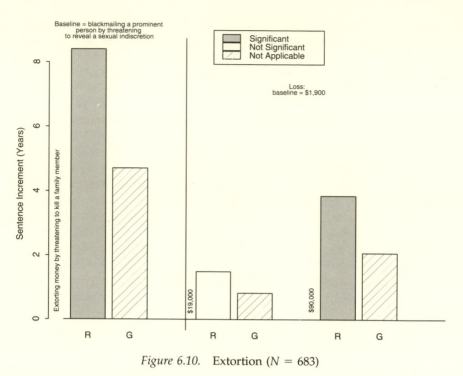

Figure 6.10.   Extortion (*N* = 683)

Extortion

Figure 6.10 shows the results for extortion in which money or other valuables are taken by threats made to a victim. Two dimensions are included: the kind of threat (left panel) and the amount of money extorted (right panel). It is clear that for the respondents and the guidelines extorting money by threatening to kill a family member is taken far more seriously than extorting money by threatening to reveal a sexual indiscretion. The increase in sentence length is around five years for the guidelines and over eight years for respondents.

The right panel clearly indicates that when more money is extorted, longer sentences result. Compared to the baseline of $1,900, extorting $19,000 increases the sentence by about a year for both guidelines and respondents. However, extorting $90,000 increases the guidelines sentence by about two years and respondents sentence about four years. There is a hint, therefore, that respondents take the amount extorted more seriously than the guidelines. This is a theme we will see repeated for a large number of crimes when economic motives predominate and when there is no actual violence.

Illegal Arms Possession

The federal laws regulating the possession of firearms prohibit the possession of certain kinds of firearms such as sawed-off shotguns and the possession of any kind of firearms by convicted felons. In the firearms possession vignettes a key descriptive dimension was the kind of possession offense involved. Thus, the comparison is between possession of a rifle or handgun by a convicted felon and possession of a sawed-off shotgun by anyone.

Figure 6.11 shows that there is general agreement between the respondents and the guidelines. Illegal possession of a handgun because of a prior felony conviction is treated more severely than illegal possession of a rifle, and possession of a sawed-off shotgun is treated the most severely

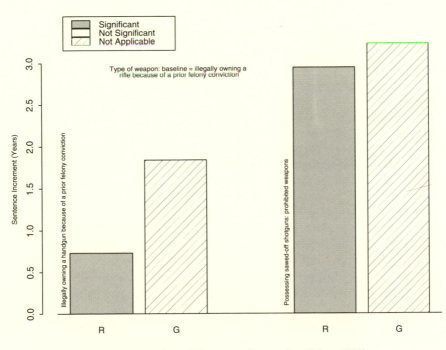

Figure 6.11. Illegal Firearms Possession (*N* = 1988)

of all. While in each case, the guidelines provide for a larger sentence
increase, the differences are about a year for illegal handgun possession
by a felon and only a few months difference for possession of a sawed-off
shotgun. Using our one-year differences as a substantive threshold, we
would characterize Figure 6.11 as showing substantial consensus.

Illegal Arms Sales

The federal statutes also regulate the sale of firearms. Firearms dealers
are required to be licensed and to keep careful sales records, and they are
prohibited from selling firearms to felons and the mentally ill. The vignettes describing illegal firearm sales have descriptive dimensions that
vary the numbers of firearms sold in illegal traffic, the knowledge the
dealer had about the illegal use of firearms sold, and how carefully sales
records were kept.

The sentence increments associated with levels of the dimensions are
shown in Figure 6.12. Overall, there is also broad agreement between the

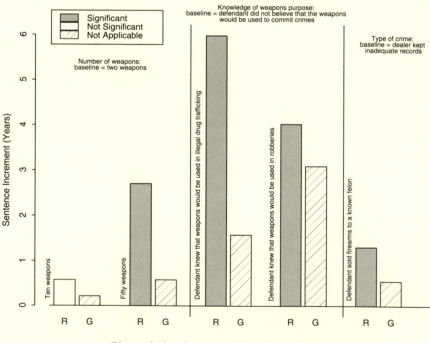

Figure 6.12. Firearms Sales (*N* = 1382)

respondents and the guidelines about the factors affecting sentences for illegal arms sales. The more weapons sold, the stiffer the sentence (left panel of Figure 6.12). But 10 weapons compared the baseline of 2 weapons makes little difference. The effects are found for sales of 50 weapons and then primarily for respondents. The guidelines increment is less than one year, while for respondents, the sentence increase is nearly three years.

An illegal transaction made when the dealer knew that the guns sold were for use in criminal activities led to longer sentences than guns sold illegally, but for lawful purposes (middle panel of Figure 6.12). For respondents, selling guns known to be used in drug trafficking leads to six more years in prison; the comparable figure for the guidelines is about one year. For respondents, selling guns known to be used in robberies leads to four more years in prison; the comparable figure for the guidelines is about three years. Clearly, the disparity between respondent and guidelines sentences is larger for guns used in drug trafficking, although in both cases the respondents take the offense more seriously. Interestingly, there is a reversal in priorities as well. Respondents worry more about guns used in drug trafficking than guns used in robberies. The guidelines are more concerned with guns used in robberies than guns used in drug trafficking.

Both respondents and the guidelines give longer sentences when the guns are knowingly sold to a convicted felon than when the guns are sold with inadequate record keeping (right panel of Figure 6.12). The sentence increase is a little more than a year for respondents and a little less than a year for the guidelines. In short, there is substantial agreement.

Perhaps the major message about sentences for firearms sales (beyond broad agreement) is the much greater variability in sentence increases given by respondents. Increments ranged from under a year to nearly six years. The increments for the guidelines ranged from under a year to about four years.

Larceny

Larceny is defined as the unlawful appropriation of property, a broad category covering a variety of property and modes of appropriation. Under the heading of larceny, we included three kinds of crime: stealing property, stealing mail and checks, and buying and selling stolen goods. While these kind of crimes are somewhat heterogeneous, they all can be broadly characterized as street crime or offenses that support street crime. The descriptive dimensions included concern the dollar value of the property stolen, the degree to which the crimes were well planned in advance, and the kind of property stolen.

Figure 6.13 shows (left panel) that the respondents and the guidelines increase sentence length with the size of the economic gain ($900, $4,000, and $400,000 compared to $200). The guidelines increases are a bit more regular, but both the guidelines increases and the respondent increases are roughly monotonic. The increments for respondents are about one year, two years, and then about four years for the largest two economic gains. The increments for the guidelines are approximately zero, six months, one year, and three years. Clearly, the respondent sentence increments are larger by between one and three years.

The middle panel of Figure 6.13 shows that there is also broad agreement about the impact on the sentence of a planned crime, compared to an unplanned one. A planned crime adds about 18 months for the respondents and about 6 months for the guidelines.

The far right panel of Figure 6.13 shows that the kind of crime has little effect for either respondents or the guidelines, but there is a hint that the

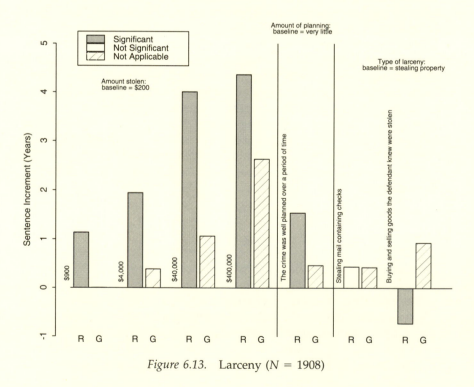

Figure 6.13.   Larceny (N = 1908)

guidelines take buying and selling stolen goods more seriously than do the respondents.

Money Laundering

In order successfully to conceal large scale economic crime, various schemes are used by criminals to make their monetary gains appear to be earnings from legitimate economic activity. These schemes are known as *money laundering*, a felony that covers both the owners of the money involved as well as those who participate in the schemes. The statutes related to money laundering also prescribe that large transactions made by banks or other firms dealing with money must be reported to the government. All the vignette descriptions are of felons who participated in money-laundering activities.

Three descriptive dimensions were used as shown in Figure 6.14. The right panel describes the instances of money laundering. The baseline offense describes a coin dealer who fails to file prescribed reports about

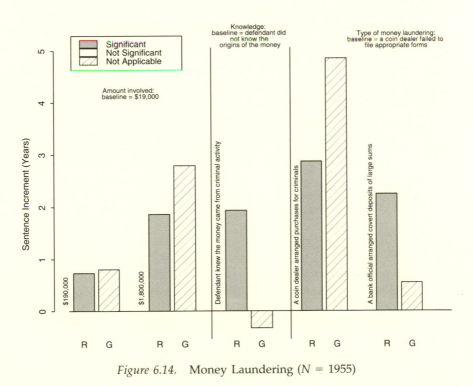

Figure 6.14. Money Laundering (*N* = 1955)

transactions. Both respondents and guidelines enhance sentences when a coin dealer arranged coin purchases for criminals, although the guidelines calls for a five-year enhancement, compared to the respondents' three years. Both also enhance sentences for bank officials who arranged to disguise large deposits which would otherwise have to be reported. In this last case, respondents want a sentence more than two years longer whereas the guidelines calls for an enhancement of about six moths.

The left panel concerns the amount of money being laundered. Compared to the baseline of $19,000, sentences are nearly a year longer if $190,000 is laundered and around two years longer if $1.8 million is laundered. The agreement between respondents and the guidelines is nearly perfect for the first figure and well within a year for the second figure.

The middle panel shows that respondents increase the sentence by about two years if the defendant knew that the money being laundered came from criminal activity. The increment for the guidelines is less than six months. Although this is a small disparity in absolute terms, it is large in relative terms.

To summarize the results for offenses supporting street crimes, while there were some very large quantitative, and even some qualitative, differences found between respondents and the guidelines for street crimes, the differences for illegal arms possession and sales, larceny, and money laundering are modest. One could easily imagine substantial public controversy around the differences surrounding street crimes, but the differences found here would probably go largely unnoticed. One possible exception would be the larger increments given by respondents for the economic gains from larceny. We will consider similar issues shortly when we examine white-collar crimes.

WHITE-COLLAR CRIMES

We turn now to white-collar crimes, which are characterized by the goal of economic gain and in which profits derive from stealth as opposed to force. White-collar crimes are also typically associated with offenders holding high positions within corporations, banks, or other business organizations or within public agencies. These white-collar managerial positions provide the opportunity to engage in illegal behavior resulting in illegal economic gains for the offender and/or the employing organization. Because economic motives dominate these crimes, ordinarily without the use of force, a key issue in sentencing is how sentences should respond to the size of the economic gain. A second key issue is how sentences should be tailored to the organizational position held by the defendant, because the higher the latter the greater the violation of the trust implicit in the position.

Forgery

Although forgery is not a white-collar crime common to the higher reaches of management, it has some of the formal characteristics of such crimes. Forgery involves the falsification of documents to obtain economic gain. Forgery is involved in the private printing of public currency, and in the unauthorized use of credit cards, checks, or other financial instruments.

Two descriptive dimensions were included in the forgery vignettes: the kind of forgery and the size of the economic gain. Figure 6.15 shows that both kinds of levels mattered, but that there are some quantitative differences between respondent sentences and guidelines sentences. With re-

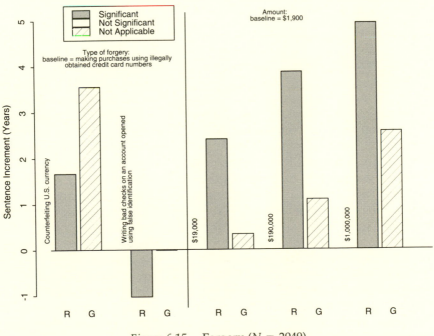

Figure 6.15. Forgery (N = 2049)

spect to type of forgery (left panel), the guidelines are a bit more punitive than respondents for the crimes of counterfeiting compared to baseline of using a stolen credit card numbers: roughly a four-year sentence increase compared to a two-year sentence increase. This is not surprising, given the special concerns that the federal government has about counterfeiting.

The results are more complicated for writing bad checks on an account opened using false identification. The guidelines treat writing bad checks in about the same manner as making purchases using stolen credit card numbers, but the respondents treated writing bad checks less sternly than using stolen credit card numbers; the sentence is about one year shorter. Perhaps because writing checks that bounce can happen to anyone, respondents were more tolerant of writing bad checks on purpose.

For both the respondents and the guidelines, greater economic gain leads to longer sentences, with the increment for the respondents about two years longer (right panel). The sentence increments for respondents are about two, four, and five years, respectively, from economic gains of $19,000, $190,000, and $1 million (compared to the baseline of $1,900). The counterpart sentence increases for the guidelines are about four months, one year, and two years. In short, much like for the crime of larceny, respondents make more of the economic gain than do the guidelines.

Embezzlement

Embezzlement involves the violation of trust that inheres in some occupational position. A company financial officer who uses company funds for personal use may be regarded as the archetypical embezzler. Three descriptive dimensions were used for the crime of embezzlement: the amount of money embezzled, how carefully the crime was planned, and the role of the defendant. As shown in the left panel of Figure 6.16, both respondents and the guidelines gave longer sentences for embezzling larger amounts of money. But the respondents' sentence increments were between one and two years longer. For example, compared to $900, embezzling $400,000 added about two years to the guidelines sentence and well over four years to the respondent sentence. Apparently, for larceny, forgery, and embezzlement, respondents seem to be taking the economic gain more seriously than do the guidelines.

In the middle panel the findings are that respondents and the guidelines increased sentences when the crime was well planned compared to when it was spontaneous. But respondents took the premeditation more seriously; they added nearly two years to the sentence, while the guidelines added far less than one year.

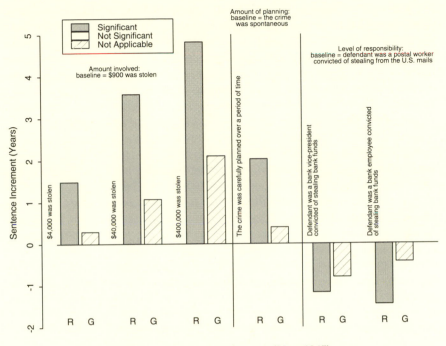

Figure 6.16. Embezzlement (*N* = 1945)

In the right panel of Figure 6.15, it can be seen that both respondents and guidelines gave greater sentence increments to a defendant who was a postal worker convicted of stealing from the U.S. mails than to a bank employee or bank vice president convicted of stealing bank funds. Perhaps the postal worker was seen as violating a more important trust. In any case, the sentence increments were around the same, about a year or less.

Fraud

The crime of fraud typically involves misrepresentation for the purpose of obtaining money from a victim. Unlike embezzlement, fraud does not usually involve the violation of trust inhering in some occupational position. Bankers may embezzle bank funds entrusted to them, but someone who successfully solicits a bank for a nonexistent charity commits a fraud. The fraud vignette descriptive dimensions involved the economic gain and kind of offense.

As shown in Figure 6.17, both respondents and the guidelines increase sentence length with increasing economic gain. However, the guidelines sentences increase in a smoother fashion, holding to a monotonic trend throughout. Still within sampling errors, the penalties given by the respondents increase monotonically too. Note also that the sentence increments for both respondents and the guidelines increase far more slowly than linearly with the size of the economic gain. Indeed, the increases in sentence length are more linear with the log of the economic gain.[7]

For each level of economic gain, respondents give longer sentences of between about one year and four years. To take a typical example, when the economic gain is $100,000, respondents add over four years to the sentence, and the guidelines add less than two years. For the greatest economic gain of $80 million, respondents add over six years, and the guidelines add about five years. The now familiar pattern for economic crimes holds: respondents give greater sentence increases than the guidelines for each level of economic gain.

The impacts for the kind of fraud are typically far less dramatic, as shown in Figure 6.18. On the average, the effects on sentence length are

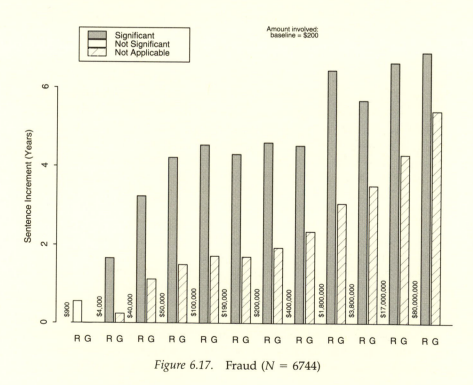

Figure 6.17.   Fraud (*N* = 6744)

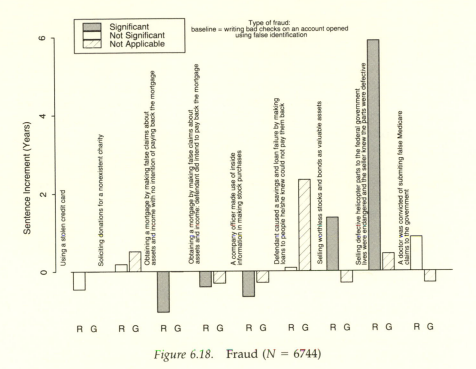

Figure 6.18. Fraud (*N* = 6744)

small for both the respondents and the guidelines. However, compared to the baseline of writing bad checks on purpose, the guidelines sentence increase for causing the failure of a savings and loan was more than two years, whereas causing the failure of a savings and loan had no noticeable impact on the average respondent sentence. In contrast, respondents gave sentence increments that were nearly two years for selling worthless stocks and bonds, whereas selling worthless stocks and bonds had no real impact on the guidelines sentence. The biggest disparity occurred for knowingly selling defective helicopter parts to the federal government. For that crime, respondents added nearly seven years to the sentence, while the increase for the guidelines was well under a year. It is important to note that the description of this crime included "endangering the lives of helicopter personnel and passengers." As noted in other crimes that result in endangering the physical safety of persons, respondents were more punitive than the guidelines.

It is difficult to tell a coherent story from Figure 6.18. For the range of crimes we considered, there is typically little impact on sentence length; all of the crimes are treated pretty in much the same fashion. In the one case where the guidelines were noticeable tougher than respondents, we may be picking up the consequences for the federal penal code of the savings and loan debacle of the last decade, which cost taxpayers billions. The two cases for which respondents were noticeably tougher than the guidelines were ones in which the public is likely to be directly hurt (selling worthless stocks and bonds) and a crime in which tax dollars are being wasted and military personnel are put in jeopardy (selling defective helicopter parts). However, there are other crimes in Figure 6.18 that share at least some of these attributes and yet do not seem to elicit longer sentences. For example, soliciting donations for a nonexistent charity might hit the pocketbooks of everyday people, and submitting false Medicare claims amounts to stealing from the public's coffers.

In short, we find once again that respondents take the amount of economic gain more seriously than the guidelines when sentence length increases are the issue. However, no clear patterns emerge for the kind of fraud committed.

Illegal Tax Shelters

The federal tax codes are notoriously complex. Some provisions make it possible for someone to enjoy a lower tax rate by investing in certain ways, for example, in the production of low-rent housing. Such tax shelters are quite legal. However, there are schemes promoted to perhaps the unwitting that purport to be legal tax shelters but are not. Selling such illegal tax shelters is a white-collar crime that makes headlines from time to time. For this crime, we included a single dimension: the size of the defendants' economic gain. Figure 6.19 shows what is now becoming a very familiar pattern. Both the guidelines and respondents increase sentence length with the size of the economic gain. The guidelines increments are more systematic, but smaller than the respondent increments. Both patterns imply that the sentence increase grows roughly as the log of the economic gain. In this case however, the differences are not as dramatic as some we saw earlier.

Income Tax Evasion

There are many ways that individuals and corporations can try illegally to evade or reduce their income taxes. Some do not file income tax returns and others file their returns but enter false information on the

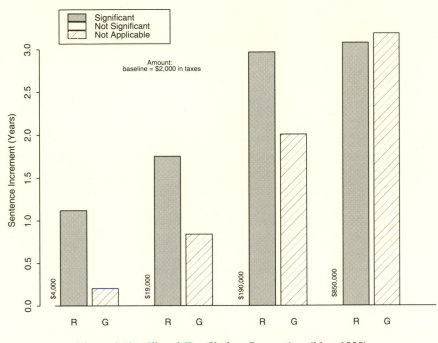

Figure 6.19. Illegal Tax Shelter Promotion (*N* = 1333)

forms. The income tax evasion vignettes include descriptive dimensions that distinguish between the two kinds of tax evasion, the amount of taxes evaded, and the extent to which the income involved was related to criminal activities of the offender. The findings are shown in Figure 6.20.

The left panel shows the sentence increments associated with the dollar amounts of evaded taxes. As in previous crimes, the expected pattern emerges. Sentencing length increases with the amount of evaded taxes for both respondent sentences and guidelines sentences. But the increase in sentence length under the guidelines goes up far more slowly than the size of the economic gain, and the respondent increases are larger.

Respondents make important sentencing decisions according to whether the offender's income was linked somehow to criminal activity. It does not matter whether that link was shown in a previous criminal conviction or was reputed to be so linked. Respondents add about two years to the sentence whether or not the criminal links are actually proved in a court of law. In contrast, the guidelines are silent on this issue: the federal courts have ruled that such matters should not affect sentencing in these cases.[8]

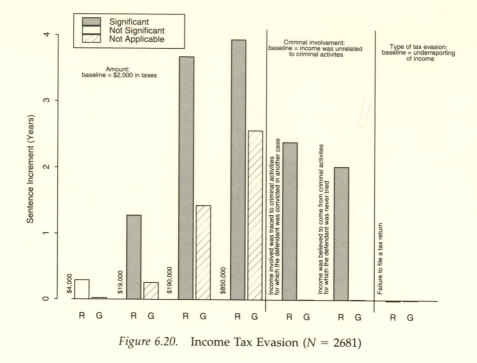

Figure 6.20. Income Tax Evasion (*N* = 2681)

As shown in the right panel of Figure 6.20, neither respondents nor the guidelines make any distinction in sentencing whether the income tax evasion results from underreporting of income or failure to file a tax return.

The summary of results from the income tax evasion vignettes is straightforward. It matters how much money is involved and whether that money is linked to criminal activities. There is broad agreement between respondents and the guidelines on the money amount but not on the source of the funds involved.

Bribery

Bribery involves the offering of rewards to a person in a decision-making position for making a decision favoring the briber. It is illegal to offer bribes and it is also illegal to accept them. Accordingly, four types of bribery were considered: (1) a government purchasing agent convicted of accepting a bribe to award a contract to the briber; (2) a county commissioner accepting a bribe to let a contract; (3) offering a bribe to a government purchasing agent; and (4) offering a bribe to a county commissioner. As shown in the right panel of Figure 6.21, respondents do not translate these different roles into important differences in sentence length. In contrast. the guidelines give them different sentences. Guidelines sentences are about a year shorter when the crime is a bribing a government purchasing agent and about two years shorter when the case involves a private purchasing agent accepting a bribe. These guidelines enhancements are all in contrast to a county commissioner accepting a bribe. The guidelines do not make any distinction between a county commissioner accepting a bribe or someone offering a bribe to a county commissioner.

The second dimension is the size of the bribe, shown in the left panel of Figure 6.21. The familiar pattern emerges. The more money involved in the crime, the larger the sentence enhancement. As usual the respondent enhancements are larger. Contrasted to the smallest bribe, $1,900, respondents add over two years to the sentence and the guidelines add about six months for the largest bribe, $90,000.

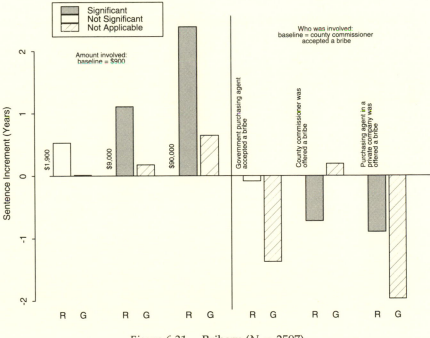

Figure 6.21. Bribery (*N* = 2597)

CORPORATE CRIME

What we call corporate crime resembles white-collar crime in being characteristic of occupations high in the managerial hierarchy of businesses. However, the white-collar crime is committed for personal gain, while the corporate crime is committed for the gain of the business enterprise. The trust being broken is not the business's trust placed in the manager, because the manager may actually be acting on behalf of the company. In addition, the economic gains are often explicitly linked to the well-being of the offender's corporation; there are potential corporate gains as well as potential individual gains. Therefore, another key difference from other white-collar crime is that the kind of organization itself matters too. Officials in public agencies may well be held more accountable than officials in private corporations and federal public officials may be held more accountable than local public officials.

Antitrust Violations

Perhaps the archetypical corporate crime consist of violations of antitrust laws. The broad goal of the federal antitrust statutes is to protect the viability and integrity of the market. Agreements among competing firms to fix prices of products or collusion in making bids in contract competitions are frequently encountered examples of antitrust violations.

Three descriptive dimensions were included in the antitrust vignettes. Figure 6.22 shows that none of the dimensions we have included move the sentences for antitrust violations by very much. The left panel of Figure 6.22 shows that both respondents and the guidelines increase sentences by small amounts (a year or less) for larger economic gains.

The role of the defendant is more important (middle panel). Compared to the role of acting under orders from a higher executive in the firm, when the defendant was personally responsible for the crime, respondents and the guidelines added an average of about two years to the sentence. For respondents, a corporate officer "just going along" with a violation that had been in place for many years added about two years to the sentence, but the increase for the guidelines was only about six months. Respondents were far more tolerant when the defendant was only a contract manager. The increase in sentence length for respondents linked to "just going along" was well under a year. The increase for the guidelines was about a year. In short, respondents are more sensitive than the guidelines to the degree of the offender's involvement in the violation.

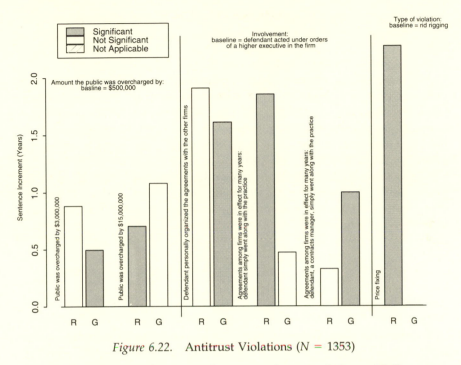

Figure 6.22. Antitrust Violations (*N* = 1353)

A major difference between the respondents and the guidelines surfaces for the kind of antitrust violation (right panel). The guidelines treat price fixing and bid rigging the same way. Respondents take bid rigging more seriously, adding about two years to the average sentence.

To summarize, what is perhaps most interesting is that economic gains do not seem to play much of a role, and certainly less of a role than the content of the crime and the role of the defendant.

Corporate Food and Drug Cases

Federal food and drug legislation regulate the manufacture and marketing of medical drugs, medical appliances, and certain food products. The two food and drug violation vignettes are both concerned with violations of medical drug marketing rules. One version described a manufacturer putting a new drug illegally on the market, by falsely claiming that the drug had been tested adequately. In the other vignette, a drug manufacturer suppressed evidence that a marketed drug had dangerous side effects. In addition, a descriptive dimension was concerned with the number of people who were harmed by the violations.

As can be seen in the right panel of Figure 6.23, respondents called for a sentence enhancement of two years for concealing dangerous side effects in comparison to the crime of inadequate drug testing. The guidelines made no distinction between the two violations.

The left panel of Figure 6.23 shows that sentence enhancements were very responsive to harm to persons who used the drugs in question. Respondents added on the average four years to the sentence if a dozen people were hospitalized and nearly twelve years if there was at least one fatality. The guidelines basically agreed with respondents with respect to a fatality, but did not respond to the hospitalizations.

In the case of this corporate crime, what matters most to both the guidelines and respondents are the health consequences of the violations. When injuries result from the violations, sentences are enhanced by substantively large amounts.

Air Pollution Violations

Federal air quality legislation is concerned to reduce the amount of pollutants released into the air. Air quality regulations govern emissions

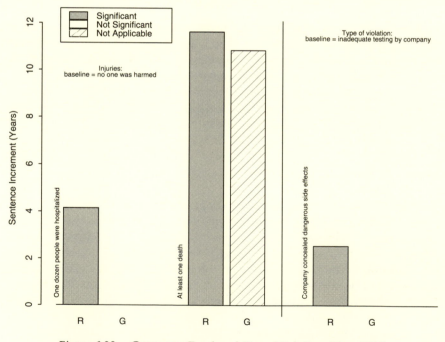

Figure 6.23. Corporate Food and Drug Violation ($N = 1308$)

from vehicles and from manufacturing activities. The air pollution violation used in the study concerned a factory that failed to install proper
antipollution devices on its smoke stacks. The one descriptive dimension
used centered on the consequences for the area surrounding the factory.

Figure 6.24 shows the sentence enhancements called for by respondents and the guidelines. Compared to no damage or health effects, respondents added between a year and two years when (1) there were foul
smells near the point of emission, (2) when paint finishes on nearby
homes and cars were damaged, (3) when local trees and birds were killed,
or (4) when respiratory illness rates were unusually high. Only for the
last condition were they any sentence increases for the guidelines; about a
year was added. It is clear that respondents were, by and large, more
concerned with the consequences of air pollution than were the guidelines.[9]

Waste Water Violations

The environmental laws and regulations also govern the discharge of
waste water into streams. Factories discharging waste water into streams

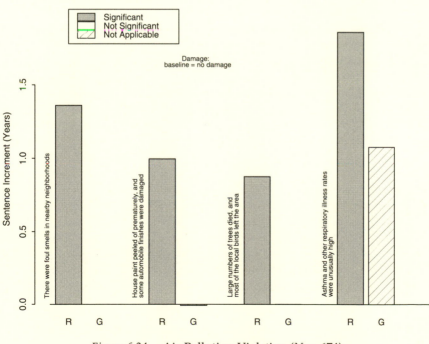

Figure 6.24. Air Pollution Violation ($N = 674$)

have to obtain permits specifying permissible waste water temperatures and compositions. Two kinds of water violations were included in the vignettes. In one vignette scenario the crime was the release of water into a local stream that was warmer than allowed and the other concerned waste water that contained toxic chemical wastes. The descriptive dimension concerned the impact of the illegal discharge on fish in the stream into which the waste water was discharged.

The left panel of Figure 6.25 shows how sentence length was affected by the consequences for fish in the stream. Compared to when no fish were killed by the illegal release of warm waste water, respondents added nearly two years to the sentence when the warm water released led to a large-scale fish kill. The guidelines contained no enhancement for this consequence. The right panel shows the sentence enhancements for discharging chemical wastes as compared to discharging warmer than allowable water. For the water discharged that contained a toxic chemical, respondents added two years to the sentence and the guidelines added nearly six years.

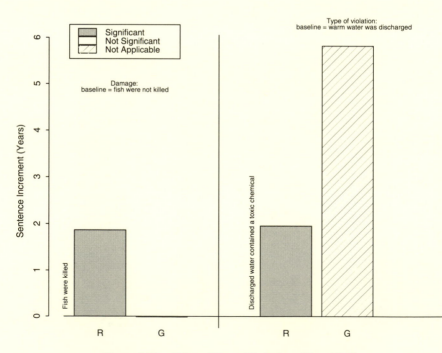

Figure 6.25.   Waste Water Violation (N = 1322)

Respondents apparently weigh the consequences for wildlife, whereas the guidelines are silent on this issue. Both guidelines and respondents give enhancements when the waste water contains toxic chemicals, but the guidelines call for a larger enhancement.

Illegal logging

Private lumber companies may harvest timber on federally owned lands but only after a permit is issued. A vignette described the crime of logging on federal lands without having obtained a permit. The descriptive dimension attached to this vignette described the consequences of the crime, as shown in Figure 6.26. For all the different consequences shown, the contrast is with no damages. Respondents did not seem especially troubled if all mature trees were illegally cut down or if, as a result, the water shed was extensively damaged. However, when, as a result of the illegal logging, habitats for local plants and animals were

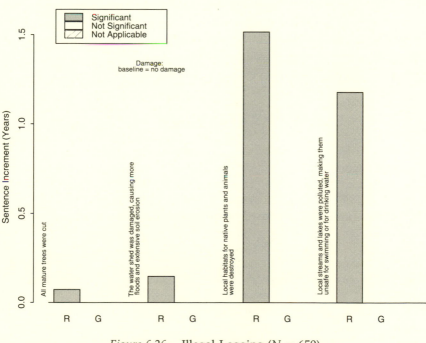

Figure 6.26.   Illegal Logging (*N* = 650)

damaged or when local streams were polluted, respondents increased sentences by about a year. Clearly, the respondents were more concerned when concrete consequences were specified. Illegal logging without apparent environmental impact seemed not to be of much concern. No comparisons with the guidelines were possible because the dimensions we included were not covered explicitly by the guidelines.[10]

In summary, perhaps the major message from our examination of corporate crimes is that the dimensions we included did not changes sentence lengths very much. Enhancements larger than two years were rare. This is in great distinction to both the street crimes and white-collar crimes we considered earlier. Perhaps corporate actors are given the benefit of the doubt, because their only "real" crime is an *overzealous* pursuit of profit. In a market society such as ours, there is certainly nothing wrong with profit maximization as long as one plays by the rules. Or perhaps there were important dimensions we (and the commission staff) missed. The exception to this general characterization is when crimes result in potential or actual physical harm to individuals, in which case sentences are enhanced both by respondents and guidelines.

A second message is that while the guidelines do not focus much on environmental crimes, they are of some concern to respondents. Crimes that destroy wildlife or wildlife habitats are punished by respondents and largely ignored by the guidelines. The difference is a major disparity between the two, although the implications for sentence length are modest.

OTHER CRIMES

In this section we deal with three kinds of crimes that did not fit into crime typology used above. They also do not form a coherent class by themselves. These miscellaneous crimes include tampering with packaged drugs, violations of laws governing immigration, and civil rights violations.

Package Tampering of Over-the-Counter Drugs

The vignette describing the crime of "package tampering" had the defendant convicted of adding poison to 17 packages of over-the-counter drugs. Although this is in fact a rarely committed crime, when committed and detected, the crime has received wide attention in the mass media. Two descriptive dimensions were included in these vignettes. The left panel in Figure 6.27 shows sentence enhancements given for the conse- quences of the crime. Compared to no resulting injuries, respondents increased the sentence an average of a little over four years when a dozen people were hospitalized, while the guidelines increased the sentence by a little less than two years. A resulting death led to over an eight-year increment to the sentence for both respondents and guidelines. Clearly, respondents took hospitalizations more seriously than the guidelines. Still the overall story is broad agreement.

When package tampering is detected, the manufacturer attempts to remove the product from the market both in order to restrict harm to consumers and to assure that consumer confidence is maintained in the drug product. The right panel shows the second descriptive dimension of the financial cost to the manufacturer of removing the drug from the market. The contrast level describes $100,000 being spent to remove the product from the market. The bars show the sentence enhancements when the firm had to spend $10,000,000. This difference had no impact on

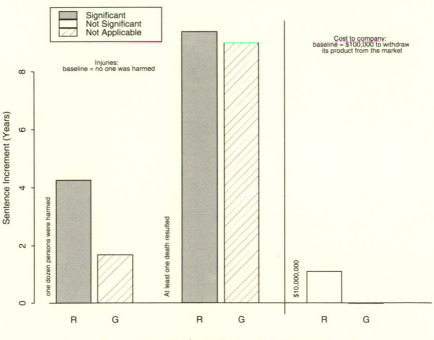

Figure 6.27. Package Tampering (*N* = 681)

the guidelines sentence and added an average of about a year to the respondent sentence (not statistically significant). There is apparently an enormous disparity between how public health and corporate health are treated.[11] Both respondents and guidelines are clearly more concerned over the threat to people.

Immigration Crimes

There has been considerable media attention over the past several years about illegal immigration. That attention is reflected in vignettes that describe persons who organize smuggling illegal immigrants into the country and persons who enter the country illegally.

A variety of immigration violations are shown in Figure 6.28, including a defendant smuggling in unauthorized aliens for profit, a defendant smuggling in family members, a defendant smuggling in unauthorized aliens for profit in a manner that risked their safety, a defendant convicted of reentry into the United States illegally, and a defendant convicted of

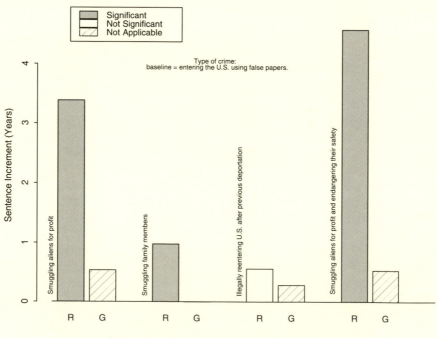

Figure 6.28. Immigration Cases ($N = 3333$)

entering the United States using false papers. The last crime is used in Figure 6.28 as the baseline.

It is clear that smuggling for profit in a dangerous manner is treated most severely by the respondents: compared to the baseline of entering the United States using false papers, over four years are added to the prison term. Smuggling aliens for profit, even if their safety is not an issue, adds over three years. Apparently the overriding issue is the smuggling for profit, not the safety of the smuggled persons. This is underscored by the finding that smuggling family members adds only about a year and reentering the United States a bit less than a year.

In contrast, the guidelines do not seem to make any large distinctions in sentencing the several scenarios. Longer sentences are given for all offenses compared to entering the United States using false papers, but the all of the sentence increases are less than a year. In short, the respondents make more significant distinctions between different kinds of immigration crimes than do the guidelines. In addition, respondents give longer sentence enhancements for each of the immigration violations.

Civil Rights Violations

Civil rights violations can occur in a variety of forms. Government officials may overstep the boundaries of authority by denying to citizens, rights to which they are entitled. Citizens may attempt to hinder other citizens while they are pursuing a legitimate activity. In other instances, property may be damaged with the intent to intimidate the property holders because of their religious or political beliefs.

Five kinds of civil rights violations were considered: police use of excessive force on a minority motorist, police use of excessive force on a motorist resisting arrest, police use of excessive force on a nonresisting motorist,[12] a neighbor attempting to force an unwanted minority newcomer to leave by harassment, and vandalism to a house of worship. Figure 6.29 shows how the guidelines and respondents would sentence persons convicted of these crimes. The baseline offense is that of a police officer who beat up a motorist found driving an unregistered car with expired license plates. The findings are that respondents would give longer sentences to all of the civil rights crimes than would the guidelines. For example, respondents would not give any different punishment (compared to baseline) to persons convicted of vandalizing a place of worship, but the guidelines would give a sentence that is three years shorter. In other words, the guidelines treat vandalism of a place of worship less seriously than the police beating up unresisting wayward motorists.

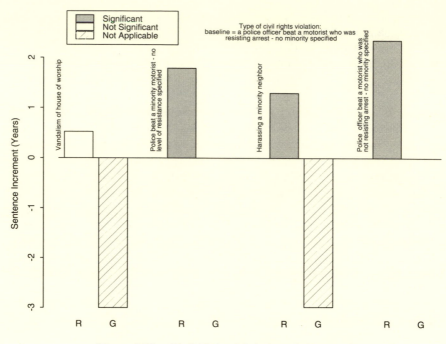

Figure 6.29. Civil Rights Violations ($N = 3343$)

When a police officer beats up a minority motorist, the guidelines would treat that incident no differently than beating up a motorist who is not described as a minority member, but the respondents would give two years more when the motorist is so described. Harassing a new minority neighbor is given an enhancement of more than a year by the respondents, but the guidelines gives this crime three years less than the baseline offense. Finally, respondents would give a sentence enhancement of more than two years to a police officer who beat up an unresisting motorist.

Figure 6.30 shows findings for two dimensions used in the police beating crime. The left panel shows sentence enhancements given when the victim is described as one of four minority groups. Neither the guidelines nor the respondents provide significant enhancements to the sentences of police officers according to the minority involved. Sentences were not significantly enhanced whether the victim was described as an African-American, a Hispanic, an Asian-American, or a homosexual. The right panel shows that respondents give sentence enhancements of more than two years when the victim does not resist arrest whereas the guidelines

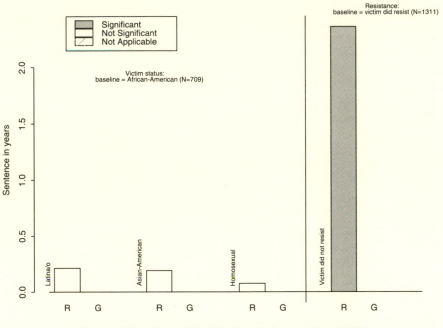

Figure 6.30. Police Civil Rights Violation (*N* = 3343)

do not give any enhancements at all. Apparently police brutality is less justifiable to respondents when there is no resistance to arrest.

Attached to the vignettes describing the vandalism of a place of worship was a dimension specifying the religious denomination involved. Figure 6.31 shows the sentence enhancements given according to the denomination specified. The baseline is a Protestant church. The guidelines sentences do not vary by denomination. In contrast, respondents tend to give sentence enhancements for each non-Protestant denomination, although only the enhancement of about 1.5 years for vandalizing a Catholic church is significant.

A descriptive dimension incorporated into the vignettes describing the harassment of minority neighbors described the minority involved. Figure 6.32 shows the results. Neither respondents nor guidelines make significant enhancements.[13] Apparently harassment is harassment whether the harassed neighbor is homosexual, African-American, Hispanic, or Asian-American.

Overall, the guidelines and respondents tend to disagree on civil rights cases. Respondents want more punishment for police officers who beat up unresisting motorists and give less punishment to officers who use

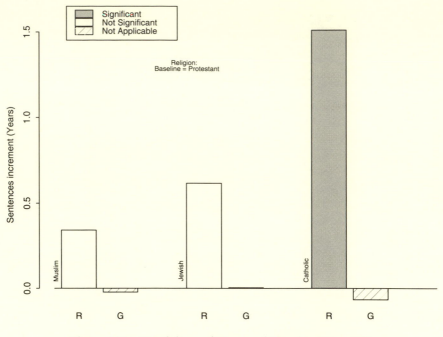

Figure 6.31.   Vandalism of House of Worship (*N* = 673)

force when a motorist resists. In addition, respondents would give more punishment to persons convicted of harassing a neighbor and for vandalizing a house of worship. The guidelines treat the latter two crimes as harassment and vandalism respectively and not as the infringement of civil rights.

OFFENDER CHARACTERISTICS

A major feature of the guidelines is the set of sentence enhancements required to be imposed according to the previous felony conviction records of the convicted person. These enhancements are added to the sentence after a baseline sentence is calculated on the basis of the crime committed. The prior-record enhancements are tailored to severity of the offense and increase with that severity.

Most other offender characteristics that are not related to the crime of conviction[14] are not taken into account as grounds for enhancement. In

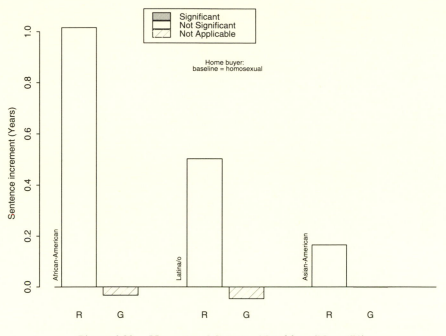

Figure 6.32. Harassing Minority Neighbor ($N = 650$)

particular, the guidelines do not recognize gender, race, family status, or employment status as factors that should be taken into account in calculating sentences.

The vignette design incorporated prior record into each of the vignettes, describing the convicted person as having no prior felony record, two prior felony convictions, or four prior felony convictions. We also included dimensions describing the sex of the offender, the offender's family status, and the offender's employment status. These dimensions were included to ascertain whether respondents took them into account in their sentences even though they are not recognized by the guidelines. There is some research indicating that these are factors that are sometimes taken into account in actual sentencing in the courts.

The right panel of Figure 6.33 contains the findings concerning sentence enhancements for prior record. Compared to no prior record, two prior convictions leads to longer sentences: both the respondents and guidelines increase average sentences by about three years. The sentence increment for respondents and the guidelines for four prior convictions is about four years. In both cases, the respondent sentences increases are a

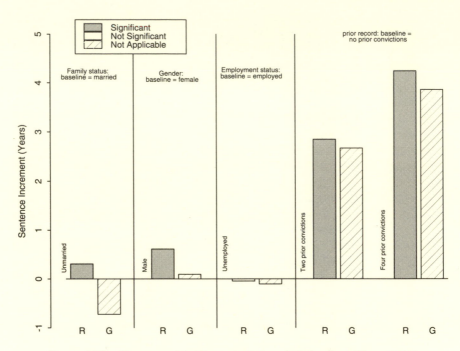

Figure 6.33. Demographic Characteristics of Defendant (*N* = 67895)

bit longer. In short, prior record matters to both the public and the guidelines. What is important in these findings is the close correspondence between the guidelines and respondents. Both give about the same level of sentence enhancements. This is an important degree of convergence because of the importance of previous record in the calculation of sentences under the guidelines.

The other background variables that we built into the vignettes are not reasons for substantively significant sentence enhancements. Although respondents give male defendants and those with no dependents slightly longer sentences, in both cases, the enhancement are well under a year (although statistically significant).[15] The respondents pay almost no attention to employment status.

The overall findings are that the guidelines and the respondents agree fairly closely about how offenders' background characteristics ought to affect sentencing. Both agree that repeat offenders should be punished more severely and they also agree about how much sentences ought to be enhanced. Although respondents would treat female offenders less harshly, the amount involved is quite small.

CONCLUSIONS

The conclusions from this chapter are straightforward. First, it is clear that there is remarkable agreement between average respondent sentences and guidelines sentences, not just overall (as shown in earlier chapters), but in sentencing determinants. Time and again, the patterns shown by the bar graphs for respondent and guidelines sentences were nearly identical. This patterning serves to underscore that the U.S. Sentencing Commission had for most crimes somehow managed to come close to how the American public thinks about sentencing for federal crimes. The patterning also serves to underscore that the respondents were able to make sense of the vignettes presented to them; the factorial survey method itself gains credibility.

Second, when there were discernible patterns in the sentence determinants, those patterns were generally more regular for the guidelines than the respondents. Perhaps the prime example is the pattern of sentencing increments for the monetary gains from crime. The guidelines sentence increases were smoother as the gains increased. This should not be surprising since the guidelines increases were not subject to sampling error and were specified by formula. What may be surprising is how closely, nevertheless, the respondents' increases corresponded to the guidelines increases.

Third, the increases associated with greater monetary gains went up far more slowly than the gains themselves. On graphs where there were enough bars to establish a pattern, linear increases in gains were roughly associated under the guidelines with the log of sentence increases. Similar but less definitive patterns were found for the respondents. Perhaps the major point is that the respondents and guidelines agree that sentence increases should not go up as fast as the monetary gains from crime.

Fourth, there were a number of crimes in which the public may be ahead of the guidelines, particularly environmental crimes. While both the guidelines and respondents did not punish such crimes very seriously, the respondents took many more factors into account. As a result, their sentences were more heterogeneous and perhaps more responsive to the facts of the case. It may be reasonable to expect that as environmental controversies continue to attract press coverage, public sophistication will continue to grow. At some point, the guidelines may need to respond.

Finally, perhaps the most striking disagreements between the respondent sentences and the guidelines revolve around how trafficking in drugs is treated. To begin, the public seems more concerned than the guidelines about the violence associated with drug trafficking. In contrast, the guidelines seem more concerned than the public with the defendant's operational role and economic gains from drug trafficking. In effect, the public seems to be focusing on drug trafficking as a crime of violence while the guidelines seems to be focusing on drug trafficking as a business enterprise. However, more important is the manner in which trafficking in crack cocaine is treated. Respondents give about equal and modest increases in sentence length to trafficking in heroin, powder cocaine, and crack cocaine (compared to marijuana). The guidelines single out crack cocaine for special treatment.

This is of course, just a restatement of a key point raised in earlier chapters, but now we see that the special treatment of trafficking in crack cocaine also stands out against other aggravating and mitigating factors. The distinction made by the guidelines between crack cocaine and other narcotics is one of the most important effects on sentence length of any of the crime dimensions we have considered in this chapter and produced what is arguably the starkest disagreement within an overall picture of remarkable consensus.

NOTES

1.   An alternative to the procedure used would have been to use the mean or median sentence for each level of each dimension. Although this alternative would have produced unbiased estimates of the sentences given to the vignettes with the levels in question, the regression weights are much more useful because they represent the *increments* given the levels rather than the total sentences. We also used quantile regressions, which are less sensitive to outlier respondent sentences. Because the results with quantile regressions were not appreciably different from the ordinary least squares approach, we do not show them here. As in the Chapter 5 analyses, the 101 respondents whose sets of responses were largely outliers were dropped from the analyses.

2.   We used linear least squares to obtain the guidelines weights because, by construction, there was no concern about outliers. The least squares procedures were just a way to produce weights for each of the sentencing factors in a form comparable to those produced for the respondent sentences.

3.   All of the R^2 for the guidelines equations were essentially 1.0, because the guidelines enhancements did not vary for each level shown in a vignette.

4.   Huber adjustments were made for the small within-person correlations for the residuals. They made no important difference. As in other factorial studies, within-person correlations for the residuals were not large enough to affect standard errors substantially.

5. The injury dimension described the person hurt as a "victim." Accordingly, it is not clear whether the victim is a store clerk or some other person who may have been present in the convenience store at the time.

6. Actually the amount of violence associated with drug trafficking is mentioned in the guidelines as an allowable grounds for departure from the guidelines. However the degree of allowable departure is not specified and hence cannot be systematically incorporated into the calculated guidelines sentences.

7. The commission staff informed us that indeed the sentence enhancements were calculated to be log linear.

8. Except, of course, when taken into account as part of the defendant's criminal record.

9. The guidelines explicitly allowed for deviations from mandated sentences if the consequences of violations were serious. However, because no specific enhancements were indicated, it was not possible to include them in the guidelines sentences used in this study. It is quite possible that in actual court sentencing violations with the consequences described in the vignettes received enhancements routinely.

10. The guidelines do allow judges to enhance sentences if the consequences of illegal logging were severe. However, because the guidelines did not give specific enhancements, we could not reflect such enhancements in the calculated guidelines sentences.

11. The vignette did not indicate whether the offender was an employee of the company involved or someone outside the firm. Perhaps respondents assumed that the felon was an employee and that the firm should bear the costs of improper supervision. But that interpretation is speculative and does not take into account that the guidelines also do not give any enhancement.

12. The differences among the three instances of police use of excessive force revolve around whether the motorist was identified as a member of a minority group and whether the motorist resisted the officer's request for identification. In all three cases, the motorist was described as driving an unregistered vehicle using false license plates.

13. The respondent enhancements appear large but they are not statistically significant.

14. For some crimes, the degree of premeditation involved in the crime commission can be cause of enhancing sentences.

15. Note that there were more than 67,000 vignettes in the analysis presented in Figure 6.33. With such a large case base, even very small differences become statistically significant.

7

Respondent Concordance with the Guidelines

Chapters 5 and 6 were concerned with how closely the guidelines and Americans agreed on the sentences to be given to convicted felons. The analyses primarily focused on vignettes and the crimes and offenders described in them centering around the means and medians of the sentences given by the national sample. However, means and medians obscure the rather wide differences among individuals. Some were close to those central tendencies and others departed considerably from them. We can also anticipate that some of our sample agreed quite strongly with the guidelines and others had preferences that departed considerably from them.

In this chapter we will shift our attention to differences among respondents in the extent to which they agree with the guidelines. The main issue addressed is: What distinguishes respondents whose sentences more closely agree with guidelines sentences from those whose sentences depart markedly from the guidelines? Looked at from the perspective of studying the American normative structure, this question can be rephrased as determining whose norms are being reflected in the guidelines.

Given the level of agreement between respondents collectively and the guidelines, as shown with means and medians in Chapter 5, we can expect a modest amount of agreement on average for an analysis on the level of respondents. We can also anticipate that there will be significant amounts of variation in levels of agreement among respondents, some whose sentencing preferences closely match the guidelines and some whose preferences are not in agreement.

There are several ways to interpret whatever level of agreement may be found in the data. One alternative centers around how respondents learn about punishment norms. For example, if we find that respondents who have had some direct contact with the courts give sentences that are more in agreement with the guidelines that might be explained by positing that their direct experience with the machinery of justice led them to be more accurate in their understanding of the normative structures that the laws and the courts represent. The alternative stresses how the commission arrived at its understanding of the norms. The same finding is then interpreted as indicating that commission members' experiences with persons who use the courts and lawyers as sources of information about American punishment norms. Accordingly, the guidelines sentences are closer to the norms as perceived by such persons.

Using the survey dataset, there is no way that evidence can be marshaled for or against either interpretation of the level of individual agreement with the guidelines. Furthermore, it seems likely that the commission had greater access to some sectors of American society and that the American normative structure was better known by some Americans.

MEASURING RESPONDENT-GUIDELINES AGREEMENT

In order to undertake the analysis of interrespondent differences in agreement with the guidelines, it is necessary to develop a summary measure of each individual's agreement with the guidelines. Because the set of vignettes printed in each respondent's booklet was an independently drawn sample of all possible vignettes that could be formed by randomly associating the levels of the vignette dimensions, each received a virtually unique set. As discussed previously, some booklets contained examples of the most serious crime, but others did not. Accordingly, it was necessary to take that fact into account.

To measure the degree of agreement between each respondent and the guidelines, we computed for each respondent the rank order correlation[1] between the respondent's sentences and the guidelines sentences for each vignette. The resulting rank order correlation coefficient (rho) measures the extent to which the respondent and the guidelines ranked the vignettes in similar ways. A rho coefficient of +1.0 for a respondent indicates that the respondent's rank order is exactly the same as the guidelines rank order; −1.0 indicates that the two rank orders are mirror images of each other; and 0.0 shows that the two are unrelated. Positive values indicate that the two orders are related positively, with higher values showing closer correspondence than lower ones.

Rho values were computed for each of the 1628 respondents,[2] with results as shown in Table 7.1 and Figure 7.1. The mean rho value was +.57 indicating that, on average, respondents ranked crimes in much the same order as did the guidelines. Only two respondents literally disagreed with

Table 7.1. Distribution of Spearman Rank Order Coefficients (rho) between Respondents' and Guidelines Sentences

Measure	Value
Mean	.57
Median	.59
Interquartile Range	.48–.67
Standard Deviation	.15
N	1628[a]

[a] Outlier respondents not included.

the guidelines as shown by their negative rho values.[3] Half had rho values between +.48 and +.69. The histogram shown in Figure 7.1 shows that most respondents' rho values clustered closely around the mean. A normal curve is superimposed upon the histogram to show how the distribution of rho values compared to the normal curve.

A mean rho value of +.57 certainly indicates that the agreement between the respondents and the guidelines was much better than chance

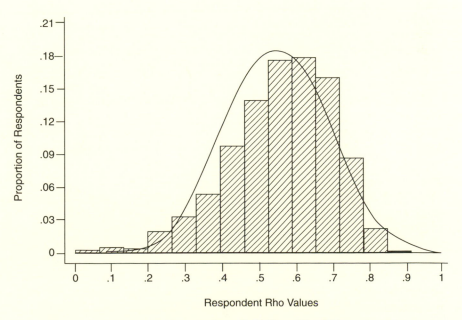

Figure 7.1. Respondent-Guidelines Rho Values

but less than perfect. Because there are no standards against which that value can be compared, it is a judgment call whether that value can be considered an indicator of high or relatively low levels of individual agreement with the guidelines.

SOCIAL AND DEMOGRAPHIC CORRELATES
OF AGREEMENT

Although there are significant differences in agreement among demographic subgroups, as shown in Table 7.2, those differences are not very large. As Panel A indicates, on average men tend to agree with the guidelines more strongly than women (.59 versus .55). Panel B shows that agreement is strongest for non-Hispanic whites (.58) and weakest for Afro-Americans (.54), Hispanics (.53), and other ethnic groups (.54).

There are also differences by marital status: as shown in Panel C, currently married respondents show a higher average level of agreement

Table 7.2. Demographic Differences in Agreement with Guidelines (N = 1628)[a]

Demographic Attribute	Rho	N
A. Gender (*p* < .0001)		
Male	.59	720
Female	.55	906
B. Race/Ethnicity (*p* < .0001		
Non-Hispanic Whites	.58	1234
Afro-American	.54	221
Hispanic	.53	127
Other	.54	36
C. Marital Status (*p* < .001)		
Currently Married, Cohabiting	.58	913
Widowed, Divorced, Separated	.54	437
Single, Never Married	.56	269
D. Age (*p* < .01)		
Under 35	.57	540
35–49	.58	511
50–64	.57	274
65 & Over	.54	283

[a] N shown in body of table differ because of missing values.

with the guidelines than either the previously married or those who have never married. Differences by respondent age, as shown in Panel D, are consistent with the marital status differences, with the highest mean agreement among respondents in "midlife" (35–49) than either the younger or older.

There are also demographic characteristics of respondents that were found to be unrelated to agreement. There are no significant differences by region or by size of place of residence. These findings are especially interesting because region played an important role as a correlate of sentencing severity, as will be shown in Chapter 8. Apparently southerners are more severe in their sentencing but do not disagree more (or less) with the guidelines, giving harsher sentences for all crimes.[4]

When we turn to socioeconomic subgroups, Table 7.3, stronger subgroup differences appear. Especially striking are the differences in agreement by education. As shown in Panel A, the mean rho for high school dropouts was .52 compared to .62 for those who had some postcollege education. Not surprisingly, there were parallel differences by annual household income, as shown in Panel B: the mean rho for those with less than $20,000 was .53, compared to .60 for those earning $50,000 or more.

Table 7.3. Socioeconomic Differences in Respondent Agreement with Guidelines

Socioeconomic Indicator	Rho	N
A. Educational Attainment ($p < .0001$)		
Did Not Finish High School	.52	266
High School Graduate	.56	561
Some College	.57	460
College Graduate	.61	222
Postgraduate Degree	.62	116
B. Household Annual Income ($p < .0001$)		
Under $20,000	.53	332
$20–37,000	.55	270
$38–49,000	.59	576
$50,000 & Over	.60	300
C. Respondent Occupation ($p < .001$)		
Manager, Proprietor	.60	136
Professional	.60	194
Semiprofessional	.57	57
Sales	.60	75
Clerical	.58	220
High-Skilled Manual	.58	150
Low-Skilled Manual	.55	272
Not employed	.55	524

Occupational differences, shown in Panel C, are consistent with the educational and income differences.

The task of setting sentences for the persons described in vignettes involves cognitive skills of the kinds that are fostered in formal education. Although we wrote the vignette levels simply, there were still words such as *habitat* that may not have been familiar to some. These are skills that are also involved in acquiring knowledge of the normative structure of our society. Accordingly, the strong effects of education on agreement can be interpreted as at least partially reflecting the fact that respondents with higher education can handle the sentencing task more easily and had more accurate knowledge concerning the normative structure.

We do not have any measures of cognitive skills. However, we did ask the interviewers to note whether respondents appeared to have difficulty performing the sentencing tasks.[5] The interviewers reported that most (87%) did not have any apparent problems. The minority (13%) who did have problems were concentrated more heavily among the poorly educated: 27% of the high school dropouts appeared to have trouble, in contrast to 3% of the respondents with postgraduate education.

There is a fairly strong relationship between the interviewers' ratings of respondent difficulty and agreement with the guidelines. The mean rho for respondents having difficulty was .51 in contrast to .58 for those who did not. These effects were independent of education: within each educational level, respondents appearing to have difficulty showed lower levels of agreement with the guidelines.

An alternative to the interpretation that points to variations in cognitive skills as strongly related to individual agreement with the guidelines looks to the commission's likely sources of knowledge about the view of the American public. The commissioners and their professional staff were all highly educated persons whose circles of acquaintances were likely to share their elevated occupational, educational, and general socioeconomic statuses. If their understanding of the public was influenced strongly by the views discerned within such circles, then the higher levels of agreement among the better educated might simply reflect the socioeconomic limits of the social circles familiar to the commissioners and the professional staff.

The survey data cannot fully uphold either interpretation. The finding concerning how strongly interviewers' ratings of respondent difficulty with the vignette task tends to lend more support to the interpretation leaning on cognitive skills.

The two sets of individual characteristics considered in the previous two tables are all interrelated. Educational attainment varies by race/ethnicity; income is related to those characteristics as well. In addition, the interviewers' ratings of respondents difficulty with the sentencing task also vary by those socioeconomic characteristics. Accordingly, we need to consider whether these relationships hold up when approached via multivariate analysis methods. Table 7.4 shows the results of a multiple regression in which the respondent demographic and socioeconomic variables discussed above are entered together as independent variables.

The most surprising outcome shown in Table 7.4 is that almost all of the variables are independently related to agreement with the guidelines, as shown by the fact that all but two of the coefficients are statistically significant. Indeed, the combined effect of the demographic and socioeconomic characteristics is quite strong. For example, the extremes contrast sharply: middle-aged married white males who had no difficulties with the sentencing tasks and who are in the highest income and educational categories have a mean rho of .65, whereas old unmarried black females in the lowest income and education categories and who had task difficulties have a mean rho of .41. The eight respondent characteristics jointly account for about 7% of the variation in agreement with the guidelines, indicating that a great amount is still unaccounted for.

Note that neither household income nor age has any significant effect on agreement with the guidelines when the other respondent attributes are taken into account. Apparently education absorbs most of the income effects and task difficulty accounts for the poor agreement among older respondents.

The overall characterization of the findings so far is that respondents

Table 7.4. Regression of Rho on Socio-demographic Variables[a]

Independent Variable	b
Education (years)	.0104***
Age	−.0004
Female	−.0244**
Afro-American	−.0240*
Hispanic	−.0350**
Annual Income[b]	.0004**
Currently Married	.0207**
Difficulty Rating	−.0378**
Intercept	.5205***
R^2	.07***
N	1606

[a] *, $p < .05$; **, $p < .01$; ***, $p < .001$.
[b] Income imputed for missing values using education, marital status and race/ethnicity.

who fit more closely the conventional definition of mainstream American society are those who agree more with the guidelines. Males agree more than females; members of minority groups less than members of the majority; the better educated and those with higher incomes more than those with limited education and lower incomes; and married persons more than those who are unmarried or formerly married.

These findings may mean that the American punishment norms as understood by the commission are those of "mainstream" America. The commission's understanding of the norms are those of the segments of American society with which members were in closest contact and association. This interpretation fits well all but one of the findings of Table 7.4, namely, the lower agreement with the guidelines for women.

LEGAL SYSTEM: EXPERIENCES AND ATTITUDES

The questionnaire administered to respondents (see Appendix B) also contained questions about personal experiences with crime either in the form of crime problems in one's environment or as direct victims of crime. These items played no important role in affecting respondent agreement with the guidelines. Those living in neighborhoods perceived as having high crime rates or who have been recently victimized did not agree more (or less) with the guidelines in their sentencing.

In contrast, respondents' direct experiences with legal institutions had a small but significant effect on agreement. As Table 7.5 shows, respondents who had several kinds of contacts with the legal system had slightly higher levels of agreement with the guidelines than those who had no

Table 7.5. Justice System Experiences and Agreement with Guidelines[a]

Number of Justice System Contacts[b]	Mean Rho	N
None	.56	457
1	.57	590
2	.57	377
3 or more	.60	204

[a] p value for table is $< .01$.

[b] The sum of number of experiences ever as a juror, reporting crime to police, having been sued, testifying as a witness in court, having been arrested, and having served time in jail or prison.

direct contacts with the legal system either as jurors or as participants in a civil or criminal case. Those who have never had any experience of reporting crime to the police or being in court as a juror or as a participant in a civil or criminal case had slightly lower mean rho (.56), as compared to those who have had three or more such experiences (.60).

We also asked questions about views on the criminal justice system. Unfortunately the only two measures available have to do with how respondents view the rights of criminals in the courts and the rights of police in using their investigative powers. As shown in Table 7.6, both measures are significantly but not strongly related to agreement with the guidelines. In Panel A it is shown that respondents who believe that police have too many rights in investigating crimes are less in agreement than those who want police powers enhanced or who believe that the police powers are sufficient. A complementary finding is shown in Panel B: Respondents who want to see the rights of criminals in the courts enhanced disagree more with the guidelines. Neither finding is very strong.

Several additional questions concerning respondent views on public affairs issues were unrelated to agreement with guidelines. Self-reported political liberals agreed with the guidelines about as much as conservatives. Views on the rights of minorities and on public welfare also were unrelated to agreement.

There are two main points to be drawn from the findings in this section. First, agreement or disagreement with the guidelines appears not to reflect general ideological stands on social issues nor on direct experience with crime in one's environs or with victimization experiences. Ideological stances that are related to such agreement are those that are directly related to the criminal justice system. Respondents who would like to see police powers curtailed and the rights of accused persons enhanced tend

Table 7.6. Views on Criminal Justice Issues and Agreement with Guidelines

Respondent Views	Rho	N
A. Police Crime Investigative Rights ($p < .02$)		
Not Enough	.57	580
About Right	.58	824
Too Much	.54	218
B. Criminal Rights in the Courts ($p < .001$)		
Not Enough	.52	127
Just Right	.57	469
Too Much	.57	1026

to disagree with the guidelines ranking of crimes. Second, persons who have participated directly in one way or another in the legal system, are more likely to agree with the guidelines ranking of sentences for criminal offenses. However, neither of the two points reveal strong correlates of agreement or disagreement with the guidelines.

SENTENCING SEVERITY AND AGREEMENT

We also developed several respondent measures of the relative severity of sentences given to groups of crimes. These measures described how far each respondent's sentencing departed from the average sentencing recorded for the entire sample. (How the measures were calculated is described in Chapter 8.) For example, a respondent with a high positive Total Severity Score was someone whose sentences for all crimes considered was higher than the average for the entire sample, whereas someone with a negative score gave sentences that were lower than those given by the total sample.

The Total Severity Score, which measures the sentencing tendencies of respondents for all crimes, was unrelated to agreement with the guidelines.[6] Respondents who tended to give longer or shorter than average sentences had sentences whose rank orders were not different from each other and both were about as highly related to the guidelines sentences. (No table is shown for these findings.)

In contrast, when we consider severity scores for classes of crimes, four of the eight of the severity scores were related to agreement with the guidelines. Table 7.7[7] presents the regression of rho on five crime-specific severity scores as well as the three measures related respectively to the use of death sentences, life sentences, and probation. The regression coefficients for the crime-specific severity scores show how a respondent's rho is increased (positive) or decreased (negative) for each additional year that the respondent's sentences for those crime exceed the average sentences given for those crimes. The coefficients for death, life, and probation represent the increments in rho for each additional percentage of such sentences given by the respondent.

The more severe a respondent's sentences for street crimes were, the more his sentences tended to agree with the guidelines. The other two significant regression coefficients were negative, indicating that increased severity scores for drug possession crimes and for white-collar crimes were associated with lesser amounts of agreement. The coefficient for Drug Possession Severity was especially large: for every additional year

Table 7.7. Regression of Rho on Sentencing Severity Measures[a,b]

Independent Variables	b
Street Crimes	.0027***
Drug Possession	−.0100***
Mixed Crimes	−.0013
White Collar	−.0069***
Drug Trafficking	.0007
Death Sentences	−.0093***
Life Sentences	−.0012
Probation	−.0000
Intercept	.5676***
R^2	.12***
N	1617

[a] *, $p < .05$; **, $p < .01$; ***, $p < .001$.
[b] See Chapter 8 for explanation of how these
measures were computed.

above the average for the sample, rho was decreased by .01. For example,
a respondent whose sentences for drug possession crimes were 5 years
longer[8] than the average for the entire sample had rho values which were
.51, .05 lower than the overall rho for the entire sample.

Among the three sentence type scores, only the Death Sentence Severity had a significant coefficient. Respondents who tended to give the death
sentences more frequently than average tended to disagree with the
guidelines. Life Sentence and Probation Severity Scores did not affect
agreement with the guidelines.

The Sentence Severity Scores accounted for a respectable amount of the
variance in rho, as indicated by the R^2 values of .12.

The findings of Table 7.7 indicate that agreement with the guidelines is
partially determined by how much agreement there is over how classes of
crimes are to be treated. Respondents who were harsher on street crimes
were in agreement with the guidelines, whereas those who gave too many
death penalties or were harsh about drug possession and white-collar
crimes tended to be in disagreement with the guidelines.

COMBINED EFFECTS

As will be shown in the next chapter, the sentencing severity scores are
related, albeit somewhat weakly, to respondent demographic and socio-

economic characteristics. In an earlier section of this chapter it was shown that many of those respondent attributes and the degree of respondent difficulty with the sentencing task are also related to degrees of agreement with the guidelines. Accordingly, it is necessary to see how severity and respondent characteristics jointly affect agreement. The findings shown in Table 7.8 address this issue.

In the combined regression most of the coefficients that were significant in earlier regressions remain significant, although in some instances reduced in size. Both sociodemographic differences in agreement and crime-specific severity differences are independently affecting respondent agreement with the guidelines. Jointly these two sets of factors account for a respectable amount of the variation among respondents in agreement with the guidelines, as indicated by the R^2 value of .17.

Perhaps the most important changes concern race/ethnicity. In the first section of this chapter, the coefficients for Afro-Americans and Hispanics were negative and significant, indicating that these members of these two groups agreed less with the guidelines. In Table 7.8, the coefficients are

Table 7.8. Regression of Rho on Sentence Severity Scores and Sociodemographic Respondent Characteristics[a]

Independent Variables	b
Total Severity	.0039
Street Crimes	.0026***
Drug Possession	−.0093***
Mixed Crimes	−.0011
White Collar	−.0052***
Drug Trafficking	.0009
Death Sentences	−.0086***
Life Sentences	−.0011
Probation	−.0001
Education (years)	.0087***
Age	−.0003
Female	−.0200**
Afro-American	−.0111
Hispanic	−.0252*
Household Income	.0003
Married	.0196**
Task Difficulty	−.0314**
Intercept	.5183***
R^2	.17***
N	1595

[a] *, $p < .05$; **, $p < .01$; ***, $p < .001$.

still negative but reduced in size and that for Afro-Americans is no longer significant. It is likely that the reduction in these effects occurs because Hispanics and Afro-Americans tended to give fewer death sentences.[9] Note also that the coefficient for household income is not significant.

SUMMARY

The analysis presented in this chapter centered around the extent to which the sentences given individual respondents agreed with the severity ordering laid out in the guidelines, as indicated by rank order correlations between respondent and guidelines sentences. Overall, there was a modest amount of agreement, the mean rank order correlation being .57. Analyses of differences among respondents uncovered several important sources of disagreement.

"Mainstream" Americans had higher levels of agreement with the guidelines. Among demographic and socioeconomic correlates of agreement, the strongest correlate was educational attainment: high school dropouts were much less likely to agree with the guidelines than college graduates. Men had higher levels of agreement than women. Whites had higher levels of agreement than either Afro-Americans or Hispanics.

Levels of agreement were also affected by the treatment of types of crime. Those who gave longer than average sentences to street crimes had higher levels of agreement, whereas those who gave relatively long sentences for drug possession and white-collar crimes and gave more death sentences had lower levels of agreement.

NOTES

1.   An alternative measure, linear correlation, was considered as a measure of agreement but was rejected in favor of rank order correlation because the former weighted too heavily extreme values in respondent sentencing, whereas rank order correlations were relatively insensitive to such values. An analysis using linear correlations was undertaken with results that were similar to those presented in this chapter but with weaker relationships.

2.   As in the analyses in previous chapters, outliers (those who gave an excessive number of death or probation sentences) were not included in the analyses presented in this chapter.

3.   This finding clearly indicates that there are no radically diverging norma-tive structures concerning punishment in American society. If anything, the di-vergences are a matter of degree rather than radical.

4.   Comparing rank orders eliminates differences in degree. For example, southerners will be shown in Chapter 8 to give significantly longer sentences than New Englanders, but both groups rank crimes in much the same ordering.

5.   The interviewers' ratings were in response to the following question to be answered after the interview was completed: "Did the respondent appear to have any problems reading or understanding the directions or the crime descriptions in the vignette booklet?"

6.   The correlation between rho and the Total Severity Score was $-.03$, not statistically significant at the .05 level.

7.   The Total Severity Score is not included in Table 7.7 or Table 7.8 because it is redundant with the specific severity scores.

8.   About 7% of all respondents had Drug Possession Severity Scores of 5 or above.

9.   When Death Sentence Severity scores are removed from the equation in Table 7.8, both coefficients become large and significant at better than the .001 level. In addition, members of these two groups also had more difficulty with the sentencing task.

Social and Individual Factors
in Sentencing Severity

INTRODUCTION

Throughout the preceding chapters, ample evidence has been presented establishing that there is considerable individual variability in the sentences given by respondents to almost every crime in the survey. Compared to the typical sentence, some gave much longer and others gave much shorter sentences. This chapter will explore the extent to which this variability is associated with social and individual characteristics of the respondents. Regional and demographic differences in sentencing behavior are shown. In addition, the findings bear on the extent to which harshness in sentencing is associated with experiences with crime and our criminal justice agencies, as well as with views held on some major political and social issues.

The issue of individual variability in sentencing is also involved in establishing whether there is a normative order concerning punishment for crimes. Although the existence of a normative order does not require that there be no individual variability in sentencing preferences, the presence of strongly structured individual variability can cast some doubt on whether a normative structure exists (Rossi and Berk, 1985). By strong structured variability we mean high correlations between sentencing tendencies and social characteristics of individuals, such as ethnicity, gender, or region. Accordingly, in line with our assumption of a normative structure of American punishment norms, we expect the differences among socioeconomic levels of American society to be relatively small. Of course, what is small is a judgment call, although we believe that most would agree that weak structured variability exists if socioeconomic differences cannot account for more than 10% of the interrespondent variability in sentencing.

We also expect that there will be some structured variability. We all vary in the extent to which we are connected to and embedded in our society. The social roles occupied by individuals affect their perspectives about the world about them, their assessments of social institutions, and their knowledge about how such institutions function. In addition, individuals vary in the kinds of experiences to which their life courses have exposed them. For example, some have been victims of crime and others have been accused and convicted of misdemeanors and felonies, all experiences that potentially can condition their views of how criminals ought to be sentenced.

As shown in previous chapters, to some appreciable extent, respondents share the same views about sentencing. Their sentencing is not totally idiosyncratic: rather, there is some modest consensus on sentencing, indicating the existence of shared norms concerning how convicted criminals should be treated. Accordingly, we can expect that the effects of the social and experiential sources of person-to-person variability will not be very strong. For example, our respondents agree with each other by and large that kidnapers should be given much longer sentences than someone found in possession of a small amount of an illegal drug. Men and women might disagree about how long sentences should be for each of crime, but we cannot expect to find that men and women would disagree over which was the more serious crime. Social and individual differences in sentencing can be properly considered as variations around the fairly well defined central tendencies in the sample.

ANALYSIS STRATEGY

The units of analysis in most of the previous chapters have been individual vignettes, Crime Types, and Crime Examples. As in Chapter 7, we shift to a different unit, the individual respondent. The data on each respondent's sentencing consist of the sentences each gave to the 42 vignettes incorporated into the survey booklet where the respondent recorded them. Data on the social and personal characteristics of the respondents were obtained from questionnaires administered orally by interviewers after the respondent filled out the vignette booklet. (A copy of the questionnaire is reproduced in Appendix B.)

Because the crimes included in each individual's survey booklet were chosen randomly, each booklet differed to some degree in the mix of crimes included. A mean or median of the sentences given by a respondent to the 42 vignettes accordingly will partially reflect the specific mix of vignettes included in his or her booklet. For example, the probability was .84 that a vignette describing someone convicted of a kidnaping would appear in any respondent vignette booklet. About three out of every five vignette booklets contained a kidnaping vignette. Because half of the kidnaping vignettes described a kidnaping incident in which the victim was killed, that means that a substantial proportion—about 42%— of the booklets contained the most serious crime studied. A respondent given a vignette booklet including a kidnaping in which the victim was killed likely would have a higher average sentence, computed across all 42 vignettes, than a respondent whose set did not include that kind of vignette.

Any measure summarizing the sentencing behavior of respondents needs to take this variability in vignette booklets into account. Although this variability is random because the respondent samples of vignettes were constructed randomly, it tends to obscure contrasts among individual respondents by masking real differences among individual respondents. Nevertheless, it is possible to adjust for the variability in vignette booklet mixes, using the method described below.

First, the overall median sentence for the entire sample given to each crime example crossed by the level of previous imprisonments was calculated, resulting in 175 median sentences[1] Second, the overall median value corresponding to the crime example and prior record of a vignette was subtracted from the sentence given by each respondent to each of the vignettes in his or her vignette set, resulting in a number that is positive when the respondent gives a higher-than-median sentence to a vignette and is negative in the opposite condition. Third, those differences were averaged over all the vignettes in a respondent's booklet, resulting in a mean difference for each respondent. The resulting mean difference for each respondent measures the extent to which his or her sentences were higher or lower than the median sentences of the entire sample for the specific set of vignettes given to that person.

Using these mean differences adjusts for sampling variations in respondent vignette sets[2] The resulting respondent sentencing difference measure has a clear meaning: it is the mean of the differences of each respondent's sentences from the overall median sentences given by the total sample to the vignettes in each respondent's vignette set. For example, a calculated mean difference measure for a respondent of +2.5 means that the respondent's sentences averaged 2.5 years longer than the median sentences of the entire sample when rating the same vignettes. A calculated mean difference measure of −1.5 means that the respondent gave sentences that averaged 1.5 years shorter than the overall median sentences.

Because it appeared likely that individual respondents would react differently to the various types of crimes included in this study, a number of sentencing measures were calculated, each based on subsets of composed of similar crimes. A set of respondent sentencing measures was constructed by calculating mean differences for each of six subsets of Crime Types, as follows:

Total Sentencing Severity: Defined as the overall mean of differences of respondent sentences from sample median sentences computed across all 42 vignettes in a respondent vignette set.

Street Crime Sentencing Severity: Defined as the mean of differences for vignettes involving the following Crime Types: larceny, bank robbery, street robbery, kidnaping, extortion, and three[3] Crime Examples involving illegal possession of weapons.

Drug Possession Sentencing Severity: Defined as the mean of differences for vignettes of the drug possession Crime Type.

Drug Trafficking Sentencing Severity: Defined as the mean of difference for vignettes of the drug-trafficking Crime Type.

White Collar Sentencing Severity: Defined as the mean of differences for vignettes of the following Crime Types: major fraud, minor fraud, embezzlement, bribery, antitrust, tax, money laundering, and forgery.

Mixed Crime Sentencing Severity: Defined as the mean of differences for the remaining Crime Types; food and drug, environment, civil rights, the remaining firearms Crime Examples,[4] and immigration.

The above indexes were the outcome of an attempt to construct groups of crime types that were similar and also contain enough crimes so that each respondent would have several vignettes of each type, producing more reliable individual respondent means for each group. The crime types that did not appear to belong to a common group were lumped together in the Mixed Crime Sentencing Severity category, admittedly a heterogeneous group.

The indexes described above all have a uniform interpretation: for example, a calculated value of 2.5 for the Drug Trafficking Sentencing Severity Index for a given respondent means that over all the drug-trafficking vignettes rated, respondent gave sentences with a mean value that was 2.5 years longer than the sample medians for those vignettes.

The distribution of Total Sentencing Severity scores is shown in Figure 8.1. Although there is a bunching of the values around 0, the fairly large number of respondents who are more severe overall in their sentencing leads to a mean Total Sentencing Severity score of 2.9 and a median of 1.3. The long right tail of the distribution indicates that a minority of respon

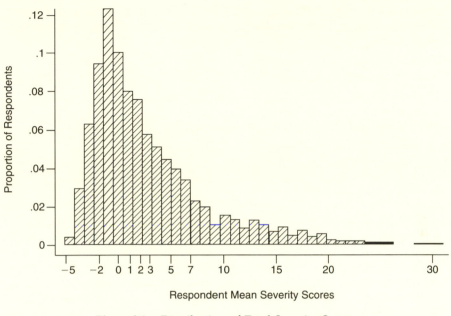

Figure 8.1. Distribution of Total Severity Scores

dents give sentences that are far more severe than the total sample. Similar distributions are characteristic of the scores for the several classes of crime. Note that the presence of many long sentences for some crimes means that a large proportion of respondents have Total Sentencing Severity scores that are positive: the sample medians, as noted in earlier chapters are almost always smaller than the means for Crime Examples.

Based on the same rationale, three additional respondent sentencing indexes were computed to measure the extent to which each respondent used probation, life, and death alternatives to sentencing. These three sentencing measures are also adjusted for the particular mix of vignettes in each respondent's vignette set. For each of 175 combinations of Crime Examples and previous imprisonment record, the overall sample mean percentages for each alternative to sentencing were calculated. For each respondent's vignettes, the overall mean percentages for the vignettes in that respondent's set were then subtracted from the respondent's mean percentages to arrive at indices indicating the extent to which a respondent departed from the overall sample. These measures also are adjusted for the particular mix of crimes including in each respondent's vignette set.

The resulting indexes should be interpreted as follows: a Life Sentence measure of 0.6% means that the respondent in question gave out 0.6%

more life sentences than the sample average. A negative number, say, −0.8%, means that a respondent gave out 0.8% fewer life sentences.

    Life Sentence Index: The difference in the percentage of vignettes given life sentences by a respondent from the overall life sentence percentage given by the entire sample to the vignettes in his or her set.
    Death Sentence Index: The difference in percentage of vignettes given death sentences by a respondent compared to the overall sample percentage of death sentences.
    Probation Sentence Index: The difference in the percentage of vignettes given probation sentences from the average percentage given by the overall sample.

The values of the life, death, and probation sentencing measures tend to be quite small, but they may represent substantial differences because the percentages giving those sentences in the entire sample are also small. Overall, 2.6% of the vignettes were given death sentences: hence a Death Sentence Index value of +0.5% means that the respondent gave out 20% more death sentences than the average respondent.

Although 1737 respondents constitute the total dataset, 101 outliers were identified, as described in Chapter 3, and excluded from the analyses presented. Accordingly, the effective sample size is 1636, although for some analyses, no answers to the questionnaire items involved may force a reduction in sample size.

The respondent characteristics each will be considered individually because of interest in the simple two-way relationships. For example, racial and ethnic differences in sentencing behavior are of policy interest even though taking other factors into account may reduce or eliminate their influence.

Because respondent characteristics tend to be intercorrelated, and are all measures taken at one point in time, it is difficult to interpret with confidence the potential causal implications of many of the findings for individual characteristics. For example, respondents who describe themselves as politically and socially liberal tend to give shorter sentences. We will also find that several views on current political issues are also related to political liberalism and to sentencing. Furthermore, both political views and sentencing tendencies may reflect other differences among respondents. Unraveling the causal threads that link political views to sentencing would be a fascinating enterprise that we cannot pursue successfully because all our measures were obtained at the same time. We cannot discern with any degree of confidence whether liberal political views lead to lesser sentencing severity or vice versa, or whether both have their roots in other causal processes.

REGION AND COMMUNITY SIZE

The contiguous United States spans an entire continent east to west and a range of climates from the tropical in Florida to the midcontinental temperature ranges found in Montana and Minnesota. Some portions of the country, such as New England and the Mid-Atlantic states, were settled territories in colonial days, whereas states such as Idaho and Nevada came into the Union only about a century ago. A brutal civil war left the country with scars that are still visible in persistent differences in regional social and political cultures, although they are declining in significance. There are also differences that arise out of the varying regional economic bases and demographic composition. The waves of immigration left behind varied demographic mixes as newcomers settled in different regions. The current waves of new immigrants are also concentrated geographically.

Countering the regional heterogeneity arising out of climatic, economic, and demographic forces are the homogenizing tendencies stemming from public schools, colleges and universities, the mass media, and internal migration. Although the public school systems vary from place to place, there is a strong tendency to uniformity in curriculum, to a large degree imposed by national college admissions standards. Television, radio, a national press, and national magazines reach into every corner of the nation.

In addition, Americans migrate frequently across county, state, and regional borders. One in five American households changes addresses every year. In the last half-century, migration streams running from east to west and north to south have made California the most populous state and Florida one of the largest. The South and Southwest have been transformed from a heavily rural and small town residential pattern into one in which much of the population lives in urbanized places, a change aided by shifts in regional industrial bases. The early childhood origins of the population of many of our regions are heterogeneous. Countering these larger migration streams are smaller ones that bring diversity to the demographic mixes in the Northeast and North-Central regions.

Tastes of all sorts are widely disseminated through an efficient consumer goods marketing system that sells much the same variety of foods, clothing, cars, and even housing everywhere in the country. Still, there are regional differences: hominy grits are hard to find in New England restaurants and Indian pudding is virtually unknown in Alabama.

Superimposed upon regional differences are community size contrasts. The United States residential patterns changed from predominantly rural to predominantly urban six decades ago, with the majority of our population currently living in urban places. Day-to-day living patterns vary by size of place. Crime rates are highest in our major central cities and lowest in small towns and rural areas, but so are also average levels of income and educational attainment. Often age compositions differ as well.

Whether the forces pushing for national homogeneity successfully overcome regional heterogeneity is problematic for a wide variety of attitudes and behavior. It is not always easy to predict whether the forces of homogenization will overbalance those fostering heterogeneity or vice versa. This is certainly the case with respect to regional differences in sentencing. The observation that crime rates vary by region might lead one to expect that where crime rates are highest, harsher punishments might be seen as desirable. An alternative prediction might be based on imprisonment rates, leading one to expect that states such as California, Florida, and Texas, states that have very high incarceration rates would have populations favoring longer sentences. Still other considerations would also lead one to expect either large regional and community size differences or the contrary.

Although on balance, the reasoning given above led us to have expectations for weak regional patterning, in fact, the regional differences in sentencing severity measures were much larger than anticipated. Table 8.1 shows the nine severity measures for each of the nine major census regions, with the regions listed in descending rank order of Total Sentencing Severity. The greatest contrast is shown between New Englanders and those living in either the West South Central or East South Central regions. New Englanders were least severe on all the severity measures and were less likely to give life imprisonment and death sentences, whereas those living in the West South Central region gave average sentences overall (Total Severity Index) that were 4.8 years longer than the median, and gave out life imprisonment and death sentences more frequently (1.6 and 0.6%, respectively). The West South Central states residents are joined by the East South Central in being on the more punitive side. On the side of leniency, those from New England gave sentences that were only 1.1 years longer than the sample medians and gave fewer life and death sentences (-1.1 and -1.2%, respectively). In leniency, New England is joined by the Mid-Atlantic states. The rest of the country, including the South Atlantic, the East and West North Central, Mountain, and Pacific states, lies between the two extremes.

Table 8.1. Sentencing Severity Scores by Census Regions. Regions Arranged in Order of Descending Total Severity Scores

Region[a]	Respondent Sentencing Severity Scores									N
	Total	Street	Drug Trafficking	Drug Possession	White Collar	Misc.	Probation	Life	Death	
W. South Central	4.8	4.4	9.6	2.0	3.4	4.0	−2.1	1.8	0.6	181
E. South Central	4.2	3.7	8.1	1.8	2.9	4.4	−0.1	1.0	0.5	96
E. North Central	3.2	2.8	6.6	1.5	2.2	2.5	−0.4	0.4	0.2	300
South Atlantic	2.9	2.7	5.3	1.2	2.3	2.5	0.8	−0.4	−0.2	283
W. North Central	2.9	2.6	6.2	1.0	2.1	2.4	0.2	−0.5	0.0	130
Pacific	2.6	2.3	4.8	0.9	2.1	2.3	−1.0	0.1	−0.0	238
Mountain	2.4	2.2	6.5	0.6	0.9	2.3	2.2	−0.5	0.6	67
Mid-Atlantic	1.8	1.1	3.8	0.6	1.1	2.2	1.2	−0.9	−0.3	225
New England	1.1	0.6	1.9	0.3	1.1	1.4	0.8	−1.1	−1.2	112
p<	0.0	0.0	0.0	0.0	0.0	0.0	0.03	0.0	0.0	1635

[a] Regions are defined, as in the U.S. Census, as follows. New England: Connecticut, Rhode Island, Massachusetts, Maine, New Hampshire, Vermont; Mid-Atlantic: New York, Pennsylvania, New Jersey; South Atlantic: Delaware, Maryland, West Virginia, the District of Columbia, Virginia, North Carolina, South Carolina, Georgia, Florida; East South Central: Kentucky, Tennessee, Alabama, Mississippi; West South Central: Texas, Oklahoma, Arkansas, Louisiana; East North Central: Ohio, Indiana, Illinois, Michigan, Wisconsin; West North Central: Minnesota, Iowa, Missouri, Kansas, Nebraska, South Dakota, North Dakota; Mountain: New Mexico, Arizona, Colorado, Utah, Nebraska, Wyoming, Idaho, Montana; Pacific: California, Oregon, Washington.

Anticipating findings that appear later in this chapter, the regional differences shown in Table 8.1 are quite robust, persisting when regional social and demographic differences are taken into account. With respect to sentencing severity, the states that constituted the Confederacy seemingly have sentencing norms that call for stronger punishment than the rest of the country, standing in sharp contrast to New England and the Mid-Atlantic states.

It is important to note that the sentencing norms of the Old South are not qualitatively different from the rest of America. Crime Types or Crime Examples that are punished severely by New Englanders are also punished severely by southerners and, as was discussed in Chapter 7, respondents from the various regions of the country have about the same levels of agreement with the guidelines about the ordering of sentencing for Crime Examples. The regional differences are mainly about the severity of sentences.

Americans' homes are located in a variety of places. Some live in the great metropolitan areas, other in smaller cities and their surrounds. And, although most Americans live in urbanized places, there are many who live in small towns and rural areas. Living conditions vary considerably by community size. In particular, crime rates are higher in the large metropolitan areas and are significantly lower in the less densely settled small towns and rural areas.

The a priori predictions that could be made about the existence of differences among residents of communities of different sizes are also contradictory. On the one hand, the mass media reach almost every corner of the country, leading to expectations that differences in sentencing would be small. On the other hand, living conditions in small towns and rural areas are quite different from those encountered in our great metropolitan areas, leading to very different expectations.

The findings concerning community size are shown in Table 8.2. The dataset allows us to distinguish among community sizes in rather gross terms. The largest community size category is Metropolitan Statistical Areas (MSAs) with over 500,000 population in 1990. MSAs are sets of contiguous urbanized counties surrounding and including a central city of over 50,000 population with a total inclusive population of more than 500,000. MSAs can be very large and cover an extensive area: For example, the Chicago MSA extends into Indiana on the south and up into Wisconsin on the north and, at places, is several counties wide east to west.

The second community size tier consist of small MSAs with inclusive populations between 50,000 and 100,000. The third consists of all counties that are not included in MSAs, typically rural counties with small cities and towns.

Table 8.2. Respondent Sentencing Severity Measures by Community Size

| Community Size | | Respondent Sentencing Severity Scores | | | | | | | | |
	Total	Street	Drug Trafficking	Drug Possession	White Collar	Misc.	Probation	Life	Death	N
Large: MSA >500,000	2.3	1.8	4.8	0.8	1.6	2.3	0.4	-0.8	0.1	669
Small: MSA 50,000–500,000	3.2	3.0	6.0	1.3	2.4	2.8	-0.5	0.4	-0.2	593
Non-MSA	3.5	2.9	7.2	1.4	2.6	2.9	0.1	0.9	0.1	370
p	0.0	0.0	0.01	0.0	0.0	0.1	0.3	0.0	0.5	

These community size measures are not very sensitive to the considerable differences in the actual living conditions that respondents face within each size class. The residents of the affluent and comfortable suburbs, such as Scarsdale, New York, or Greenwich, Connecticut, live in the same New York MSA as those who live in the economically depressed areas such as the South Bronx or Harlem. Unfortunately, the dataset does not permit any finer residential classification.

Respondents living in the smallest places are almost consistently more severe in their sentencing, desiring longer sentences overall and for each particular types of crime. For example, as shown in the first column of Table 8.2, the Total Sentencing Severity score for respondents living in large MSAs is 2.3, whereas those living in non-MSA areas have a mean Total Severity Score of 3.5, with those living in the intermediate size places having a mean of 3.2. This difference means that those living in the non-MSA places want convicted felons generally to serve sentences that are more than a year longer. Similar differences can be found in Table 8.2 for the severity measures for street crimes, drug-trafficking, drug possession, and white-collar crimes, and for the giving of life sentences. However, place size differences with respect to death sentences, probation and mixed crimes are not statistically significant.

These community size differences are not large, but they are robust. They obtain within each of the nine regions.[5] However, as will be discussed below, the community size differences appear to be a consequence of associated differences in the mix of resident social and demographic characteristics: community size differences are considerably attenuated when such factors are taken into account.

GENDER DIFFERENCES IN SENTENCING

Do men and women differ in their sentencing proclivities? Previous studies of attitudes toward those convicted of crimes typically have shown that women are likely to be more lenient in their views of desired punishments, although these reported gender differences were rarely very large (Roberts, 1992; Rossi et al. 1985).

For the six crime sentencing measures, sentencing differences by gender are shown in Table 8.3. Note that the entries for the mean sentencing severity measures are in terms of years: For example, the entries in the first row indicate that men gave sentences that averaged 2.9 and women 2.8 years longer than sample medians, but these differences are not signif-

Table 8.3.   Gender Mean Differences in Sentencing Behavior—
            Outliers Omitted

Sentencing Measure	Men	Women	p^a
Total Sentencing	2.9	2.8	.56
Drug Trafficking	6.1	5.4	.29
Drug Possession	1.0	1.3	.09
Street Crime	2.9	2.2	.02
White Collar	1.9	2.2	.20
Mixed Crime	2.6	2.6	.79
Death	0.2	−0.2	.03
Life	−0.2	−0.2	.31
Probation	0.6	−0.4	.06
Approximate N^b	[722]	[911]	

[a] This column contains the *p*-values for the differences between the mean differences between men and women.

[b] The *N* for each of the measures vary slightly, depending on missing values in the variables used. In this table and most others in this chapter, there were missing values in less than 5 cases.

icantly different. The entries in the last column of the table are the *p*-values for statistical tests of gender differences.

Although, women were generally slightly less severe in their sentencing when compared to men, those differences were not large enough to be statistically significant: all but two of the gender differences are not significantly different. Men and women differ significantly with respect to sentencing for street crimes, with women preferring slightly shorter sentences than men. On the qualitative sentencing measures, women give fewer death sentences. Only on drug possession crimes are women more severe than men, but not enough so to reach statistical significance.

Overall, there is some weak evidence than women are slightly more lenient than men but in general what women report as their views of sentencing norms are about the same as those reported by men.

AGE DIFFERENCES IN SENTENCING

In studying social and psychological phenomena, age differences are often encountered, sometimes in complicated forms. Age differences arise through three main processes: First, an individual's age is an indicator of certain developmental and aging processes, at least partially physiological in character. Physical strength and endurance peak in late adolescence

and early adulthood, and advanced age often is accompanied by frail-
ness. The fact that street crime offense rates peak in late adolescence and
early adulthood is often attributed to developmental origins, because the
peaks coincide with maximum strength and endurance. Despite some
evidence that cognitive abilities change with age, there appear to be no
simple implications of these processes for sentencing behavior.

Second, age is an indicator of where in the life course an individual
may be. Entry into the labor force, marriage, parenthood, changes in
employment, retirement, and other status changes are all associated with
stages in the life cycle. A person's primary concerns vary with age, a life
course condition than can affect one's views on many issues. Third, age is
a marker for the experiences that living through a given historical period
can bring. Those who have lived through periods in which there was
widespread unemployment are often different in their views on social
and political issues when compared to those who did not experience such
historical periods.

It is difficult to disentangle the effects of these processes, each of which
may have different effects. For example, engaging in crime is largely a
young man's activity but so is soldiering, participation in professional
athletics, and being the victim of a violent crime. Age experiences also
vary by historical period: if a man was on the threshold of adulthood in
the early years of World War II, his chances of becoming a soldier was
magnitudes greater than if he entered adulthood in the 1980s. The
chances of engaging in crime were also different, but in opposite ways.

Life course experiences also matter: For most, income is at a peak in the
middle years along with family responsibilities. For young single adults,
social responsibilities may be at a minimum. For the aged, whose world of
peers may be rapidly shrinking, social responsibilities may also be on the
decline.

For all the reasons cited above, it is not easy to anticipate age differences in sentencing severity, although it is a good wager that some differences will be found. The relevant data from the sample are to be found in
Table 8.4. The sample has been divided into four age groups; 18–34 (late
adolescence and early adulthood), 35–49 (the early middle years often
coinciding with the rearing of children through adolescence), 50–64 (the
late middle years), and 65 and over (old age, accompanied by retirement
and often physical decline).

Table 8.4 shows that significant age differences appear with respect to
five of the sentencing severity measures. Typically, the two intermediate
age groups, 35–49 and 50–64, show the highest severity scores, with the
youngest group, under 35, and the oldest group, 65 and older, showing
lower scores. Indeed, for some of the severity measures, the age trend
appears to be increased severity up to age 65 and then a decline. Some of

Table 8.4.   Age Group Mean Differences in Sentencing—Weighted Data

Sentencing Measure	Age Group				p
	<35	35–49	50–64	65+	
Total Sentencing	2.4	3.2	3.6	2.6	.01
Drug Trafficking	4.4	6.1	8.2	5.4	.001
Drug Possession	1.0	1.2	1.7	0.9	.01
Street Crime	2.3	3.0	3.4	1.4	.001
White Collar	1.7	2.2	2.4	2.4	.09
Mixed Crime	2.6	3.1	2.7	1.7	.007
Death	−0.1	0.0	0.3	−0.2	.33
Life	−0.2	0.5	0.3	−0.7	.09
Probation	−0.2	0.6	−0.2	−0.4	.54
Approximate[a] N	[541]	[514]	[277]	[284]	

[a] Actual N varies in minor ways because of missing values for some of the indices.

the age group differences are quite large: for example, persons aged 50–64 give sentences for drug trafficking that are almost four years longer than those under 35 and almost three years longer than those over 65.

There are no significant age related differences with respect to the giving of death, life, or probation sentences, although the trend noted above appears in a weak form.

Overall, age differences are not very strong: younger and older respondents are not very different in their sentencing.[6]

RACE AND ETHNIC DIFFERENCES IN SENTENCING[7]

Despite legal and behavioral changes in American society over the past few decades, our society is still clearly structured along ethnic and racial lines. This may be nowhere more evident than in the criminal justice system. Although African-Americans and Hispanics are numerical minorities within our society, as defendants in the criminal courts and as inmates in prisons, they often are majorities and almost always overrepresented. Accordingly, the persons who are more likely to be subject to the sentencing of the both the state and federal courts are African-American. Differential exposure to the criminal justice system may affect sentencing behavior. There are other relevant racial and ethnic differences as well: The incomes of minority households are lower on the average. There are political and ideological differences as well as geographical concentration. In short, there are several strong reasons to expect some racial and ethnic differences.

Table 8.5 presents the sentencing measures computed for three groups; whites (composed of all non-Hispanic whites), self-identified Hispanics, and black non-Hispanics[8], Asians, American Indians, and other races are not shown because case bases for the those groups were too small. There are significant mean differences in drug-trafficking sentencing severity: whites preferred sentences that were more than two years longer than those preferred by blacks and more than one year longer than Hispanic preferences. A weaker contrast of the same sort holds for sentences for street crimes, with whites asking for sentences that were more a year longer than those of blacks.

Similar racial/ethnic contrasts can be seen for the use of life sentences and probation. Whites were more likely to give out life sentences and less likely to give probation. The overall patterning of racial/ethnic group differences appears to be one in which whites are inclined to give longer sentences, Hispanics somewhat shorter sentences than whites, with African-Americans tending to give the shortest sentences.

SENTENCING DIFFERENCES BY EDUCATIONAL ATTAINMENT

Most people's educational experiences were received during the first two decades of life. Nevertheless, the effects of those experiences persist throughout the life course. In a wide variety of behavior and attitudes,

Table 8.5. Race and Ethnic Mean Differences in Sentencing—Weighted Data[a]

Sentencing Measure	Ethnic/Racial Group			
	White (Non-Hispanic)	Hispanic	African-American	p
Total Sentencing	3.0	2.5	2.4	.21
Drug Trafficking	6.2	5.0	3.7	.03
Drug Possession	1.1	1.2	1.4	.40
Street Crimes	2.7	1.8	1.7	.06
White Collar	2.1	2.1	2.2	.96
Mixed Crimes	2.6	2.9	2.6	.88
Death	−0.0	0.4	−0.1	.46
Life	0.2	−1.1	−0.7	.02
Probation	0.1	−2.8	1.7	.000
Approximate N	[1240]	[127]	[222]	

[a] Because case bases were inadequate, Asians, American Indians, and other races are omitted from this table. Hispanics are defined as self-identified and the white and African-American categories do not contain any Hispanics.

there are persistent differences between Americans according to the number of years spent in formal education. In part, these persistent educational effects reflect cognitive skills and substantive knowledge acquired in school. Those with greater educational attainment more readily absorb and assimilate information about the world around them. In particular, those with greater amounts of education may have found the task of assessing vignettes easier to do and to understand.[9] In addition, greater educational attainment facilitates greater socioeconomic attainment, leading to higher incomes and occupational attainment. Finally, education, especially at the college and university levels, is often a liberalizing experience leading to social ideologies that foster tolerance for differences. For these reasons, we can expect that sentencing behavior will vary by educational attainment levels.

Table 8.6, containing mean sentencing severity differences by education, fulfills the expectations described above. For all but one of the sentencing severity measures, educational differences are regular and statistically significant. For the other measure, the findings are irregular and not strong enough to reach statistical significance. The regular pattern is that those who did not graduate high school give much longer than median sentences, whereas those who received college degrees give shorter sentences. The differences are not only consistent statistically but also substantively significant: the mean sentencing difference between the lowest and highest educational attainment level is about two years in total sentencing and at least a year for the other crime categories. Those who were not graduated from high school gave death sentences to 150% more of their vignettes compared to those who were college graduates. Note

Table 8.6. Mean Sentencing Differences by Levels of Educational Attainment—Weighted Data

Sentencing Measure	Educational Attainment				
	No High School Graduation	High School Graduate	Some College	College Graduate	*p*
Total Sentencing	3.7	3.3	2.8	1.8	.000
Drug Trafficking	7.1	6.4	5.7	3.9	.01
Drug Possession	1.9	1.2	1.0	0.6	.000
Street Crimes	2.8	2.9	2.7	1.4	.000
White Collar	3.0	2.4	2.0	1.1	.000
Mixed Crimes	3.2	3.0	2.6	1.6	.000
Death	0.7	0.1	−0.1	−0.6	.000
Life	−0.2	0.5	−0.1	−0.4	.25
Probation	−1.4	−0.1	−0.1	1.5	.007
Approximate *N*	[269]	[562]	[463]	[339]	

also that college graduates were more likely to give probation, especially when compared to the group with the lowest educational attainment.

The most dramatic severity differences concern drug-trafficking sentences: those who did not finish high school gave sentences that were 7.1 years more than the median, whereas those who earned the B.A. degree gave only 3.9 years, a difference of more than 3 years. Similar differences hold for the other sentencing severity measures as well.

As will be shown, educational attainment is a fairly consistent correlate of sentencing severity, persisting as negatively correlated with severity when other respondent characteristics are considered in multivariate analyses. For example, respondents who have earned the bachelor's degree give lower sentences than high school dropouts whether they are liberal or conservative, whether they live in the South or in other regions, and no matter what views they hold on criminal justice issues. Each additional year of formal education leads to a decline of about three months in the Total Sentencing Severity measure and similar declines in other severity measures.[10]

We can only speculate on the reasons for this finding. We conjecture that formal education and accompanying higher levels of cognitive skills and knowledge lead the better educated to have clearer perception and knowledge of differences among crimes and their associated degrees of seriousness, as well as a better understanding of American sentencing norms. (Additional evidence bearing on this interpretation also appears in Chapter 7.)

HOUSEHOLD INCOME, OCCUPATION, AND SENTENCING

To measure the respondent's economic well-being, each was asked to estimate his or her household's income in 1993, using rather broad income categories, as shown in Table 8.7. The table shows that household income effects were neither pronounced nor consistent. Although there were statistically significant household income effects on six of the nine sentencing measures, these effects were small and irregular. For example, the total sentencing measures show the lowest severity for the highest income group, but the longest sentencing was given by the next to highest. Similar irregularities exist for most of the other severity measures. The only regular effects of any note were those on probation. With increased income, respondents consistently gave out more probation sen-

Table 8.7. Differences in Sentencing by Household Income

Sentencing Measure	1993 Household Annual Income[a] ($000)				*p*
	<$21	$21–37	$38–49	$50+	
Total Sentencing	1.5	1.1	1.7	0.8	.03
Drug Trafficking	8.8	6.2	8.1	7.1	.45
Drug Possession	0.5	−0.2	−0.1	−0.3	.04
Street Crimes	1.6	2.0	2.7	1.4	.03
White Collar	1.9	1.4	1.7	0.6	.005
Mixed Crimes	1.6	1.6	1.3	1.0	.37
Death	0.5%	−0.2%	−0.1%	0.1%	.10
Life	−0.2%	−0.2%	0.1%	0.1%	.70
Probation	−1.2%	−0.3%	0.5%	1.3%	.03
Approximate *N*	[332]	[272]	[579]	[309]	

[a] About 9% of the respondents did not provide answers to the income questions. For these cases we imputed household incomes based on the regression of household income on education, gender, and age, calculated over those cases where we had information on those variables.

tences. Overall, the most consistent trend is that respondents in the highest income group ($50,000 and over) gave the least severe penalties.

The household income findings bolster the interpretation of educational effects as stemming from the educational experience itself, given that high educational attaining is a frequent base for high household incomes. This interpretation is further supported by findings concerning occupational effects. None of the estimates of occupational effects showed any significant differences among occupational groups, although respondents holding down highly trained professional positions typically gave the shortest sentences on most of the sentencing measures. In the interest of saving space, the occupational tables are not presented.

NET EFFECTS OF RESPONDENT REGIONAL, COMMUNITY SIZE, AND DEMOGRAPHIC CHARACTERISTICS

All of the respondent characteristics discussed above are related to each other. Household income and educational attainment are both related to age. There are considerable racial and ethnic differences in household income and educational attainment and in region of residence. Interrelationships obtain among the entire list of respondent characteristics discussed so far in this chapter. This pattern of interrelated characteristics raises the issue of the extent to which these characteristics contribute independently to sentencing behavior.

To unravel the interrelatedness of respondent sociodemographic characteristics, we will utilize a multiple regression approach, regressing each of the sentencing measures on the variables discussed so far in this chapter plus regional location and community size. The regression model used for the nine sentencing severity measures holds each characteristic constant so that each regression coefficient estimates the effect of the associated variable independent of the others used in the equation. For example, the coefficients for gender will be the independent contribution of gender to sentencing severity, net of all the other characteristics entered into the equation. The results of the nine regression equations—one for each of the sentencing severity measures—are shown in Table 8.8.

Each of the respondent characteristics is entered as a dummy variable, except for educational attainment, which is represented as the number years of education completed, and household income, entered as thousands of dollars. Because age typically had an irregular effect on sentencing, it is represented as three dummy variables, one for each of the age groups used in Table 8.4. Each of the regression coefficients has a direct interpretation. For example, the entry in the first cell of the table, $-.25$, means that women gave sentences that were about three months shorter (0.25 years) than men, independent of all the other respondent characteristics in that column. Asterisks after the regression coefficients show whether the coefficients are statistically significant: the absence of an asterisk indicates that the coefficient is not significant.

Table 8.8 is divided into three panels. Panel A contains the regression coefficients for the sociodemographic respondent characteristics. Panel B contains the regression coefficients for census regions, all shown in contrast to the New England region as the omitted region. Panel C displays the regression coefficients for community size. Each column displays the regression coefficients resulting from regressing the sentencing measure shown at the head of each column on the variables in that column. In the last row are shown the adjusted R^2 for each of the regression equations.

Reviewing the findings in Panel A concerning respondent sociodemographic characteristics, we find that the patterning of the coefficients is quite similar to those shown so far when those characteristics were considered singly. However, fewer are statistically significant. Although women tended to be less severe in their sentencing (with the exception of drug possession crimes) only the coefficients for street crimes and death sentences are significant. African-Americans also tend to be less severe in the penalties they give to crimes of most types. However, African-Americans have significant coefficients for lower sentences overall (Total

Table 8.8. Regressions of Sentencing Measures on Respondent Demographic Characteristics, Region, and City Size[a]

Respondent Characteristics	Respondent Sentencing Measures								
	Total Sentencing	Drug Trafficking	Drug Possession	Street Crimes	White Collar	Mixed Crimes	Death Sentence (%)	Life Sentence (%)	Probation (%)
A. Respondent Sociodemographic Characteristics									
Female	-0.25	-0.83	0.22	-0.80*	0.20	-0.13	-0.46*	0.28	-0.84
Black[b]	-0.92*	-3.08**	0.12	-1.30*	0.11	-0.67	-0.43	-0.82	2.03*
Hispanic[b]	-0.88	-1.60	-0.10	-1.49*	-0.27	-0.30	0.02	-1.65*	-1.67
35–49[c]	0.74*	1.68*	0.27	0.63	0.59*	0.79*	0.19	0.69	0.31
50–64[c]	0.78	3.04**	0.59*	0.60	0.45	0.00	0.32	0.15	-0.23
65+[c]	-0.29	0.28	-0.24	1.45**	0.42	1.03*	-0.15	-0.76	-0.02
Education (years)	-0.23**	-0.36*	-0.11**	-0.24**	-0.20**	-0.22***	-0.18***	-0.04	0.25*
Income ($000s)[d]	-0.01	-0.02	-0.00	-0.00	-0.00	-0.01*	0.00	0.00	0.03
B. Census Region (New England Region Omitted)									
Mid-Atlantic	1.2	3.06*	0.42	1.11	0.23	1.03	1.11*	0.54	-0.16
N.E. Central	2.00**	4.68**	1.01**	2.09**	1.04*	0.94	1.26**	1.40	-1.12
W.N. Central	1.60*	3.82*	0.65	1.77*	0.92	0.80	1.12*	0.38	-0.65
S. Atlantic	2.06**	4.02**	0.84*	2.46**	1.22*	1.22*	1.05*	0.91	-0.38
E.S. Central	3.10***	7.12***	1.33**	2.97***	1.54*	2.94***	1.94***	1.85	-1.04
W.S. Central	3.58***	7.64***	1.59***	3.76***	2.12***	2.37***	1.75***	2.89***	-2.52*
Mountain	1.41	4.90*	0.43	1.66	-0.04	0.81	1.93**	0.67	1.36
Pacific	1.91**	3.65*	0.80*	2.24**	1.36**	0.90	1.17**	1.78*	1.66
C. MSA Size (MSA over 500,000 Omitted)									
Small MSA	0.54	0.13	0.33	0.83*	0.75**	0.24	-0.38	0.98*	-0.82
Non-MSA	0.41	0.55	0.25	0.29	0.61*	0.11	-0.29	1.19*	0.33
Intercept	4.4***	7.83***	1.37	5.02***	2.92***	4.92***	2.10**	-1.26	1.82
Adjusted R²	0.05***	0.03***	0.03***	0.04***	0.04***	0.03***	0.02***	0.02***	0.02**

[a] Approximate $N = 1610$.
[b] The omitted category is whites.
[c] The omitted age category is under 35.
[d] Household income imputed for respondents who did not answer income questions.

*, $p < .05$; **, $p < .01$; ***, $p < .001$.

Sentencing Severity), lower sentences for drug trafficking and street crimes, and more probation awards. The significant coefficients for Hispanics involve giving shorter sentences for street crimes and a lower proportion of life sentences.

The coefficients for age groups all show the contrast between the age group in question and those respondents who were under 35 years of age. The age group 35–49 tends to be more severe in sentencing than the contrast group, giving significantly longer sentences overall for drug trafficking, white-collar crimes, and "mixed" crimes. Respondents in the age group 50–64 show a similar pattern of greater severity, giving significantly longer sentences for drug trafficking and drug possession. As we saw earlier, the oldest age group, 65 and over, is not significantly different from the youngest age group in most measures, but gave longer sentences for street crimes and "mixed" crimes.

With the exception of giving a slightly lower sentences for "mixed" crimes, the coefficients for household income are not significant.

Of all the respondent characteristics, education has the most consistent effect pattern: Respondents' educational attainment is significantly negative in eight out of the nine equations, clearly indicating that the more education a respondent had, the lower the sentence given. Indeed, education is the strongest and most consistent correlate of sentencing of all of the respondent characteristics. The impact of educational attainment can be very large even though the coefficients are small because they represent decrements in sentencing for each additional year of education. Accordingly, for the six-year educational difference between a high school dropout and a college graduate the difference in total sentencing is almost 1.4 years.

Perhaps the most striking finding in Table 8.8 is the robustness of regional differences. Because the omitted region is New England, one way of interpreting the many significant regional coefficients is that every region differs from New England in some respect over and above regional differences in age, sex, educational attainment, and household income. Especially striking are the strong differences shown by the three southern regions in total sentencing: The southernmost tier of states ranging from Texas and Oklahoma on the west to the Atlantic Ocean on the east gave sentences that were almost four years longer than those given by New Englanders, indicating significant proportions of southerners giving much longer than usual sentences. The West South Central regions, stands out in greatest contrast to New England by having significant coefficients on all nine sentencing measures, in each case indicating greater severity of sentencing. This region is closely followed by the East South Central region—Mississippi, Alabama, Kentucky, and Tennessee—with significant coefficients in the same direction on seven of the nine sentencing measures. Note that the Pacific region also shows many significant coefficients indicating greater severity than New England.

Looked at in another way, New England is different from most other regions in being lower on punitiveness for street crimes and in giving death sentences. This is shown by all eight other regions having positive coefficients on street crimes and having positive coefficients on death sentences. In addition all of the eight regions have all of their coefficients, significant or not, positive, indicating that their residents are more severe than New Englanders in their sentencing.

In Panel C, the effects of community size detected earlier in this chapter have almost disappeared when other variables are taken into account. Only 5 of 18 coefficients are significant and positive. In short, when sociodemographic factors and region are held constant there are few strong differences among residents of large, medium, and small communities.

THE EFFECTS OF EXPERIENCES WITH CRIME AND CRIMINAL JUSTICE

For many citizens, crime consists of events and actions that are outside their immediate ken and experience. Crimes are events that have happened to others or happenings that are noted in the press or in television news broadcasts. For many others, criminal actions are more immediate because either they or someone in their households have been victims or even perpetrators. In addition, crime rates vary considerably by location. Even if the impact of crime is not immediate and close, living in a neighborhood with a high crime rate might noticeably affect sentencing behavior.

Many of the same differentials in direct exposure exist with respect to the legal institutions and the criminal justice system. Many, but not all Americans have served on juries. A smaller proportion have been involved in the courts in other ways such as being plaintiffs, defendants, or witnesses. Even smaller proportions have ever been embroiled in the criminal justice system by having been arrested and having served time in jail or prison.

One might expect that those who have been victims of a criminal action would be more severe in the punishments they would like to see given to convicted felons. However, such expectations are not borne out by the survey data, as shown in Table 8.9. About one in four respondents report-

Table 8.9.   Crime Victimization[a] and Mean Sentencing Differ-
        ences

Sentencing Measures	Nonvictim	Victim	p
Total Sentencing	2.9	2.8	.65
Drug Trafficking	6.1	4.7	.05
Drug Possession	1.1	1.1	.55
Street Crimes	2.5	2.6	.84
White Collar	2.1	2.2	.56
Mixed	2.5	3.0	.09
Death	0.1	−0.2	.72
Life	0.0	0.1	.93
Probation	−0.1	0.2	.67
Approximate N	[1217]	[418]	

[a] A respondent was classified as having been victimized if he or she
reported someone in his or her household was the victim in 1993 of a
burglary, a purse or wallet snatching, consumer fraud, an assault, or
had property stolen.

ed that some person in their households had been victimized in 1993, but
those who were victimized were not likely to give longer or shorter
sentences as measured by the measures shown in the table, only one of
the measures being statistically different when victimized respondents
are compared to others. If anything, victimized respondents desired
slightly shorter sentences for the convicted felons described in the vignettes rated, as shown in the significantly shorter sentences for drug-
trafficking crimes.

Perhaps part of the explanation for the findings of Table 8.9 lies in the
demographic characteristics of those who are most prone to be victims of
crime. As shown repeatedly in victimization surveys, the highest probabilities of being victimized are associated with minority group member-
ship, and being a young male. As has been shown in earlier sections of
this chapter, these demographic groups are not among the more punitive
segments of our population.

Although one might also expect that persons living in what they per-
ceive to be high crime areas would be more punitive toward convicted
felons, that is also not the case. Using the combined answers to five
questions about how serious respondents believed to be the problems
presented by several kinds of crimes in their neighborhoods (or communities), Table 8.10 shows no consistent relationship between perceived
seriousness of neighborhood crime problems and mean sentencing behavior for most of the sentencing measures. For example, on the Total
Sentencing Severity measure, respondents living in high crime areas gave

Table 8.10 Perceived Seriousness of Community Crime and Mean Sentencing
Differences

Sentencing Measures	Perceived Seriousness of Community Crime Problem[a]				p
	Highest	High	Low	Lowest	
Total Sentencing	3.1	3.0	2.7	2.8	.70
Drug Trafficking	6.0	5.9	4.9	6.1	.54
Drug Possession	1.0	1.2	1.2	1.3	.89
Street Crimes	2.7	2.6	2.3	2.4	.78
White Collar	2.2	2.1	1.9	2.1	.82
Mixed Crimes	2.8	2.4	2.8	2.4	.47
Death	1.2	−0.3	0.1	−0.1	.27
Life	−0.1	0.8	−0.4	−0.2	.08
Probation	0.2	−0.5	0.1	0.8	.77
Approximate N	[370]	[349]	[391]	[422]	

[a] Sum of answers to 5 questions about the seriousness of neighborhood crime, each concerned with one variety of crime: street crime, property crime, white-collar crime, drug trafficking, and drug usage. The scores were divided into approximately equal groups.

sentences that averaged 3.1 years higher than median sentences but those living in very low crime areas gave sentences that are about 3 months shorter, a difference that was not statistically significant.

Crime may be experienced as a local problem but that experience does not lead persons to want higher or lower sentences for convicted felons. It should be noted that these findings are consistent with those stemming from other studies of crime seriousness and sentencing, which also do not find that the seriousness of local crime problems and personal victimization affect judgments about seriousness or sentencing behavior.

One of the reasons why the findings concerning victimization and local crime conditions do not affect sentencing behavior as one might have expected, is provided in the earlier findings of this chapter concerning the effects of community size. Victimization rates are higher in larger places and neighborhood crime problems are more serious in large communities. However, as shown, residents of smaller places consistently gave longer sentences. Much the same can be said for demographic categories: Young people are more likely to be crime victims, but they also give shorter sentences. Clearly direct or community experiences with crime does not override the demographic determinants of sentencing behavior.

How does contact with legal institutions affect sentencing severity? The respondent questionnaire contained a battery of items concerned with personal participation in legal institutions in various roles, including jury service, reporting crimes to the police, being a participant in litigation as a defendant or witness, being arrested, and serving time in jail or prison[11] Overall, almost three in four (72%) of the respondents had at least one such contact. The most frequent contact (55%) was reporting crimes to the police.

A priori expectations were that the effects of such contact would vary with the kind of experience involved. Serving on a jury and thereby participating in a court trial as a decision-maker seemed to be worlds apart from having been arrested or sentenced to jail or prison. Perhaps people who had been sentenced themselves might be more lenient in sentencing others who had been convicted. However, initial analyses indicated that all the measures of contact affected sentencing behavior similarly. Any kind of contact led respondents to be more severe in their sentencing. Accordingly, we formed an index that was a simple count over all the six forms of contact.

Table 8.11 presents the findings. On six of the nine sentencing measures, the greater the number of contacts, the longer and harsher the sentences given, all differences that were statistically significant. The greater the number of contacts the more severe the sentences given. The mean sentencing differences for drug-trafficking crimes are especially large: those with three or more contacts gave sentences that were 2.7 years longer than those with no contacts.

Searching for a firmly defensible interpretation of the findings in Table 8.11 has not proved successful. For most contacts, one can make arguments for effects that would shorten sentences and other arguments that would lead one to expect longer sentences. For example, it is easy to

Table 8.11   Contact with Criminal Justice System and Sentencing[a]

Sentencing Measure	Number of Contacts with Legal System				
	0	1	2	3+	p
Total Sentencing	2.4	2.7	3.5	3.4	.01
Drug Trafficking	4.6	5.6	6.5	7.3	.06
Drug Possession	1.2	1.0	1.3	1.1	.06
Street Crimes	1.6	2.3	3.3	3.5	.001
White Collar	1.8	1.8	2.8	2.2	.002
Mixed Crimes	2.3	2.4	3.2	2.8	.04
Death	−0.4	−0.0	0.1	0.6	.02
Life	−0.7	−0.3	0.9	0.1	.05
Probation	−0.6	0.4	−0.5	1.3	.10
Approximate N	[460]	[592]1	[379]	[204]	

[a] Based on a count of positive answers to items asking whether the respondent has ever served on a jury, reported crimes to the police, been sued in court, testified as a witness in court, been arrested, and served time in jail or prison.

argue somewhat convincingly that participation in jury decision-making might lead to longer sentences because learning the details of a crime that are revealed in a trial could lead to feeling more strongly about punishing criminals. However, much of jury service does not involve criminal cases, and some criminal trials may lead jurors to of being arrested and serving time in jail or prison. What may be the best explanation is that any direct contact with the legal system leads to more intimate knowledge of the normative system involved.

POLITICAL AND SOCIAL ATTITUDES AND SENTENCING

The respondents' views on sentencing express primarily how they would punish those who transgress federal criminal laws. Secondarily they may also reflect other associated attitudes about a variety of political and social topics, some conceivably quite removed from the arena of crime and criminal justice. This section explores a limited number of such possibly related topics.

The first attitude measure considered refers to the general political division in our society that pits conservatives against liberals. This is a fuzzy division that is associated with political party preference, views on the role of the state in the economy and on individual rights, and a host of specific issues ranging from gun control, immigration, government role in health care, to legalized abortion. To measure that ideological split respondents were asked to classify themselves as conservatives, moderates, or liberals, a classification that ignores the many subtle divisions within each of these broad ideological groupings.[12]

The mean sentencing severity measures for the liberals and conservatives are shown in Table 8.12. In six of the nine sentencing measures there are statistically significant differences. Especially dramatic are the differences on sentencing for drug trafficking: The very conservative give sentences that are seven years longer than those given by the very liberal. Strong differences are also shown for total sentencing (2.5 years), drug possession (1.2 years), street crimes (3.2 years) and the percentages given death sentences (1.8%).

Interestingly, on white-collar and mixed crimes, the very conservative and the very liberal do not occupy the extreme positions. Apparently the very liberal were also punitive toward persons convicted of these crimes. A likely explanation for this pattern is that the mixed-crimes category

Table 8.12.   Political Leanings and Mean Sentencing

| Sentencing Measure | Leanings on Political and Social Issues[a] | | | | | p |
| | Conservative | | Moderate | Liberal | | |
	Very	Somewhat		Somewhat	Very	
Total Sentencing	4.6	3.2	2.7	2.2	2.1	.000
Drug Trafficking	9.1	6.6	5.4	4.4	2.1	.000
Drug Possession	1.9	1.0	1.2	0.8	0.7	.01
Street Crimes	4.5	2.9	2.1	2.1	1.3	.000
White Collar	3.3	2.3	1.9	1.5	2.0	.000
Mixed Crimes	3.4	2.8	2.4	2.0	3.6	.06
Death	0.8	0.0	−0.1	−0.2	−1.0	.11
Life	1.3	0.6	−0.3	−0.4	−1.0	.01
Probation	−0.2	−0.5	0.0	0.3	2.8	.22
Approximate N	[157]	[413]	[728]	[247]	[68]	

[a] Based on answers to the item "People often classify their views on political and social issues as conservative, moderate, or liberal. In general, would you say that your views usually tend to be very conservative, somewhat conservative, moderate, somewhat liberal, or very liberal?"

contains violations of civil rights and environmental laws, and white collar crimes committed by the affluent, for which the very liberal may desire stronger sentences.

Although the very conservative were very different from the very liberal, the intermediate groups were not far as far apart in their sentencing behavior. The somewhat conservative respondents were usually closer to the moderates than they were to the very conservative. Similarly, the somewhat liberal were also closer to the moderates than they were to the very liberal.

In summary, views on sentencing also reflect more general ideological positions on social and political issues, those on the far right contrasting especially strongly with those on the far left. It is important to keep in mind that these contrasting views are decidedly minority voices: 9.6% of the sample identified themselves as very conservative and 4.2% as very liberal with the remaining 85% occupying the middle positions, which differed more moderately.

Although the conservative-liberal ideological split is related to sentencing behavior, as we have seen, it is nevertheless a general stance on social issues. Other views on public issues may be more closely related to the criminal justice system. Respondents were asked whether they believed that persons accused of serious crimes were accorded too many, too few, or just about the right amount of legal rights. Most (63%) thought that the accused had too many rights, with a respectable minority (29%) believing that the rights accorded to the accused were about right and a very small minority (8%) believing that the accused had too few legal rights. Apparently the balance of public opinion is that the current set of legal rights for the accuse[13] accords too many rights to that group.

There are strong relationships between views on the rights of accused person and sentencing behavior. Table 8.13 shows the sentencing severity measures for each of the three viewpoints on the rights of accused persons. Significant differences are shown on eight of the nine sentencing measures. In addition, some of the contrasts in measures are very large. Overall, on the total sentencing measure, those who believed that accused persons had too many rights wanted sentences that were about two years longer than those desired by respondents holding the opposite views. On sentences for drug-trafficking crimes the differences were even greater, 5.1 years, and on street crimes, 2.6 years.

Arguably, the reverse of sympathy for the those accused of crimes is support for the criminal justice system. To tap that dimension of social attitudes, respondents were asked whether police departments had too much, too little, or about the right amount of freedom to investigate crimes, a question we believed would be interpreted as dealing with the investigative rights and responsibilities of the police. The balance of public opinion clearly was against the view that the police had too much freedom, a minority view held by 13% of the sample. About half of the sample thought that police had about the right amount and a fair-sized minority believed the police did not have enough freedom.

Table 8.13. Views on the Proper Balance of Rights for Criminally Accused and Sentencing

| Sentencing Measures | Legal Rights for Accused[a] | | | p |
	Too Few	About Right	Too Many	
Total Sentencing	1.5	2.0	3.5	.000
Drug Trafficking	2.1	3.9	7.2	.000
Drug Possession	0.7	1.3	3.3	.01
Street Crimes	0.7	1.3	3.3	.000
White Collar	1.4	1.0	2.4	.000
Mixed Crimes	2.3	2.2	2.9	.054
Death	−0.1	−0.4	0.2	.02
Life	−1.6	−0.7	0.6	.000
Probation	0.3	0.9	−0.5	.05
Approximate N	[127]	[470]	[1032]	

[a] Based on item "People accused of serious crimes: Would you say they have too few, about the right amount of, or too many legal rights?"

The findings in Table 8.14, are the mirror images of those in Table 8.13. In eight of the nine severity measures, the differences are significant, with those holding the view that the police have too few investigative powers giving longer sentences. Indeed, the severity differences are about as great as in Table 8.13.

In the discussion above, we treated the attitudinal measures concerning accused persons and the police as if they were related as causes to sentencing behavior. Because the data are derived from a cross-sectional survey, this interpretation is clearly not warranted. Using the data presented here there is no way we can tell whether sentencing behavior affects attitudes toward the police and accused persons or the other way around. However, we can say that views on the police and views on the legal rights of the accused are not one and the same attitude, the correlation between the two being quite small ($-.22$), indicating that there were some respondents who favored both strengthening the powers of the police and more rights for accused persons.

The two attitudinal items considered above focus on issues that are closely related to criminal justice practices and institutions. When we consider other social attitudes, as in the next two attitudinal measures presented, we can expect that such attitudes will not be strongly related to sentencing behavior even though they are often thought of as clearly dividing the liberal from the conservative camps in American society.

Views on whether protecting the environment against pollution was receiving too much, too little, or about the right amount of attention were

Table 8.14. Sentencing and Respondent Views on Police Freedom
to Investigate Crimes

Sentencing Measures	Investigative Rights of Police[a]			p
	Too Few	About Right	Too Many	
Total Sentencing	3.9	2.3	2.3	.000
Drug Trafficking	8.1	4.6	3.8	.000
Drug Possession	1.5	1.0	0.9	.007
Street Crimes	3.6	1.9	1.7	.000
White Collar	2.6	1.7	1.9	.000
Mixed Crimes	2.8	2.4	2.9	.23
Death	0.4	−0.3	0.1	.003
Life	0.5	−0.1	−1.1	.008
Probation	−1.5	0.6	1.6	.000
Approximate N	[582]	[828]	219]	

[a] Based on item "Police departments and the freedom they have in investigating crimes: Would you say they have too little, about the right amount of, or too little freedom?"

also measured in the respondent questionnaire. Views on this statement of environmental issues were virtually irrelevant to sentencing measures to the point that we did not think it worthwhile to present any numerical results.

In stark contrast to environmental issues, public views on civil rights for minorities were found to be quite strongly related to sentencing behavior, as shown in Table 8.15. Public opinion is about evenly divided on the civil rights issue: About half (48%) thought that minorities had about the right amount of civil rights and the remainder was almost evenly divided between those thinking minorities had too many civil rights (27%) and those who thought they had too few (26%).

Respondents who thought the civil rights movement had won too many victories consistently gave significantly longer sentences on six of the nine severity measures. However, the two groups were not significantly different on drug possession and mixed crimes, as well as life sentences or probation. At the other extreme, respondents who thought minorities had too few civil rights gave shorter sentences for most crime types, as well as fewer death sentences.

Some of the differences are substantively quite large. On total sentencing, the difference in sentencing was 1.8 years, on street crimes 2 years, and on drug-trafficking crimes 5.4 years. Those believing that minorities had too many civil rights were almost twice as likely to give out death sentences. Given the considerable overrepresentation of minorities among arrestees, indicted persons, and prison inmates, the connection between sentencing behavior and attitudes toward minority civil rights appears obvious. Under this interpretation, those prejudiced against

Table 8.15. Sentencing and Views on the Civil Rights of Minorities

| Sentencing Measures | Minority Rights[a] | | | *p* |
	Too Few	*About Right*	*Too Many*	
Total Sentencing	2.0	2.9	3.8	.000
Drug Trafficking	3.4	5.4	8.8	.000
Drug Possession	1.0	1.0	1.4	.12
Street Crime	1.4	2.6	3.4	.000
White Collar	1.6	2.2	2.5	.007
Mixed Crimes	2.3	2.7	2.9	.28
Death	−0.5	−0.2	0.8	.000
Life	−0.4	0.4	−0.2	.17
Probation	0.9	−0.4	−0.2	.12
Approximate *N*	[420]	[775]	[433]	

[a] Based on answers to item "Minority groups in the United States: Would you say that they have too few, about the right amount of, or too many civil rights?"

Blacks and Hispanics would prefer longer sentences for offenders, many of whom are Black or Hispanic. However, there is also an alternative explanation, namely, those who are more punitive to felons are also more conservative in general and hence would not favor extending the civil liberties of minorities. Perhaps both processes are at work. Respondents who are more conservative and those who are opposed to the aspirations of minorities both find that their views converge in giving longer sentences to convicted felons.

In another set of questions on broad social issues, respondents were asked whether they thought poor people in the United States had too few, too many, or about the right number of welfare benefits. Public sentiment clearly did not favor more benefits for the poor: Close to half (44%) thought poor people had too many benefits, more than one-third (36%) thought the poor had about the right amount, and only one-fifth (20%) thought the poor should have more benefits.

A weak tendency can be discerned in Table 8.16 for those who were in favor of more benefits for the poor to give shorter sentences, but of the nine sentencing measures there were only three in which that tendency was strong enough to reach statistical significance: For street crimes, the mean sentencing difference for the two extreme groups was 0.9 years, significant at the .01 level, with those opposed to more benefits giving the longer sentences. The same group also gave a more severe sentences overall and to drug-trafficking crimes.

In general, views on political and social issues are related to sentencing

Table 8.16.   Public Views on the Adequacy of Public Welfare Benefits and Sentencing

	Welfare Benefits for the Poor[a]			
Sentencing Measures	*Too Few*	*About Right*	*Too Many*	*p*
Total Sentencing	2.8	2.5	3.3	.03
Drug Trafficking	5.1	4.8	6.8	.02
Drug Possession	1.3	1.0	1.2	.29
Street Crimes	2.2	2.0	3.1	.01
White Collar	2.2	1.8	2.3	.13
Mixed Crimes	3.0	2.2	1.7	.11
Death	−0.1	0.2	0.2	.15
Life	0.1	−1.2	0.2	.59
Probation	0.3	0.1	−0.3	.68
Approximate *N*	[330]	[575]	[715]	

[a] Based on answers to the item "Poor people in the United States and their public welfare benefits: Would you say they have too few, about the right amount of, or too many welfare benefits?"

behavior, especially when the issues in question are substantively closely to criminal justice. When, as in the cases of environmental issues and welfare benefits, the tie between views on issues and sentencing becomes quite attenuated.

INDEPENDENT EFFECTS OF DEMOGRAPHIC, EXPERIENTIAL, AND ATTITUDINAL FACTORS

There is a strain toward consistency among attitudes producing what can be called ideological syndromes. Those who identify themselves on the conservative side of the American political spectrum tend to hold similar views on a wide variety of specific issues. Those on the liberal end of the political continuum tend to hold similar views, although different from those held by the conservatives. Furthermore, such views are also structured along demographic and along regional and community size lines, as shown earlier in this chapter.

Unraveling the resulting entangled web of interrelationships is the task of this section. Multiple regression analyses will be used to do so. Each of the nine sentencing measures was regressed on all of the measures discussed in this and the preceding chapter. The resulting coefficients show the effects of each of the respondent characteristics independent of all the other characteristics in the regression equation. For example, if a coefficient on total sentencing for residents of the West South Central region is 2.5, that means that respondents living in that region gave sentences that were 2.5 years higher than the median sentences when compared to residents of the New England region[14], regardless of their own experiences, attitudes on various social issues, and their age, education, gender, and so on throughout the entire list of characteristics included in the equation.

The presentation of regression coefficients follows the same conventions used in Table 8.8: each coefficient represents the increment ($+$) or decrement ($-$) in a severity score associated with each unit of the respondent characteristic of that row and the presence of asterisks marks a coefficient as statistically significant.

The findings from the nine regressions are shown in Table 8.17. Each column of the table contains the results of a regression equation in which the sentencing measure described at the top of the column was the dependent variable. Each row of the table contains findings concerning one of the respondent characteristics discussed earlier in this chapter.

To facilitate discussion, Table 8.17 is divided into five panels, each composed of respondent characteristics of the same general type. How-

Table 8.17. Sentencing Measures Regressed on Respondent Characteristics and Place of Residence (Approximate N = 1563)

Respondent Measures	Total Sentencing	Drug Trafficking	Drug Possession	Street Crimes	White Collar	Mixed Crimes	Death (%)	Life (%)	Probation (%)
A. Personal Experiences with Crime and Legal Institutions									
Justice Contacts	0.45**	0.98**	0.04	0.59**	0.31**	0.29**	0.29**	0.31	0.09
Victimization	−0.12	−0.99	−0.04	0.27	0.14	0.24	−0.26	0.10	0.06
Local Crime Problem	−0.06*	−0.08	−0.00	−0.07*	−0.03	−0.05	−0.02	−0.06	0.01
B. Attitudes on Political and Social Issues									
Wants Fewer Rights for Accused	0.73***	1.64***	0.06	1.09***	0.39*	0.26	0.20	0.78**	0.41
Fewer Welfare Benefits	0.03	0.16	−0.02	0.15	−0.03	−0.08	0.56	−0.07	−0.20
Liberal on Social and Political Issues	−0.33*	−0.74*	−0.12	−0.26	−0.30*	−0.15	0.02	−0.46*	0.47
Fewer Civil Rights for Minorities	0.53*	1.15*	0.14	0.40	0.36*	0.31	0.54***	−0.39	−0.25
Less Police Freedom to Investigate Crimes	−0.69**	−1.67**	−0.31*	−0.76*	0.38*	0.03	−0.16	−0.51	1.5***
Too Much Attention to Environment	0.12	0.62	0.07	0.39	−0.21	−0.26	0.20	−0.12	0.50
C. Demographic Characteristics									
Female	0.07	−0.18	0.26	−0.42	0.43	0.06	−0.22	0.34	−1.0
Single	−0.30	−0.74	−0.19	−0.05	−0.21	0.36	−0.06	−0.07	−0.45
Education (years)	−0.20**	−0.26	−0.10*	−0.20*	−0.19**	−0.22**	−0.15**	−0.05	0.25

Age 35–49[a]	0.43	1.06	0.32	0.91*	0.34	1.04**	0.14	0.76	0.23
Age 50–64[a]	0.32	2.1*	0.66**	0.73	0.19	0.18	0.17	0.25	−0.21
Black[b]	−0.11	−0.91	0.44	−0.41	0.52	−0.25	0.19	−0.73	1.1
Hispanic[b]	−0.49	−0.47	0.04	−0.93	−0.07	−0.01	0.29	−1.3	1.7
Income ($000s)	−0.01	−0.03	−0.00	−0.00	−0.00	−0.00	−0.00	−0.00	−0.03
D. Region[c]									
Mid-Atlantic	1.1	3.0	0.41	1.0	0.23	1.06	1.1*	0.44	−0.48
East North Central	1.6**	3.8**	1.0**	1.7*	0.87	0.92	1.1*	1.1	−1.36
West North Central	1.5*	3.5*	0.69	1.7	0.87	0.97	1.0*	0.39	1.38
South Atlantic	1.7**	3.3**	0.77*	2.0**	0.99*	1.02	0.87**	0.60	−0.62
East South Central	2.8***	6.6***	1.3**	3.0**	1.4*	2.4**	1.8**	1.8	−1.3
West South Central	3.1***	6.7***	1.5***	3.3***	1.8**	2.2**	1.6**	2.5**	−2.5
Mountain	1.3	5.1*	0.45	1.5	−0.11	0.83	1.9**	0.70	0.52
Pacific	1.8**	3.4*	0.83*	2.1*	1.2**	0.91	1.1*	1.5	−2.5
E. Community Size[d]									
Medium MSA	0.72*	0.31	0.48	0.76	0.95***	0.56	−0.33	1.11**	−1.1
Non-MSA	0.58	0.73	0.31	0.33	0.89**	0.38	−0.21	1.5**	0.18
Intercept	3.1	3.5	1.4	1.4	2.8*	3.8*	−0.51	0.41	−3.6
Adjusted R^2	0.08	0.06	0.04	0.07	0.06	0.03	0.03	0.03	0.03

201

[a] Omitted age categories are respondents under 35 and respondents 65 and over.

[b] Omitted race/ethnic categories are whites, Asians, Native Americans and "others."

[c] The omitted region is New England.

[d] Metropolitan areas 500,000 and over constitute the omitted category.

*, $p < .05$; **, $p < .01$; ***, $p < .001$.

ever, the panels do not mark off separate regression equations: All of the coefficients in a given column derive from a single regression.

In Panel A are collected the three measures dealing with respondent experiences with crime and legal institutions, including the criminal justice system. With respect to theses measures, the findings shown earlier hold up quite strongly. The more contacts with legal institutions, the more significantly severe are the sentences given, the exceptions being sentences for drug possession, and the giving of life sentences and probation. The differences can be quite large. For example, for every additional contact with legal institutions, respondents gave an addition 0.45 years on the total sentencing measure. That means that a respondent who has had four kinds of contacts—perhaps served on a jury, reported a crime to the police, was a witness in a court case, and was arrested for some cause— gave sentences that were overall 1.8 years longer than the median for all crimes. For drug-trafficking crimes, the same respondent gave sentences 3.9 years longer than the median. In contrast, for respondents who had been crime victims in 1993 (or if someone in their household had been a victim) there were no significant differences in sentencing: victims gave sentences that were no more severe than those given by nonvictims.

Experiences with serious crime in one's neighborhood also modestly affected sentence severity. Overall, as shown in significant coefficients for the total severity and street crimes measures, respondents living in neighborhoods in which crime problems were not serious were prone to give longer sentences.[15] In Panel B, the findings concerning social and political attitudes are shown. Two measures were found to be unrelated or very weakly related to sentencing. None of the coefficients associated with views on welfare benefits or environmental issues were significant. Clearly these are issues at some remove from those affecting punishment for convicted felons.

In contrast, there were several social attitudes that affected many of the sentencing measures, even when other things were held constant. Those wanting fewer rights given to accused persons desired more severe sentences on the total sentencing, drug-trafficking, street crime, and white-collar crime measures, as well as giving out proportionately more death sentences. Those who wanted to restrict the investigative powers of the police also wanted shorter sentences on three of the nine measures, desiring shorter sentences for total sentencing, drug-trafficking, drug possession, street crimes and white-collar crimes, and giving out proportionately more probation awards.

The remaining attitudinal measures also affect sentencing severity measures although not as many as the attitudes more directly concerned with criminal justice issues. Those who thought minorities had too many civil rights gave longer sentences than the average on the total sentencing measure, drug-trafficking, and white-collar crimes, and were more likely to give out death sentences. Surprisingly, holding other things constant diminished strongly the influence of self-identification as conservatives or liberals: Liberals gave shorter sentences on the total sentencing measure, drug-trafficking, and white-collar crimes, and gave out fewer life sentences, but were not significantly different from conservatives on the other measures. This finding suggests that generalized political predispositions are not as important as rather specific views on a topic, with the latter's effects swamping those of the more general views.

The effects on sentencing of respondent demographic characteristics are shown in Panel C. For most of the demographic variables, their effects on sentencing are reduced. For example, none of the coefficients for African-Americans or Hispanics were significant. Household income and gender also did not have significant coefficients.

In contrast, higher educational attainment leads to more leniency on total sentencing, drug possession, street crime, mixed crime, and white-collar measures, and to slightly fewer death sentences. Only drug trafficking and the giving of life sentences and probation is unaffected by educational attainment. The sentencing differences associated with education can be quite large. For example, the difference between those with less than high school education and those with college degrees is 1.2 years for total sentencing.

The age group differences that appeared earlier in this chapter are also considerably diminished. Respondents between the ages of 35–59 gave longer sentences for street crimes and mixed crimes but were not significantly different on others measures. Members of the age group 50–64 also were significantly different on just two severity measures, drug trafficking and drug possession.

The coefficients in Panel D are those associated with region, over and above regional differences in demographic composition, in attitudes on social and political issues, and personal experiences with crime and legal institutions. Because it was necessary to omit one region from the regression equations, the coefficients refer to the differences of each included region as compared with the omitted region, New England.

There are several important features of regional coefficients given in Panel D. First, every one of the eight included regions differs in the direction of giving longer sentences or harsher punishments on one or more of the sentencing measures. Clearly the residents of New England are the least punitive. At the other, harsher end of the sentencing continuum are the residents of the East and West South Central States, a band of states that runs from Texas to Alabama on the south and from Oklahoma to Kentucky in the north. These two regions gave significantly longer sentences on most of the sentencing measures. The differences for some measures are quite large, amounting to sentences 6.6 and 6.7 years longer sentences for drug trafficking for residents of East South Central and West South Central regions, respectively. Between these contrasts are regions that are closer to New England in sentencing tendencies. The Mid-Atlantic, Mountain and Pacific regions are closer to New England, and the remaining regions occupy what appears to be middle ground between New England and the South Central states.

Regional differences in sentencing are clearly strong enough to survive, holding many other things constant. For example, although liberals in general tend to give short sentences, these findings indicate that liberals in the South Central states give longer sentences than liberals in New England. We can speculate that these results reflect the strength of cultural regional differences that might also be seen in other ways, for example, in the nature of religious beliefs and in the political conservatism of the South.

Panel E is concerned with city size differences that appeared earlier in this chapter. However, holding other things constant, community size differences were greatly diminished, with only six of the coefficients for community size reaching statistical significance. However, all of the coefficients show that respondents living outside the major metropolitan areas desire more severe sentences for convicted felons.

In the next to last row of Table 8.16 the R^2 for each of the nine regression equations are shown. Despite the presence of many significant coefficients in most of the columns, the value for each equation is very modest, the largest being .07 for the street crimes severity measure. In short, of all the variation among respondents in their sentencing behaviors, the characteristics presented account for small amounts.

SUMMARY

Using measures that showed the extent to which each respondent's sentences differed from the median sentences given by the total sample to the same crimes, the chapter searched for those characteristics that lead respondents to depart from the sample medians. Overall, social and individual characteristics of respondents were not strongly related to sentencing behavior. However, several salient findings emerge:

1.   There were only minor differences among respondents along gender lines. Men and women did not differ strongly in the sentences each gave.

2. Although blacks and Hispanics tended to be more lenient in sentencing than others (mainly whites), those differences were neither strong or consistent.
3. The strongest demographic correlate of sentencing was educational attainment. The better educated tended to give shorter sentences and less harsh punishments.
4. Although personal experiences with being a crime victim or living in high crimes areas were not related to sentencing, personal experiences with legal institutions did have effects. Respondents who had been in the courts as juror, plaintiff, or witness, or had been arrested and convicted were inclined to give longer sentences.
5. Respondent attitudes affect sentencing if the substance of those attitudes is closely related to criminal justice issues. Those concerned that accused persons did not have sufficient legal protection were more likely to give shorter sentences, whereas those who thought the police ought to have greater freedom in investigating crime tended to give longer sentences. Although respondents identifying with liberal politics tended to give shorter sentences than conservatives, those differences were considerably diminished when other factors were taken into account. Attitudes toward welfare issues and environment issues were not related to sentencing.
6. Regional differences in sentencing persisted when other personal and attitudinal factors were taken into account. At one extreme, New England respondents were the most lenient in sentencing, whereas those living in the South consistently gave out longer sentences.

Overall, differences among respondents were not strongly structured. That is, the amounts of variation in sentencing accounted for by the individual characteristics studied was quite small, less than 10%. Members of the sample responded strongly to the crime descriptions in the vignettes and their social coordinates affected their views only weakly. In short, the norms were more important in their sentencing than their positions on major public issues or their positions in American society.

NOTES

1. Medians are used because, as shown in earlier chapters, these measures are more representative of respondent central tendencies.
2. This adjustment does not take into account the other dimensions in the

vignettes, for example, the dollar amounts lost by reason of the crime. However, as shown in earlier chapters, the crime dimension and previous record dimension are available for each crime sample and are the strongest overall determinants of sentences given by the respondents. The R^2 of the regression of respondent sentences on Crime Examples and previous record, each considered as a set of binary variables, is .24.

3.   These are firearms crime examples, two involving a felon illegally possessing firearms and the third involving possession of a sawed-off shotgun.

4.   These involving firearms dealers' violations of firearms laws.

5.   Table not shown.

6.   Although not shown here, we also investigated the relationship of marital status to the sentencing severity measures, finding that married persons were consistently more punitive and the single (never married) were the least punitive. However marital status differences disappeared once age and gender were taken into account.

7.   The vignette dimensions did not include any racial or ethnic descriptions of the convicted offenders. The main reason for this omission is that previous studies of crime seriousness and sentencing consistently showed that offender race or ethnicity played no role in the studies (Rossi et al. 1985). And, of course, neither race nor ethnicity plays any role in the guidelines.

8.   Any respondent, regardless of skin color, was classified as Hispanic if he or she indicated identification with that group.

9.   There is some weak evidence supporting this statement. Calculating the regression of sample sentences on guidelines sentences separately for educational groups, the higher the educational attainment the higher the resulting R^2 for the equation, the difference between the lowest and highest attainment groups being .05. See also the findings in Chapter 7 concerning education.

10.   This estimate is based on the regression of severity scores on years of formal education completed.

11.   Levels of contact so measured were as follows: 22% had served on a jury, 21% had been witnesses in court cases, 55% had reported crimes to the police, 7% had been sued, 15% had been arrested, 4% had served time in jail or prison.

12.   Despite the crudity of the item, only 21 respondents refused to answer the question and another 66 claimed they were unable to fit themselves somewhere among the five groupings given, amounting in total to 5% of our respondents.

13.   Views on this issue are also quite general. The survey did not ascertain what the American public thought were the rights of the accused nor which of them were objectionable and which were acceptable.

14.   For categorical characteristics, such as region, one of the categories is used as a contrast and is omitted from the equation. The coefficients for the categories included in the equation then become the difference between each included category and the omitted one.

15.   Although the coefficients are not large, at the extremes, sentencing differences can be quite large. The Neighborhood Crime Seriousness Index has a range running from 5 (most serious) to 25 (least serious), which could lead to sentencing differences of 2.0 years on street crimes between the two ends of the scale.

9

Summing Up

This book has presented a rather large number of empirical findings, sometimes in great detail. The survey we reported on was complicated and the book reflects that complexity. The purpose of this chapter is to stand above such details, to provide a synthesis and interpretation of those findings.

The central focus of our book has been on comparing the sentences prescribed for federal criminal offenders in the guidelines written by the U.S. Sentencing Commission with the sentences preferred for the same crimes by the American public. The guidelines are published in the Sentencing Manual (U.S. Sentencing Commission, 1987–1993) in the form of an elaborate set of rules for arriving at prescribed ranges of sentences for persons convicted of each of the many federal felony offenses. The public's views are represented by the sentences given by a national probability sample of adult Americans to short vignettes, each describing a convicted offender and the crime of which the felon was convicted.

The vignettes were constructed using the factorial survey approach, a blending of experimental design and sample survey methods. We included the major factors identified in the guidelines so that there were close parallels between the guidelines and the vignettes. We believe that the findings presented here demonstrate how well suited the factorial survey approach is to the study of how decisions are made in complicated circumstances. Conventional surveys using simple, one-dimensional questions yield simplistic responses. Factorial surveys allow for differentiated responses that are sensitive to complexities. In particular, we were able to show the extent to which that factors used in the guidelines rules to arrive at prescribed sentences were recognized by respondents in coming to their sentencing decisions.

Sifting through the findings presented in previous chapters, three major themes emerge:

First, and most important, there is a fair amount of agreement between sentences prescribed in the guidelines and those desired by the members of the sample. The agreement is quite close between the means and the medians of respondents' sentences and the guidelines prescribed sentences. There is also quite close agreement between how individual respondents rank crimes and the way in which the guidelines rank the same crimes. However, on the level of the sentences given to individual vignettes, there was only a very modest amount of agreement between the sentences given by individual respondents and those prescribed by the guidelines. Of course, we do not claim that the agreement was perfect, but only that it is high enough to support the conclusion that the degree of agreement is far greater than can be accounted for by chance.

In addition, our findings show that our respondents tended to use much the same rules as the guidelines in modifying sentences according to how crimes were committed and according to the previous felony record of the convicted felon. Even when we included factors ignored by the guidelines, such as the gender of the felon, respondents also tended to give minor weight to them. As with other findings, the correspondence was not perfect but there were also no instances of wide divergences.

We interpret this major finding to mean that the ideas about sentencing in the guidelines and the interviews with respondents reflect societal norms concerning punishment for those who violate the criminal laws. Both the commission and the public converge on roughly the same sentences, because the commission sought to write guidelines that would be acceptable to major constituencies. As Nagel's account (Chapter 2) relates, the commission relied heavily on the central tendencies in past sentencing practices in the federal courts as a kind of template for its sentencing rules, a strategy that used those practices as a proxy for public preferences. Using this template, the commission avoided both overly lenient and overly harsh sentences and wrote sentencing rules that came close to mainstream consensus.

The crimes causing major departures from close agreement are those crimes for which the commission was forced to disregard past sentencing practices. In particular, the Congressional mandates concerning sentences for drug-trafficking crimes led the commission to impose far higher sentences than found in past sentencing practices. Of course, why the Congress imposed sentences that were far higher than could be supported by the American public is a question that cannot be addressed in this research.

Other than the penalties of drug trafficking, about the only other consistent disagreement concerns crimes that result in physical harm to persons or have the potential of inflicting such harm. The American public would give persons convicted of such crimes longer sentences than would the guidelines. We have no explanation for this kind of disagreement.

The fact that closer agreement was found when summary measures were used to represent public opinion means that the normative structure concerning sentencing is not sharply defined. We interpret the very considerable variation in sentencing around the means and medians to mean that respondents were uncertain about the exact sentence magnitudes that corresponded to the norms. The evidence that supports this view is the modest reliability of responses given to the vignettes. When respondents rated the same vignette twice, they often gave different sentences. The differences were not very great but enough to indicate that respondents acted as if sentences that were not exactly the same were equivalent. It is as if the American sentencing norms were phrased in magnitude terms rather than in specific numbers of years of imprisonment. Further evidence for this interpretation comes from the much closer agreement between individual respondents' rank ordering of crimes and the guidelines ordering of the same crimes.

The second major theme is that there is very little, if any evidence that there exist subgroups within the American population with radically different views about sentencing norms. There are few who would condone homicide or kidnaping and there are few who would punish marijuana users with 10 or more years of imprisonment. There is no evidence for a normative order that is an alternative to what the overwhelming majority of the American population believe.

What subgroup differences exist are matters of degree. Southerners prefer harsher punishment across the board than New Englanders. The better educated give shorter sentences than those of lesser educational attainment. All of these differences of degree account for little of the variation among respondents. The sharp regional differences epitomized by the contrast between New England and the old South are similar to regional dialects. Most Americans can understand the various dialects because they are all minor variations on mainstream American English. In the same way, the regional differences in sentencing are variations on a national consensus.

The third major theme concerns whether the patterning of respondents' sentences constitutes evidence of the existence of a normative structure concerning punishment for criminals. We believe that the preponderance of evidence favors the view that there is a set of norms that guided both the respondents and the commission to converge on roughly the same set of sentences. Such norms are apparent to members of the society as the expressed views of people they come into contact with and in the content of the mass media. Because such messages are variable in content, the normative structure is fuzzy and not well defined. That fuzziness is apparent in the less than perfect reliability of the sentencing preferences of individuals and in the difficulties experienced by the commission in writing the guidelines.

Accordingly, the empirical evidence shown in this volume tends to support the Durkheimian view that the laws of a society tend to reflect that society's normative consensus. In writing the guidelines, the U.S. Sentencing Commission tried to write sentencing rules that would conform to the mandates given to it by the Congress and that would also be acceptable to the federal judiciary, the federal prosecutors, the criminal defense bar, and the other stakeholders concerned. The end result was a set of guidelines that were also close to the views of the general public. The commission may not have had that convergence as its explicit goal, but the ways in which the commissioners went about writing the guidelines assured that the guidelines would converge on those views.

A

Dimensions and Levels

This Appendix contains lists of the dimensions and levels used in constructing the vignettes used in this study. A computer program, VIG WRITE,[1] was used to compile the vignettes by randomly selecting levels from within each of the relevant dimensions. Note that once a level from Dimension A is picked, the program then proceeds to randomly choose levels from within all of the dimensions relevant to that crimes.

Levels are listed after the heading for each dimension. Dimensions that are used contingent on the selection of other dimensions are designated as such in parenthetical statements after the title for each dimension.

Dimension A: Crime Dimension (All Vignettes)

[Note: This dimension has 96 levels total over 20 crime categories. Each of the 96 levels has a 1/96 probability of being selected.]

    I.   Drug Trafficking (20 levels listed below)

        has been convicted with several others of taking part over a four-month period in the selling of *[this stem to be added to each of the crimes listed below]*

        $100 of powdered cocaine, about 15 doses.
        $1,000 of powdered cocaine, about 300 doses.
        $20,000 of powdered cocaine, about 16,000 doses.
        $100,000 of powdered cocaine, about 30,000 doses.
        $1,000,000 of powdered cocaine, about 300,000 doses.
        $100 of crack, about 10 doses.
        $1,000 of crack, about 300 doses.
        $20,000 of crack, about 6,000 doses.
        $100,000 of crack, about 30,000 doses.
        $1,000,000 of crack, about 300,000 doeses.
        $100 of heroin, about 3 doses.
        $1,000 of heroin, about 50 doses.

$20,000 of heroin, about 1,000 doses.
$100,000 of heroin, about 5,000 doses.
$1,000,000 of heroin, about 50,000 doses.
$100 of marijuana, about 60 doses.
$1,000 of marijuana, about 900 doses.
$20,000 of marijuana, about 18,000 doses.
$100,000 of marijuana, about 90,000 doses.
$1,000,000 of marijuana, about 900,000 doses.

II.   Type A Frauds—Minor frauds (4 levels listed below)

has been convicted of writing bad checks on an account opened using false identification. The bad checks amounted to

has been convicted of using a stolen credit card. The purchases amounted to

has been convicted of soliciting donations for a nonexistent charity. Victims lost

has been convicted of obtaining a mortgage by making false claims about assets and income. The defendant had no intention of paying back the mortgage. The mortgage was for

III. Type B Frauds—Major frauds (6 levels listed below)

has been convicted of obtaining a mortgage by making false claims about assets and income. The defendant intended to pay back the mortgage. The mortgage was for

, a company officer, has been convicted of making personal gain from inside information learned before the information was made public. The officer bought stocks for HIS/HER personal account knowing that the stock price would go up when the information was made public. The profits amounted to

has been convicted of being responsible for the failure of a savings and loan association by lending money to borrowers HE/SHE knew could not pay back their loans. Losses amounted to

has been convicted of selling worthless stocks and bonds as valuable assets. Customer losses amounted to

has been convicted of selling defective helicopter parts to the federal government, thus endangering the lives of helicopter personnel and passengers. The seller knew the parts to be defective. The sales amounted to

, a doctor, has been convicted of submitting false Medicare claims to the government. The false claims amounted to

IV.   Firearms (5 levels listed below)

has been convicted of illegally owning a handgun because of a prior felony conviction for theft. (Use only "bb" ($p = .5$) or "cc" ($p = .5$) of Dimension OO.)

has been convicted of illegally owning a hunting rifle because of a prior felony conviction for theft. (Use only "bb" ($p = .5$) or "cc" ($p = .5$) of Dimension OO.)

has been convicted of possessing sawed-off shotguns, prohibited weapons. (Equal probability ($p = 1/3$) of assigning "aa," "bb," or "cc" of Dimension OO.)

xx has been convicted of selling firearms to a known felon. (Do not use any level of Dimension OO.)

xx , a licensed dealer, has been convicted of selling firearms without maintaining required sales records. (Do not use any level of Dimension OO.)

V. Larceny (3 levels listed below)

has been convicted of stealing property worth
has been convicted of stealing mail containing checks worth
has been convicted of buying and selling goods HE/SHE knew were stolen worth

VI. Immigration (5 levels listed below)

has been convicted of smuggling unauthorized aliens into the U.S. for profit.

has been convicted of smuggling family members who were unauthorized aliens into the U.S. has been convicted of illegally entering the U.S. using false papers.

has been convicted of illegally reentering the U.S. after a previous deportation.

has been convicted of smuggling unauthorized aliens into the U.S. for profit in a way that endangered the safety of the aliens.

VII. Bank Robbery (6 levels listed below)

has been convicted of robbing a bank. The robber gave a note to the teller demanding money but did not threaten any harm. The robber did not have a weapon.

has been convicted of robbing a bank. The robber pointed a handgun at a teller and demanded money. The gun was not fired.

has been convicted of robbing a bank. The robber pointed a handgun at a teller and demanded money. The robber fired the gun at the ceiling, but no one was hurt.

has been convicted of robbing a bank. The robber pointed a handgun at a teller and demanded money. The robber fired the gun at the teller, who suffered a minor wound.

has been convicted of robbing a bank. The robber pointed a handgun at a teller and demanded money. The robber fired the gun at the teller, who was seriously wounded.

has been convicted of robbing a bank. The robber gave a note to a teller demanding money and threatening to blow up the bank. No one was hurt.

VIII. Street Robbery (2 levels listed below)

y   has been convicted of robbing a convenience store
z   has been convicted of taking a car by forcing the driver out of the car

IX. Embezzlement (3 levels listed below)

, a bank employee, has been convicted of stealing bank funds.
, a bank vice president, has been convicted of stealing bank funds.
, a postal worker, has been convicted of stealing from the U.S. mails.

X. Civil Rights (5 levels listed below)

, a police officer, has been convicted of beating [STATUS I] motorist who was found driving a car with no registration and with expired license plates. (Do not use any level of Dimension OO.)
, a police officer, has been convicted of beating a motorist who was found driving a car with no registration and with expired license plates. The motorist resisted the police officer's attempts to examine HIS/HER license and registration. (Do not use any level of Dimension OO.)
, a police officer, has been convicted of beating a motorist who was found driving a car with no registration and with expired license plates. The motorist did not resist the police officer's attempts to examine HIS/HER license and registration. (Do not use any level of Dimension OO.)
has been convicted of trying to get [STATUS I] couple who just moved into the neighborhood to move out by burning a cross on their lawn. (Equal probability ($p = 1/3$) of assigning "aa," "bb," or "cc" of Dimension OO.)
has been convicted of painting threats and obscenities on a [STATUS II]. (Equal probability ($p = 1/3$) of assigning "aa," "bb," or "cc" of Dimension OO.)

XI. Antitrust (2 levels listed below)

has been convicted of conspiring with other companies to fix prices for soft drinks.
has been convicted of agreeing with competitors to rig bids for government contracts in order to control the market and guarantee higher profits for the companies involved.

XII. Food & Drug Violations (3 levels listed below)

ww   has been convicted of adding poison to 17 packages of over-the-counter drugs (Equal probability ($p = 1/3$) of assigning "aa," "bb," or "cc" of Dimension OO.)

has been convicted of putting a drug on the market, falsely claiming that the drug was adequately tested and had no dangerous side effects. (Do not use any level of Dimension OO.)

has been convicted of putting a new drug on the market, concealing evidence that the drug had potentially dangerous side effects in users. (Do not use any level of Dimension OO.)

XIII. Environmental Violations (5 levels listed below)

1   has been convicted of illegally logging on federal lands.
2   has been convicted of failing to install proper antipollution devices on factory smoke stacks.
3   has been convicted of killing a bald eagle, protected by law as an endangered species.
4   , a plant manager, has been convicted of violating the terms of the plant's water discharge permit by discharging waste water that was 20 degrees warmer than allowed into a stream.
5   , a plant manager, has been convicted of violating the terms of the plant's water discharge permit by discharging waste water containing a toxic chemical.

XIV. Tax (6 levels listed below) *[Note: Crime stems appear twice.]*

uu   has been convicted of tax evasion for under-reporting income on tax returns
uu   has been convicted of failing to file income tax returns
     has been convicted of promoting an illegal tax shelter to the public
uu   has been convicted of tax evasion for under-reporting income on tax returns
uu   has been convicted of failing to file income tax returns
     has been convicted of promoting an illegal tax shelter to the public

XV. Extortion and Blackmail (1 level listed below)

has been convicted of

XVI. Bribery (4 levels listed below)

, a government purchasing agent, has been convicted of accepting a bribe to award a supply contract. (Do not use any level of Dimension OO.)

has been convicted of bribing a county commissioner to obtain a contract. (Equal probability ($p = 1/3$) of assigning "aa," "bb," or "cc" of Dimension OO.)

has been convicted of bribing a company purchasing agent to obtain a supply contract. (Equal probability ($p = 1/3$) of assigning "aa," "bb," or "cc" of Dimension OO.)

, a county commissioner, has been convicted of accepting a bribe to award a contract. (Do not use any level of Dimension OO.)

XVII. Drug Possession (8 levels listed below) *[Note: Drugs appear twice]*

has been convicted of possessing a small amount of [DRUG] for personal use. *[Insert DRUG title as listed below]*
powdered cocaine
crack cocaine
heroin
marijuana
powdered cocaine
crack cocaine
heroin
marijuana

XVIII. Forgery / Counterfeiting (3 levels listed below)

has been convicted of counterfeiting U.S. currency. The counterfeit currency amounted to
has been convicted of writing bad checks on an account opened using false identification. The bad checks amounted to
has been convicted of making purchases using illegally obtained credit card numbers. The purchases amounted to

XIX. Money Laundering (3 levels listed below)

, a rare coin dealer, has been convicted for failing to file forms required when receiving a cash payment of more than $10,000. (Equal probability ($p = 1/3$) of assigning "aa," "bb," or "cc" of Dimension OO.)
, a rare coin dealer, has been convicted of arranging large cash purchases by criminals. The dealer provided the criminals with rare coins, which they could then sell and appear to have earned the money lawfully. (Equal probability ($p = 1/3$) of assigning "aa," "bb," or "cc" of Dimension OO.)
, a bank official, has been convicted of arranging deposits of large sums of money in ways that avoided the requirement that cash transactions of more than $10,000 be reported. (Do not use any level of Dimension OO.)

XX. Kidnapping (2 levels listed below)

has been convicted of kidnapping a person and demanding ransom. The kidnapped person was not harmed.
has been convicted of kidnapping a person and demanding ransom. The kidnapped person was killed.

Dimension B: DRUG TRAFFICKING—Role

[Note: Contingent on Drug Trafficking as CRIME. This dimension appears in all Drug Trafficking vignettes.]

The defendant allowed HIS / HER apartment to be used for drug sales.
The defendant was a courier who was paid to transport drugs from overseas to dealers for a fee.

The defendant was a street-level dealer who bought drugs from a wholesale dealer and sold directly to users.

The defendant was the leader of a drug-dealing organization that hired 6 people.

The defendant was a bodyguard for a wholesale drug dealer.

The defendant was the leader of a drug-dealing organization that hired 50 people.

The defendant was the financial backer of a drug-dealing network run by others.

Dimension C: Drug Trafficking—Weapons & Violence

[Note: Contingent on Drug Trafficking as CRIME. This dimension appears in all Drug Trafficking vignettes.]

In HIS/HER criminal work, the defendant did not carry or use any weapons or engage in violence.

The defendant usually carried a handgun but was not known to have used the weapon or to have engaged in violence.

Although the defendant did not carry any weapons, the people he worked with did.

The defendant carried a handgun and was known to threaten others with it.

The defendant carried a handgun and was known to have shot and wounded others.

The defendant and HIS/HER co-defendants were known to have shot and seriously wounded several people.

The drug-dealing organization was known to use weapons and violence as a way of doing business.

Dimension D: Type A Frauds—Loss

[Note: Contingent on Fraud Type A as CRIME. This dimension appears in all Fraud Type A vignettes.]

$200.
$900.
$4,000.
$40,000.
$190,000.
$400,000.

Dimension E: Type B Frauds—Loss

[Note: Contingent on Fraud Type B as CRIME. This dimension appears in all Fraud Type B vignettes.]

$50,000.
$100,000.
$200,000.
$400,000.
$1,800,000.
$3,800,000.
$17,000,000.
$80,000,000.

Dimension F: Firearms—Number of Weapons

[Note: Contingent on Firearms as CRIME. This dimension appears ONLY in the two Firearms dealer/seller vignettes, as marked with "xx" in IV. Firearms.]

Two weapons were involved.
Ten weapons were involved.
More than fifty weapons were involved.

Dimension G: Firearms—Weapon Use

[Note: Contingent on Firearms as CRIME. This dimension appears ONLY in the two Firearms dealer/seller vignettes, as marked with "xx" in IV. Firearms.]

The defendant knew the weapons were to be used in illegal drug trafficking.
The defendant knew that the weapons were to be used in robberies.
The defendant did not believe that the weapons were going to be used in committing any crimes.

Dimension H: Larceny—Amounts

[Note: Contingent on Larceny as CRIME. This dimension appears in all Larceny vignettes.]

$200.
$900.
$4,000.

$40,000.
$400,000.

Dimension I: Larceny—Planning

[Note: Contingent on Larceny CRIME. This dimension appears in all Larceny vignettes.]

The crime was carefully planned over a long period of time.
The crime was done on the spur of the moment.

Dimension J: Bank Robbery—Loss

[Note: Contingent on Bank Robbery as CRIME. This dimension appears in all Bank Robbery vignettes.]

$900 was taken.
$4,000 was taken.
$19,000 was taken.
$50,000 was taken.

Dimension K: Street Robbery—Weapon Use

[Note: Contingent on Street Robbery as CRIME. This dimension appears in all Street Robbery vignettes.]

at gunpoint, but the gun was not fired.
at gunpoint, and the gun was fired.
by threatening harm, but a weapon was not shown.

Dimension L: Street Robbery—Personal Injury

[Note: Contingent on Street Robbery as CRIME. This dimension appears ONLY in the two vignettes indicating gun use, as marked with "vv" in Dimension K Street Robbery— Weapon Use.]

The victim was not hurt.
The victim received a minor injury.
The victim was injured seriously.

Dimension M: Street Robbery—Convenience Store

[Note: Contingent on Street Robbery as CRIME. This dimension appears ONLY in the convenience store vignette, as marked with "yy" in VIII. Street Robbery.]

$400 was taken.
$900 was taken.
$9,000 was taken.

Dimension N: Street Robbery—Carjacking

[Note: Contingent on Street Robbery as CRIME. This dimension appears ONLY in the car jacking vignette, as marked with "zz" in VIII. Street Robbery.]

The car was worth $20,000.
The car was worth $50,000.

Dimension O: Embezzlement—Amounts

[Note: Contingent on Embezzlement as CRIME. This dimension appears in all Embezzlement vignettes.]

$900 was stolen.
$4,000 was stolen.
$40,000 was stolen.
$400,000 was stolen.

Dimension P: Embezzlement—Planning

[Note: Contingent on Embezzlement as CRIME. This dimension appears in all Embezzlement vignettes.]

The crime was carefully planned over a period of time.
The crime was done with very little planning.

Dimension Q: Civil Rights—Status I

[Note: Contingent on Civil Rights as CRIME and designated Status I.]

an African-American
an Hispanic-American

an Asian-American
a homosexual

Dimension R: Civil Rights—Status II

[Note: Contingent on Civil Rights as CRIME and designated Status II.]

Protestant church.
Catholic church.
Jewish synagogue.
Muslim mosque.

Dimension S: Antitrust—Amount

[Note: Contingent on Antitrust as CRIME. This dimension appears in all Antitrust vignettes.]

As a result, the public was overcharged about $500,000.
As a result, the public was overcharged about $3,000,000.
As a result, the public was overcharged about $15,000,000.

Dimension T: Antitrust—Role

[Note: Contingent on Antitrust as CRIME. This dimension appears in all Antitrust vignettes.]

The defendant acted under orders of a higher executive in the firm.
The defendant personally organized the agreements with the other
    firms.
The agreements among firms were in effect for many years. The defen-
    dant simply went along with the practice.
The agreements among firms were in effect for many years. The defen-
    dant, a contracts manager, simply went along with the practice.

Dimension U: Food & Drug—Injury

[Note: Contingent on Food & Drug as CRIME. This dimension appears in all Food & Drug vignettes.]

No one was injured.
About a dozen people were hospitalized as a consequence.
At least one death resulted.

Dimension V: Food & Drug—Financial

[Note: Contingent on Food & Drug as CRIME. This dimension appears ONLY in the vignette involving drug tampering, as marked with "ww" in the XII. Food & Drug Violations.]

> The drug firm involved spent $100,000 in withdrawing its product from the market.
> The drug firm involved spent $10,000,000 in withdrawing its product from the market.

Dimension W: Environmental—Aesthetics

[Note: Contingent on Level 1 of Environmental as CRIME.]

> All of the mature trees were cut down.
> Some mature trees were cut but not all.

Dimension X: Environmental—Physical

[Note: Contingent on Level 1 of Environmental as CRIME.]

> The water shed was damaged, causing more floods and extensive soil erosion resulting in the filling in of local lakes with silt.
> The water shed was not significantly damaged.

Dimension Y: Environmental—Habitat

[Note: Contingent on Level 1 of Environmental as CRIME.]

> The local habitats for native plants and animals were destroyed.
> The local habitats for native plants and animals were not significantly damaged.

Dimension Z: Environmental—Human

[Note: Contingent on Level 1 of Environmental as CRIME.]

> Local streams and lakes were polluted, making them unsafe for swimming or for drinking water.
> Local streams and lakes were not polluted.

Dimension AA: Environmental Urban—
Aesthetics

[Note: Contingent on Level 2 of Environmental as CRIME.]

There were foul smells in nearby neighborhoods.
There were no bad smells in nearby neighborhoods.

Dimension BB: Environmental Urban—
Physical

[Note: Contingent on Level 2 of Environmental as CRIME.]

House paint peeled off prematurely, and some automobile finishes
were damaged.
There was no visible damage to house paint or automobile finishes.

Dimension CC: Environmental Urban—
Habitat

[Note: Contingent on Level 2 of Environmental as CRIME.]

Large numbers of trees died, and most of the local birds left the area.
Local trees and birds were unaffected.

Dimension DD: Environmental Urban—
Human

[Note: Contingent on Level 2 of Environmental as CRIME.]

Asthma and other respiratory illness rates were unusually high.
Asthma and other respiratory illness were not higher than in nearby
neighborhoods.

Dimension DDD: Environmental—
Level 4 or 5

*[Note: Contingent on Level 4 or Level 5 of Environmental as CRIME. Name of
dimension is DDD, not DD.]*

As a result, thousands of fish were killed.
But there was no damage to fish in the river.

Dimension EE: Tax—Loss

[Note: Contingent on Tax as CRIME. This dimension appears in all Tax vignettes.]

> involving $2,000 in taxes.
> involving $4,000 in taxes.
> involving $19,000 in taxes.
> involving $190,000 in taxes.
> involving $850,000 in taxes.

Dimension FF: Tax—Criminal Involvement

[Note: Contingent on Tax as CRIME. This dimension appears ONLY in the personal tax vignettes, as marked with "uu" in XIV. Tax.]

> The income involved was traced to criminal activities for which the defendant was convicted in another court case.
> The income involved was believed to come from criminal activities for which the defendant was never tried in court.

Dimension GG: Extortion and Blackmail—Amount

[Note: Contingent on Extortion and Blackmail as CRIME. This dimension appears in all Extortion and Blackmail vignettes. Apply dimension PP prior to dimension GG.]

> $1,900 was demanded.
> $19,000 was demanded.
> $90,000 was demanded.

Dimension HH: Bribery—Amount

[Note: Contingent on Bribery as CRIME. This dimension appears in all Bribery vignettes.]

> $500 was offered.
> $1,900 was offered.
> $9,000 was offered.
> $90,000 was offered.

Dimension II: Forgery—Amount

[Note: Contingent on Forgery as CRIME. This dimension appears in all Forgery vignettes.]

> $1,900.
> $19,000.
> $190,000.
> $1,000,000.

Dimension JJ: Money Laundering—Amount

[Note: Contingent on Money Laundering as CRIME. This dimension appears in all Money Laundering vignettes.]

> $19,000 was involved.
> $190,000 was involved.
> $1,800,000 was involved.

Dimension KK: Money Laundering—
Knowledge

[Note: Contingent on Money Laundering as CRIME. This dimension appears in all Money Laundering vignettes.]

> The defendant knew the money came from criminal activity.
> The defendant did not know the origins of the money.

Dimension LL: Gender

[Note: This dimension appears in all vignettes.]

> A man ($p = .8$)
> A woman ($p = .2$)

Dimension MM: Family Ties

[Note: This dimension appears in all vignettes.]

> The defendant is not married. ($p = .8$)
> The defendant is married and has a spouse and two children. ($p = .2$)

Dimension NN: Employment

[Note: This dimension appears in all vignettes.]

The defendant is currently unemployed ($p = .8$)
The defendant is currently employed ($p = .2$)

Dimension OO: Previous Record

[Note: This dimension appears in all vignettes EXCEPT those listed below:

Type B Frauds
Embezzlement
Antitrust
Firearms (assign aa, bb, cc, or none as indicated in IV. Firearms)
Civil Rights (assign aa, bb, cc, or none as indicated in X. Civil Rights)
Food & Drug (assign aa, bb, cc, or none only as indicated in XII. Food & Drugs)
Bribery (assign aa, bb, cc, or none as indicated in XVI. Bribery)
Money Laundering (assign aa, bb, cc, or none as indicated in XIX. Money) Laundering)]

aa   and has never been imprisoned before.
bb   and has served 2 previous prison sentences, each more than a year.
cc   and has served 4 previous prison sentences, each more than a year.

Dimension PP: Extortion and Blackmail—
Type

[Note: Contingent on Extortion and Blackmail as CRIME. This dimension appears in all Extortion and Blackmail vignettes.]

extorting money from a victim by threatening to kill a family member.
blackmailing a prominent person by threatening to reveal a sexual indiscretion.

NOTE

1.   VIG WRITE is a DbaseIII procedure written by Eleanor Weber, Deborah Sellers, and Peter H. Rossi and published by the Social and Demographic Research Institute of the University of Massachusetts at Amherst.

Questionnaire Used in Study

---

*Bates*_____ *101-4*

Just Punishment for Convicted Criminals

Questionnaire

Conducted for

United States Sentencing Commission

JUST PUNISHMENT FOR CONVICTED CRIMINALS

Questionnaire

Now I have a few questions to ask.

1. First, let's talk about some things that people say are problems in their neighborhood. As I read each one, please tell how serious a problem it is in <u>your</u> neighborhood. I'll ask you whether you think it's a very serious problem, somewhat serious, not a serious problem, or not a problem at all. Let's start with . . .

    (READ ITEM) Is that a very serious problem, somewhat serious, not a serious problem, or not a problem at all in your neighborhood or the general area in which you live?

		VERY SERIOUS PROBLEM	SOMEWHAT SERIOUS PROBLEM	NOT A SERIOUS PROBLEM	NOT A PROBLEM AT ALL	DON'T KNOW	REFUSED	
a.	Purse-snatching, robbery, assault, and other street crimes	1	2	3	4	7	8	130
b.	Burglary, automobile stealing, shoplifting, and other property crimes	1	2	3	4	7	8	31
c.	Embezzling, consumer fraud, passing bad checks, and other white collar crimes	1	2	3	4	7	8	32
d.	Selling illegal drugs	1	2	3	4	7	8	33
e.	Using, but <u>not</u> selling illegal drugs	1	2	3	4	7	8	34

2. Now I want to ask you about some crimes that may have been committed against you or another member of your household in the last year – that is, anytime in 1993.

    First, was your household burglarized at any time during 1993?

    35   1 YES
             4 NO
             7 DON'T KNOW
             8 REFUSED

3. In the past year – that is, anytime in 1993 – have you or another member of your household had your purse or wallet snatched or been robbed while out in a public place? (IF YES: Did that happen to **you** or to another member of your household?)

    136   1 YES, RESPONDENT
             2 YES, OTHER HOUSEHOLD MEMBER
             3 YES, REFUSED TO SPECIFY
             4 NO
             7 DON'T KNOW
             8 REFUSED

4. Were you or another member of your household cheated in a purchase at anytime in
    1993?
    (IF YES: Did that happen to **you** or to another member of your household?)

37   1 YES, RESPONDENT
         2 YES, OTHER HOUSEHOLD MEMBER
         3 YES, REFUSED TO SPECIFY
         4 NO
         7 DON'T KNOW
         8 REFUSED

5. In the past year – that is, anytime in 1993 – has anything such as a car, bicycle, or car
    radio been stolen from you or another member of your household?
    (IF YES: Was that item stolen from **you** or from another member of your household?)

38   1 YES, RESPONDENT
         2 YES, OTHER HOUSEHOLD MEMBER
         3 YES, REFUSED TO SPECIFY
         4 NO
         7 DON'T KNOW
         8 REFUSED

6. Were you or another member of your household assaulted or raped at anytime in 1993?
    (IF YES: Did that happen to **you** or to another member of your household?)

39   1 YES, RESPONDENT
         2 YES, OTHER HOUSEHOLD MEMBER
         3 YES, REFUSED TO SPECIFY
         4 NO
         7 DON'T KNOW
         8 REFUSED

7. Now, I'd like to ask you about the amount of influence or power different groups have.
    Let's start with . . . ?

	TOO LITTLE/ FEW	RIGHT AMOUNT	TOO MUCH/ MANY	DON'T KNOW	REFUSED	
a. Minority groups in the United States and their civil rights – Would you say that they have too few civil rights, about the right amount, or too many civil rights?	1	2	3	7	8	*140*
b. People accused of serious crimes and their legal rights – Would you say they have too few legal rights, about the right amount, or too many legal rights?	1	2	3	7	8	*41*
c. Police departments and the freedom they have in investigating crimes –						

	YES	NO	REFUSED	

Would you say they have too little free-dom, about the right amount, or too much freedom?	1	2	3	7	8	*42*

d. Poor people in the United States and their public welfare benefits –

Would you say they have too few welfare benefits, about the right amount, or too many welfare benefits? — 1 2 3 7 8 *43*

e. The environment and the attention given to protecting it against sources of pollu-tion –

Would you say that protecting the envi-ronment receives too little attention, about the right amount, or too much attention? — 1 2 3 7 8 *44*

8.   People often classify their views on political and social issues as conservative, moderate, or liberal. In general, would you say that **your** views usually tend to be . . . (READ LIST)?

45   1 Very conservative,
            2 Somewhat conservative,
            3 Moderate,
            4 Somewhat liberal, or
            5 Very liberal
            7 DON'T KNOW
            8 REFUSED

9.   Most people have some contact with the police or the court system at some time in their lives. The next few questions are about contacts that **you** personally may have had with the police or the court system. Please tell me whether or not you have had any of the following experiences.

		YES	NO	REFUSED	
a.	Have you ever served on a jury?	1	2	8	*146*
b.	Have you ever reported a crime to the police?	1	2	8	*47*
c.	Have you ever been sued?	1	2	8	*48*
d.	Have you ever testified as a witness in court?	1	2	8	*49*
e.	Have you ever been arrested?	1	2	8	*50*
f.	Have you ever served time in jail or prison after having been convicted of a crime?	1	2	8	*51*

10.   Now, I have a few additional questions to ask you about yourself.

       How old were you on your last birthday?

52-54   _____ YEARS OF AGE
               998 REFUSED

11.   Are you currently . . . ? (READ LIST.)

55   1Married,
          2Divorced,
          3Separated,
          4Widowed,
          5Living with a partner, or
          6Single and never married
          8REFUSED

12.   What is the highest grade or year that you completed in school or college?

56   1 LESS THAN 12 YEARS
          2 12 YEARS/HIGH SCHOOL GRADUATE/G.E.D
          3 1 OR 2 YEARS OF COLLEGE OR JUNIOR COLLEGE
          4 3 OR MORE YEARS OF COLLEGE BUT NO DEGREE
          5 COLLEGE GRADUATE
          6 ADVANCED DEGREE
          8 REFUSED

13.   Are you currently employed for pay – either full-time or part-time? (FULL-TIME IS 30 OR
      MORE HOURS PER WEEK.)

157   1   YES, FULL-TIME
          2   YES, PART-TIME – CONTINUE
          3   NO, NOT EMPLOYED – SKIP TO Q. 15
          8   REFUSED – SKIP TO Q. 17

IF "YES" IN Q. 13, ASK:
14. Last week were you . . . ? (READ LIST.)

58   1   At work all week,
          2   Out on vacation or sick leave all week, or
          3   At work part of the week and out part of the week   – SKIP TO Q. 16
          8   REFUSED

IF "NO" IN Q. 13, ASK:
15. Are you . . . ? (READ LIST.) (CIRCLE ALL THAT APPLY.)

59   1   Looking for work,   – CONTINUE
          2   **Not** currently looking for work,
          3   A homemaker,
          4   Retired, or   – SKIP TO Q. 17
          5   Something else (SPECIFY):_____ 60-
          8   REFUSED

IF "YES" IN Q. 13 **OR** "1 OR 2" IN Q. 15, ASK:
16. What is your usual occupation? What kind of work do you usually do? (PROBE TO
      CLARIFY.)
                                                                            61-
                                                                            62-

ASK EVERYONE

17.   Are you of Hispanic, Latino, or Spanish descent?

63   1 YES
          2 NO
          7 DON'T KNOW
          8 REFUSED

18.   Which of these groups best describes you? (READ LIST.)

164   1 White,
          2 Black or African-American,
          3 American Indian/Alaskan Native,
          4 Asian or Pacific Islander, or
          5 Something else (SPECIFY):   *65-*
          7 DON'T KNOW
          8 REFUSED

19.   Would you say that your total annual household income from all sources before taxes is
      above or below $25,000? (IF AMOUNT IS ON BORDERLINE, CODE IN HIGHER
      CATEGORY.)

66   1 ABOVE – CONTINUE
          2 BELOW – SKIP TO Q. 21

          7 DON'T KNOW
          8 REFUSED   – SKIP TO Q. 22 (VERIFY)

IF "ABOVE" IN Q. 19, ASK:
20. Is it . . . ? (READ LIST.) (IF AMOUNT IS ON BORDERLINE, CODE IN HIGHER CATEGORY.)

67   1 $25,000 up to $50,000
          2    $50,000 up to $75,000, or
          3    $75,000 or more   – SKIP TO Q. 22 (VERIFY)
          7   DON'T KNOW
          8   REFUSED

IF "BELOW" IN Q. 19, ASK:
21. Is it . . . ? (READ LIST.) (IF AMOUNT IS ON BORDERLINE, CODE IN HIGHER CATEGORY.)

68   1   Less than $5,000
          2    $5,000 up to $15,000, or
          3    $15,000 up to $25,000

          7   DON'T KNOW
          8   REFUSED

ASK EVERYONE

22.   (VERIFY QUESTION) My supervisor may want to verify that our interview was conducted
      in a courteous and businesslike manner and that the information was collected properly.
      May I have your . . . ?

      Name:

      Street Address/Apt No.:

City/State/ZIP Code:

Telephone Number: (___)

That's all the questions I have for you. Thank you very much for your time and cooperation.

INTERVIEWER: PLEASE ANSWER THE FOLLOWING QUESTIONS ABOUT THIS INTERVIEW.

23.   RECORD SEX OF RESPONDENT.

169   1 MALE
            2 FEMALE

24.   Did the respondent appear to have any problems reading or understanding the directions
      or the crime descriptions in the vignette booklet?

70   1 NO PROBLEMS
            2 MAYBE SOME SLIGHT PROBLEMS
            3 SOME PROBLEMS
            4 MANY PROBLEMS
            7 NOT SURE

25.   Did the respondent have any interruptions while working on the vignette booklet?

71   1 NO INTERRUPTIONS
            2 A FEW SLIGHT INTERRUPTIONS
            3 SOME INTERRUPTIONS
            4 MANY INTERRUPTIONS
            7 NOT SURE

26.   If **REFUSED** Q. 17 (HISPANIC ORIGIN), please estimate:

72   1 YES, IS HISPANIC, LATINO, OR SPANISH
            2 NO, IS NOT
            7 CAN'T TELL/DON'T KNOW

27.   If **REFUSED** or **HISPANIC** in Q. 18 (RACE), please estimate: (NOTE: DO <u>NOT</u> ANSWER
      "HISPANIC" TO THIS ITEM.)

73   1 WHITE,
            2 BLACK OR AFRICAN-AMERICAN,
            3 AMERICAN INDIAN/ALASKAN NATIVE,
            4 ASIAN OR PACIFIC ISLANDER, OR
            5 SOMETHING ELSE (SPECIFY):   *74:*
            7 CAN'T TELL/DON'T KNOW

INTERVIEWER SIGNATURE: _____   ID #:

END TIME:	a.m.
	p.m.

C

"Standard" Vignettes Used in Study

The two vignettes shown below were presented to the respondent before the respondent was handed the vignette booklet. The interviewer observed the respondent as he or she marked answers to these vignettes to make sure that the respondent understood the task and had sufficient reading comprehension skills to fill out the vignette booklet.

A man has been convicted of possessing a small amount of marijuana for personal use.

The defendant is unmarried. The defendant is currently unemployed and has never been imprisoned before.

What sentence should be given in a case like this? **CIRCLE EITHER 1, 2, 3 OR 4:**

1	2	3	4
PROBATION No time in prison	**PRISON** Less than 1 year # Months ___	**PRISON** 1 Year or more # Years ___	**DEATH** Penalty

---

A man has been convicted of robbing a bank. The robber pointed a handgun at a teller and demanded money. The robber fired the gun at the ceiling, but no one was hurt. $19,000 was taken.

The defendant is married and has a spouse and two children. The defendant is currently unemployed and has served 2 previous sentences, each more than a year.

What sentence should be given in a case like this? **CIRCLE EITHER 1, 2, 3 OR 4:**

1	2	3	4
PROBATION No time in prison	**PRISON** Less than 1 year # Months ___	**PRISON** 1 Year or more # Years ___	**DEATH** Penalty

References

Berk, Richard A., and Rossi, Peter H. 1977. *Prison Reform and State Elites.* Cambridge, MA: Ballinger.

Davis, James A., and Smith, Tom W. 1994. *General Social Surveys, 1972–1995: Cumulative Codebook.* National Data Program for the Social Sciences. No. 14. Chicago: National Opinion Research Center.

Doble, John, Immerwahr, Stephen, and Richardson, Amy. 1991. *Punishing Criminals: The People of Delaware Consider the Options.* New York: Edna McConnell Clark Foundation.

Durkheim, Emile. 1953. *Suicide.* Glencoe, IL: Free Press.

Hart, H. L. A. 1968. *Punishment and Responsibility.* New York: Oxford University Press.

Innes, Christopher A. 1993. "Recent Public Opinion in the United States Toward Punishment and Corrections." *Prison Journal* 73(2):220–36

Jacoby, Joseph E., and Cullen, Francis T. 1994. "The Structure of Punishment Norms: Can the Punishment Fit the Crime?" Department of Sociology, Bowling Green State University, Ohio.

Jasso, Guillermina, and Rossi, Peter H. 1977. "Distributive Justice and Earned Income." *American Sociological Review* 42(4):639–51.

Lipton, Douglas, Martinson, Robert, and Wilkes, Julia. 1975. *The Effectiveness of Correctional Treatment: A Survey of Treatment Evaluation Studies.* New York: Praeger.

Manski, Charles F. 1988. *Analog Estimation Methods in Econometrics.* New York: Chapman Hall.

Martin, Susan A. 1983. "The Politics of Sentencing Guidelines in Pennsylvania and Minnesota." In *Research on Sentencing: The Search for Reform,* Volume II, edited by Alfred Blumstein, Jacqueline Cohen, Susan A. Martin, and Michael E. Tonry. Washington: National Academy Press.

Nagel, Ilene. 1990. "Structuring Sentencing: The New Federal Sentencing Guidelines." *Journal of Criminal Law and Criminology* 80(4):883–943.

Roberts, Julian V. 1992. "Public Opinion, Crime and Criminal Justice." In *Crime and Justice: A Review of Research,* Volume 16, edited by Michael Tonry. Chicago: University of Chicago Press.

Rossi, Alice S., and Rossi, Peter H. 1990. *Of Human Bonding: Parent-Child Relations Across the Life Course.* Hawthorne, NY: Aldine deGruyter.

237

Rossi, Peter H., and Berk, Richard A. 1985. "Varieties of Normative Consensus." *American Sociological Review* 50(5):333–46.

Rossi, Peter H., and Berk, Richard A. 1995. *Public Opinion on Sentencing Federal Criminals: A National Sample Survey Conducted by the U. S. Sentencing Commission.* Washington: U.S. Sentencing Commission.

Rossi, Peter H., Bose, Christine, and Berk, Richard A. 1974. "The Seriousness of Crimes: Normative Structure and Individual Differences" *American Sociological Review* 39:224–37.

Rossi, Peter H., and Henry, Patrick J. 1980. "Seriousness: A Measure for all Purposes?" In *Handbook of Criminal Justice Evaluation,* edited by Malcolm W. Klein and Katherine S. Teilman. Beverly Hills, CA: Sage.

Rossi, Peter H., and Nock, Steven L. 1978. "Ascription Versus Achievement in the Attribution of Family Status." *American Journal of Sociology* 84(3):565–90.

Rossi, Peter H., and Nock, Steven L. 1982. *Measuring Social Judgments: The Factorial Survey Approach.* Beverly Hills, CA: Sage.

Rossi, Peter H., Simpson, Jon E., and Miller, JoAnn L. 1985. "Beyond Crime Seriousness: Fitting the Punishment to the Crime." *Journal of Quantitative Criminology* 1(1):59–90.

Rossi, Peter H., and Weber-Burdin, Eleanor. 1983. "Sexual Harassment on the Campus." *Social Science Research* 12(2, June):131–58.

Sellin, Thorsten, and Wolfgang, Marvin E. 1964. *The Measurement of Delinquency.* New York: John Wiley.

Stinchcombe, Arthur L., Adams, Rebecca, Heimer, Carol A., Scheppele, Kim L., Smith, Tom L., and Taylor, D. Garth. 1980. *Crime and Punishment—Changing Attitudes in America.* San Francisco: Jossey-Bass.

Thurstone, Louis L. 1959. *The Measurement of Value.* Chicago: University of Chicago Press.

U.S. Sentencing Commission (USSC). 1987–1993 (updated annually). *Guidelines Manual.* Washington: USSC.

Von Hirsch, Andrew. 1993. *Censure and Sanction.* New York: Oxford University Press.

Walker, Nigel, and Hough, Mike (Eds.) 1988. *Public Attitudes To Sentencing: Surveys from Five Countries.* Cambridge Studies in Criminology, 59. Aldershot, UK: Gower.

Weber, Eleanor, Sellers, Deborah, and Rossi, Peter H. 1988. *VIG-WRITE: The PC Vignette Generating Program.* Amherst, MA: Social and Demographic Research Institute.

Will, Jeffry A. 1993. *The Deserving Poor.* New York: Garland.

Wolfgang, Marvin E., Figlio, Robert E., Tracey, Paul E., and Singer, Simon I. (1985) *The National Survey of Crime Severity.* Washington: U.S. Department of Justice, Bureau of Justice Statistics.

Zimmerman, Sherwood, Van Alstyne, David J. and Dunn, Christopher. 1988. "The National Punishment Survey and Public Policy Consequences." *Journal of Research in Crime and Delinquency* 25(2):120–49.

Index